AF827969

Human Services and Information Technology: An International Perspective

Edited by

Jan Steyaert, David Colombi and Jackie Rafferty

arena

© ENITH 1996

All rights reserved. No part of this publication may be reproduced, stored in a retrieval system, or transmitted in any form or by any means, electronic, mechanical, photocopying, recording or otherwise without the prior permission of the publisher.

Published by
Arena
Ashgate Publishing Limited
Gower House
Croft Road
Aldershot
Hants GU11 3HR
England

Ashgate Publishing Company
Old Post Road
Brookfield
Vermont 05036
USA

British Library Cataloguing in Publication Data

Human Services and information technology: an
international perspective
1. Human services - Data processing
2. Social service - Data processing
I. Steyaert, Jan, 1962-. Colombi, David, 1945-
III. Rafferty, Jackie
361'.00285

Library of Congress Catalog Card Number: 96-83635

ISBN 1 85742 365 8 (paperback)
ISBN 1 85742 364 X (hardback)

Printed and bound in Great Britain by
Hartnolls Limited, Bodmin, Cornwall

Contents

Preface

The aims of *Human Services and Information Technology: An International Perspective* are firstly to provide academics and practitioners engaged in the provision of human services with a structured overview of how information technology (IT) is shaping the work of their professions, and secondly to facilitate the exchange of information and ideas between countries about these important developments.

This book presents a picture of progress in using IT in social work and allied professions in seventeen countries. The range of countries is shown on the contents page and we have been delighted to receive three contributions from the Pacific Rim, two from Eastern Europe, two from North America, one from the near East as well as nine from Western Europe. Our principal thanks must go to the author(s) in each country for their contributions which are the heart of this book and its *raison d'etre*. It has been a collaborative effort, facilitated by e-mail but wholly dependent on their ability and willingness to undertake the difficult task of providing a structured overview of rapid changes in a complex area of work in each country.

The strength of the European contribution reflects this book's origins in the earlier *Human Services and Information Technology: A European Perspective* which was launched at the third Human Service and Information Technology Applications (HUSITA 3) conference at Maastricht in the Netherlands in 1993. This wider perspective is written to a new framework that is explained in Chapter 1 which sets the scene for the country reports. The final chapter provides an analysis of what has gone before and cautiously attempts the always tricky task of 'future watching'. While some contributions inevitably draw on the earlier work, they show a new perspective on developments in each country as well as reflecting the rapid changes of the last three years. These changes include the dramatic rise in the use and importance of the Internet and the World Wide Web - a change that has so far impacted on the lives of academics far more than practitioners - and continuing development of hardware and software standards. We see also the inexorable progress of how computers are becoming an intrinsic part of the lives and functioning of organisations. This is not only about numbers of computers but the range of ways in which they are used. The book reflects many of the continuing tensions that exist in this area as well as the frustrations, failures and conflicts that are an inevitable concomitant of the profound changes involved. This book is about the fundamental collective commitment to use the technology for human ends, for human needs. That commitment is the ultimate yardstick by which progress must be judged.

Internationalism is a feature not only in the range of countries covered and in the editorship, but also in the planning and production process. This book is a unique collaboration of ENITH and STAKES with Arena and their roles are explained and acknowledged.

ENITH

The European Network for Information Technology in the Human Services is an association of individuals and organisations throughout Europe. Inaugurated in Antwerp in 1992, ENITH encourages the use of information technology in the human service. It pursues this aim through exchanging information and ideas, and providing opportunities for networking. Its most recent conference, at Eindhoven in the Netherlands in September 1995, was on the impact of information technology on social policy. The editors act on behalf of, and as members of ENITH, to contribute to achieving its aims.

STAKES

The Finnish National Research and Development Centre for Welfare and Health (STAKES) has played a major role in the developing use of information technology in welfare and health services in Finland. It has contributed financially and in planning to the production of this book. STAKES hosted the HUSITA 4 conference, where *Human Services and Information Technology: An International Perspective* was launched.

Jan Steyaert, David Colombi and Jackie Rafferty
March 1996

The editors

The editors co-edited *Human Services and Information Technology: A European Perspective* launched at the HUSITA 3 conference. They also co-edited *The Human Services in the Information Age,* a collection of HUSITA 3 conference papers.

Jan Steyaert is senior lecturer at Causa, Faculty of Health Care and Social Work at Eindhoven in the Netherlands. He is secretary of ENITH and co-editor of the international journal *New Technology in the Human Services.* He has published extensively on client information systems in social work and social policy and recently edited *Information Technology and Human Services, More than Computers?* (1996).

David Colombi, PhD, is a research fellow in the Centre for Human Service Technology at the University of Southampton and formerly worked for the Probation Service. He has published *The Probation Service and Information Technology* (1993), based on his doctoral thesis. His particular interest is in developing software for social work education and practice and he publishes programs as *Passada Software*.

Jackie Rafferty is a senior research fellow in the Centre for Human Service Technology at the University of Southampton and Director of the Computers in Teaching Initiative for Human Services. She has undertaken research in the ethical and community use of information technology and has developed courseware for social work and nursing education. Other publications cover equal opportunities and technology, and educational technology. The most recent publication is *Both Sides: Technology and Human Services* as an electronic book on the world wide web.

All books referred to above are included in the appendix.

Editor contacts

Jan Steyaert
Hogeschool Eindhoven
Causa
Postbus 347
5600 AH Eindhoven
The Netherlands

Telephone: +31 40 2605940
Fax: +31 40 2435274
E-mail: j.steyaert@fz.hse.nl
WWW: http://www.fz.hse.nl/ca/causa.htm

David Colombi and Jackie Rafferty
Centre for Human Service Technology
Department of Social Work Studies
University of Southampton
Southampton SO17 1BJ
UK

Telephone: +44 1703 593536
Fax: +44 1703 592779
E-mail: david@chst.soton.ac.uk
jr@chst.soton.ac.uk

1 Setting the scene

Jan Steyaert, David Colombi and Jackie Rafferty

Human Services and Information Technology: An International Perspective is published ten years after *The Human Edge: Information Technology and Helping People* (Geiss and Viswanathan, 1986). That book described itself as 'the first comprehensive attempt to look at where we are and what questions we must answer to move forward'. It was undoubtably a seminal work that clearly marked the beginning of a collaborative effort in social work and the helping professions to harness technology to the needs of the human services and people served by them. It is not our aim to provide a formal analysis of how far the hopes, fears and ambitions articulated in *The Human Edge* have been fulfilled but it is apt to now provide an international perspective on how far along the road we have travelled in the last ten years.

The tasks of this chapter are to provide a framework and to set the scene for what follows in the individual country reports. They in turn provide the basis for the final chapter. The first of these two tasks is a relatively simple one. The framework for this chapter and for each country report is -

- Human services and information technology
- Information for citizens
- Vocational education and training
- Provision of services
- Conclusion and future developments

Within this broad framework each chapter uses a common approach to address key issues and areas of work. However it is a framework, not a strait-jacket or a catalogue. The author(s) of each chapter highlight progress and issues in distinctive ways according to the circumstances of their country. Our second task of using this framework to set the scene for what follows is a more complex one of identifying topics and articulating issues at a general level.

Since *The Human Edge* was published computers have become an established part of the work environment in the helping professions. The debate has long since shifted from questioning their introduction. The more interesting task is seeking to define and develop their role in ways that are consistent with the values, aims and effectiveness of social work and assessing their impact at a time of profoundly changing social policies and priorities. In these ten years we have seen astonishing progress in the technology itself, in software, in the imaginative application of IT and in its penetration into many aspects of our lives at work and at home. This has culminated in the multi-media PC and the explosive popularity of the Internet for communication and accessing information, even if it has impacted more on the lives of academics than on those of professionals working in agencies. See *http://www.fz.hse.nl/hsandit/* for web information on this book and links to web sites mentioned in the book[1].

A networked multi-media PC using Windows and CD-ROMs is a far cry from a stand-alone 286 or 386 DOS based PC of only a few years ago. Software has become increasingly sophisticated, requiring faster and higher capacity machines on which to run effectively. Windows programs and multi-media are becoming de facto standards with voice recognition and virtual reality as expensive but increasingly effective tools. In amongst these changes we have seen faltering starts such as interactive-video disks and PDAs (Personal Digital Assistants) and endemic problems of applying concepts such as expert systems and neural networks.

With increasing technological sophistication, the gap between insiders and outsiders in the information revolution remains a powerful reality. It is ameliorated by continuing downward pressure on prices, making technology more accessible, at least in developed countries. However this book offers reminders on how different the provision and opportunities are in and between countries.

The changes are not just in technology but in its impact on social organisations and our personal lives. A key shift is how technology change has opened up debate on the nature and role of information itself and its importance and role within the community, organisations and government. This shift is manifest in the concept of ‘the information society’. Issues of how and what information is used has led to organisations developing information strategies that are distinct from IT strategies and the rise of academic disciplines such as ‘social informatics’ concerned with information per se.

Increasingly we have the concept of information as a commodity that is manufactured (by data collection) and distributed, shared or sold like other commodities. It has distinctive features of the raw ingredient (data) being available in literally unlimited quantities (albeit at a cost) and of being endlessly reproducible so that it grows exponentially rather than being consumed. Commoditisation of information is seen not only in more organisations collecting, processing and distributing information but in our understanding and use of it as a resource that has to be organised, managed, distributed and maintained. There are contradictory pressures between commoditisation and democratisation of information - sitting uneasily alongside each other on the Internet and elsewhere.

The way in which the technological, social and organisation changes impact on human service organisations is the focus of the first element in our framework.

HUMAN SERVICES AND INFORMATION TECHNOLOGY

In this section each country report provides a brief contextual overview of how human services are organised and provided. They then examine the broad impact of technology in that process, including reference to ethical issues such as data protection and discrimination. Provision of services depends on geographic, economic, historic and cultural factors, with a key dimension being the extent to which a country can be meaningfully described as a welfare society. Despite political, economic and demographic pressures that have seemed in many countries to threaten the very roots of the concept of social responsibility for the welfare of citizens, those ideals have often shown resilience in the face of determined onslaught. There has however often been severe damage inflicted on the most vulnerable members of society.

The impact of technology on the provision of services is in some respects quantitative, with computers no longer seen as mysterious and esoteric but part of the furniture of everyday office life in organisations. Its use is widely accepted for word-processing and managing information about staff, clients and the core business or services of organisations. In this respect human service organisations have been engaged in catching up with the commercial sector. A frequent starting point therefore is to attempt to quantify that progress. The quantity issue is important in the consequences for social work practice of having computerised systems. However it also affects the availability of technology for what managers usually see as secondary provision - meeting the practice needs of professionals and clients.

Technology has begun to affect the nature of service provision and social policy (Steyaert, 1966). Better communication and coordination between services enables 'one stop' service points - accompanied by greater threats to confidentiality and privacy. Increasing use of technology for client records and case management promises better services through efficiency and improved evaluation of services - but imposes greater control and accountability on previously 'autonomous' professionals. Perhaps most profoundly, new technology facilitates radically new patterns of 'social market' or 'market economy' organisation of welfare services. Internal markets and privatisation of service provision reduces the role of social work staff to assessors and purchasers (and rationers) of services within tightly controlled budgets.

Ethics

The ethical dimensions of new technology are varied with confidentiality, control of worker and client lives, unemployment, discrimination and empowerment as important elements of the debate. As resisting the introduction of IT into human services has never been a serious option, seeking to shape its use to ethical and human ends has been the hallmark of work in this area. Ethical perspectives have been central for organisations like ENITH, in the aims of HUSITA conferences, in the earlier literature and in the individual country reports in this book.

Confidentiality and control

For many social workers confidentiality has been a profound concern with the creation of client databases and exchanging data between agencies seen as a threat to client interests. That there are substantial threats is certain given the extent to which links between databases are being established and information disseminated. This is not just between agencies at a local level, but also between local, regional and national levels of organisations. However the promise or possibility of more effective services, with changes that are in the genuine interests of clients, makes the debate a complex one. Traditional paper based systems were often ineffective at maintaining confidentiality, which is further undermined through requirements for inter-agency liaison in child protection, mental illness and other areas of work. There are also benefits of computer records, through data protection laws which initiated 'open access' policies giving clients rights to see what is recorded about them. Open access restrains the use of prejudicial and discriminatory secretive comments in records that can be devastating for the interests of the clients involved.

Given these factors it is perhaps not surprising that social workers have often accepted the threat of loss of confidentiality, or at least felt powerless to oppose large scale new systems that are based on national policies as much as on local agency policies. Data protection legislation and procedures offer safeguards such as password protection, data encryption (coding) and 'audit trails' that show who has looked at a record. However, without effectively enforced data security policies, the safeguards can be more apparent than real with sloppy password procedures and audit trails that are inadequate or not checked. Another dimension to the confidentiality debate is the need for researchers to access confidential records in order to carry out much needed research into patterns of social problems and the effectiveness of social policy and social work intervention. The extent to which this is a problem depends on the rigour of data protection policies with some countries allowing access to most of the record but not to 'identifiers'. The issues around confidentiality are examined in detail by Glastonbury and LaMendola (1993) who argue for a 'Bill of Rights for the Information Age' and the concept of data ownership by the data subject.

As with confidentiality, the arguments for increased control through technology over the work of practitioners is an incremental one based on individually rational steps of increasing accountability and effectiveness. The cumulative effect however may be erosion of individual autonomy and professional judgement through political changes that are assisted by technology rather than its inevitable consequence. We have used technology to empower policy makers and managers rather than professionals or clients. With loss of autonomy may come de-skilling or sifting processes that mean that most clients are dealt with by less qualified but more generic front line workers, with qualified social workers playing a more consultative role for 'difficult cases'.

Unemployment

The extent to which the rise of IT contributes or will contribute to increasing unemployment remains uncertain in human service organisations, complicated by financial cuts and external reviews of functioning. The picture includes establishment of new computer support posts and new information and statistical departments which may use existing staff acquiring new skills. Expansion in these areas may be accompanied by erosion of clerical staff posts or threats to their job security. There are also indications of middle management posts rather than front line worker posts being most under threat from the information provided and decision making ability of computers. We not yet have seen wholesale job losses through technology as in banking and other sectors, often disguised as recession related. However continuing pressures for greater efficiency of service provision make unemployment of enduring concern.

Moving on to the issue of discrimination, one benefit of the use of computer assessment and provision of services to clients is that in many areas computers are less able or likely to directly discriminate. For example on grounds of colour, age, gender and many aspects of disability. These are gains not lightly to be dismissed and in the area of disability, a computer with associated 'assistive devices' can enable some people to compete in a dramatically improved fashion. However there may be indirect discrimination related to culture or gender as well as direct discrimination relating to access to the technology, poverty, skills, knowledge and ability. What is required is a continuing sensitivity and awareness to the issues. The question of disability, which was highlighted above, is addressed as a sub section in the next part of our framework.

INFORMATION FOR CITIZENS

Information for citizens has to do with how countries use technology to provide social information through different media to their citizens, both in their normal day to day lives, and as recipients or providers of personal or fiscal welfare services. We are concerned with a wide range of types of information and means that range from teletext; public service broadcasting; services such as Minitel in France; the Internet, provision of information on CD-ROMs and CD-i; to 'information pillars' in streets, libraries and other public buildings. A common development is 'one stop' information services that inform people on welfare and financial assistance and provide direct access to a range of welfare services. These sources may include information on cultural and tourist amenities, local political and governmental proceedings, library information, welfare services and job and training opportunities. Commercial enterprises such as 'cybercafes' have sprung up where users can pay to access the

Internet, other electronic services or games. The issues raised are addressed under headings of 'Individual and Community Support', 'Employment and Training', and 'Independent Living'.

Individual and community support

In examining IT for 'citizen information' we are dealing with a complex and shifting scenario not only about differential provision between and within countries. A useful starting point is to examine the concept of 'information needs', which are pivotal in the evolution of information strategies. Within social work agencies, needs can be identified as the information needed for particular decision making and to undertake defined tasks. Thus needs vary according to people's level and role in an agency. In academic settings the focus is not just on needs but on generation and transmission of information and knowledge ('higher level information') as a 'core business' of the organisation. Information is not a just a means to other ends, it is the currency of daily life - a major 'product'.

For citizens we can identify information needs for 'tasks' such as obtaining work, travel by public transport or use of health and welfare services. Citizens also need education and information to participate fully in a democratic society and its culture. As in universities, information and knowledge is of value for its own sake, but without the limits of academic disciplines and frameworks. As the needs of citizens widen into social, cultural, sporting and entertainment fields, so the concept of 'information need' dissolves into the potent and important areas of desires, wishes, interests, whims and pseudo-needs mediated by advertising.

Identifying citizen needs is thus a more complex task with diverse mixes of social and commercial provision vying for attention. Traditional pragmatic compromises, such as public service broadcasting alongside regulated commercial channels come under threat as funding cuts prevent the former from competing effectively. Commercial services become global, powerful and committed to maximising revenue at the expense of standards. However the forces of internationalism and deregulation can lead to different and potentially beneficial outcomes as shown through the rise of the Internet.

The period of 1994-96 has been dominated by the phenomenal growth of the Internet as the carrier and of the World Wide Web (WWW) as its shop window. They have revolutionised the ability of users to share and access information across national and organisational boundaries. This unprecedented change has wide ranging consequences and a future which remains speculative and unknown. Key tensions within the WWW will shape its future, relating to its economic basis, capacity, freedom of access, content and issues of control. For many academics use of the WWW is free and the concept of free, easy access to world wide information is a potent emblem of an ideal and attainable future. Can we hope for access to a new generation of multi-layered information superhighways regarded as a fundamental right, financed through rational self-interest of governments and business, as freely available as language itself and regarded as essential to civilised life as clean air and water supplies? The threat to this vision is not just primarily from rationing through charging, but of commercialisation so that the Internet is destroyed by advertising, 'junk mail' and narrow protectionism of government and commercial interests.

If the Internet is the revolution of the last half-decade, then perhaps television is next. It is the potential fusion of television, CD-i, computer, telephone and networking technologies that presents new opportunities and uncertainties. The defining factors are not primarily technological but about commercial power, opportunism and consumer preferences. The commercial stakes are huge and competition to define standards intense, but at the core is the extent to which television is redefined as an interactive rather than as a passive medium. If television can make that leap of popular imagination then the prospects for a genuine information revolution for all citizens are transformed. However commerce, like power, always corrupts and the social cohesion that television offers through shared viewing experiences is a factor inhibiting change.

Regardless of such opportunities, the concept of information services for citizens at low or zero cost is increasingly accepted. Existing provision is patchy, diverse in content, lacks uniformity in how systems are used and with an overall lack of coherence and integration. In consequence many services are under used to the point of not being viable. For those with Internet access, finding out about events on the far side of the world may be easier than in their own community. It is not enough for information to be available, the challenge is how to encourage people to use it as widely as possible so citizens are not polarised into insiders and outsiders.

Employment and training

Earlier reference has been made to information about jobs and training opportunities in community information systems. The wider subject of the role of technology in provision of vocational education and training for the human services is covered later in this chapter, but what we can note is the steady increase in the availability of on-line information about job and training vacancies. This includes the availability of information on the World Wide Web about vacancies, which of course has an important equal opportunities dimension in that only those with access to the Web learn about opportunities.

At a local level different patterns are emerging with information commonly available in unemployment centres but also in public libraries and the like. Individual country reports show these and other variations in action. As well as information about job vacancies, software is available for assessing people's skills and interests to match them to particular vacancies or to provide vocational or training guidance. This can take the form of PC stand alone packages for vocational guidance or use of expert systems to manage the needs of unemployed claimants, such as described byHančlová (1996) in the Czech Republic.

Independent living

The role of information technology in enhancing the capacity of people with physical or mental disabilities to live fuller lives and contribute economically to society is characterised by dramatic and profound individual positive instances but also by wide disparity in the level of progress and achievement. The individual examples include people whose lives have been transformed by technology so that even very minimal bodily movement has been the route to communication, to increasing control of their personal environment and to greater economic and other independence.

The extent to which the potential of technology is fulfilled depends on two critical factors. The first is whether the rights of people with disabilites to participate fully in social life are acknowledged and established. This framework that determines whether access to technology aids are on a 'grace and favour' basis, often mediated through charity. The alternative is the right for all people with disabilities to an assessment of the extent to which technology can assist them in achieving independence and provision, within available resources, of that technology. Such rights to an assessment are coupled with rights of access to public facilities and legal responsibilities on those who provide public services to cater for the needs of people with disabilities.

The second critical factor is the level of available economic resources. The application of technology in a society such as India (Vargese, 1996) is very different from the sort of issues addressed in Germany or in North America. While the appropriate level of technology may vary, the basic principle that technology can enhance the quality of life of citizens in different countries remains constant. Much of the endeavour involved is about equipping people with disabilities to take their place in the workplace alongside the 'temporarily abled'. However people with disabilties may be identified as 'ideal' candidates for home working for transport reasons and non-duplication of expensive technological resources and other facilities. However this plays all too easily into them remaining socially isolated and as a hidden social problem rather than becoming an integral part of part of our work and social environment. Coupled with this is a narrowness of perception of suitable jobs for people with disabilites. Computer programming and data processing are high on the list rather than competing on equal terms for the widest possible range of career options.

VOCATIONAL EDUCATION AND TRAINING

The changing face of social work education

Social work education and training has long been the subject of debate as to whether it is an art, a science; a body of knowledge, or a set of skills to be learnt and practised (Schön, 1991). The patterns of social work education and training mirror this debate. It is possible to become a qualified social worker either within an academic setting or, as in the UK, whilst in practice linked to part time education and training, possibly using open or distance learning.

The implementation of 'community care' in the US and the UK places greater emphasis on delivering 'a complex network of services and supports which enable people with needs or with a loss of independent functioning to continue to live in their own homes' (Orme and Glastonbury, 1993). This lessening reliance on residential care and the growth of community care type policies has and will continue to require a change in the curricula of social work schools but has also meant an expansion and focus on the education and training of unqualified or less qualified social workers and 'care' workers. The plethora of qualifying routes has resulted in the term 'social worker' being applied to a diversity of care workers. In this section we look at the place and impact of IT in the less than clear cut arena that is social work education and training. But first a detour to set the context of what is happening in higher education in terms of teaching methodologies and the study of how students learn.

Higher education teaching and learning

Recurrent features of higher education in the 1990s are the increasing numbers of people wishing to enter higher education and the decreasing level of resources per student. This combination of features has been a strong motivator for higher education to increase student numbers dramatically to maintain income levels, with predictable results of overflowing campuses and pressured staff and students. Consequently managers of higher education have re-examined teaching methodologies in order to make efficiency gains without sacrificing quality. Meanwhile educationalists have questioned the quality of the learning experience, looking at what makes for an effective learning environment.

> *The tradition of pedagogy that stretches back to Dewey's rejection of the classical tradition of passing on knowledge in the form of unchangeable ideas, has always argued for the active engagement of the learner in the formation of their ideas. More recent exponents of the latter tradition are Vygotsky, Piaget, Bruner, all of whom argue for the active engagement of the learner rather than the passive reception of given knowledge. These psychologists have had an effect in schools, but in universities, with their continued reliance on lectures and textbooks, the classical tradition of imparting knowledge still flourishes.*
> (Laurillard, 1993, p.15)

Laurillard advocates what she calls a principled teaching strategy. This is constituted as a dialogue between teacher and student which is characterised as being discursive, adaptive, instructive and reflective. Laurillard sees most of these characteristics being provided through the teaching methods of lectures, reading for acquisition, exercises and problems for practice, seminars and tutorials, through discussion, through discovery and practicals. In social work education teachers will and do incorporate different teaching methods often under the most difficult of circumstances: for example providing groupwork experience in a lecture theatre for over a hundred students at a time. In many ways Laurillard's remarks are more appropriate to disciplines other than social work yet the lecture still remains a core component of a social work teaching strategy and becomes more central as the numbers of students grow and the physical space more cramped. Yet the lecture is neither interactive nor adaptive and does not encourage reflection by the student. 'For the individual learner, the lecture is a grossly inefficient way of engaging with academic knowledge. For the institution it is very convenient, and so it survives' (Laurillard, p109).

But as educationalists debate how students learn, the funders of higher education and training have forged ahead with encouraging additional routes for delivering teaching and learning materials that address the numbers/resources problems outlined above. The largest expansion is in modularisation of the curricula and the development of 'open' and 'distance' teaching. The Open University in the UK pioneered this approach and their methods have been tried and tested in several countries. The Open University has gained the advantage that all its courses were originally developed in modular open learning form and its staff were recruited with this particular expertise in mind. Higher education is attempting to make the transition whilst teaching its current courses. Lecturers are often reluctant to take on external teaching materials because of the prevalence of the 'not invented here syndrome' which is rife in universities where each lecturer has a strong sense of autonomy. Yet not every good lecturer makes a good content author for open and distance learning methods or for authoring courseware (software for learning).

Incorporating information technology into higher education

Linked to open and distance learning, yet always distinct from them, is the commitment in higher education to incorporating the newest information technologies. Since the teaching machines of the 1960s, there have been individual enthusiasts who have envisaged computer technology making a valuable contribution to student learning. Despite numerous experiments and isolated success stories the promised potential was never quite delivered. The promises are now bigger, the experiments more wide ranging and yet the holy grail still seems to be just around the corner. Through national development and research initiatives for example in the UK, the Netherlands and Sweden, the reasons why the promises have not yet been fulfilled are better understood.

As noted above educational technology is not new, audio-visual technology teaching aids such as the overhead projector or the video player are now integral to many courses. They pose no threat to existing teaching methods, the teacher is in control, the same physical spaces can be used. The same cannot be said of the current swathe of educational technologies such as multi-media courseware, simulations, virtual reality, video-conferencing and use of the Internet for teaching. They require fundamental rethinking of the nature of higher education, the role of teachers and students, the physical environment and ownership of intellectual property.

> *Higher education needs to undergo a radical change in its structure and values. Institutions of higher education have often adopted what Hammond and Trapp (1992) call a 'minimalist approach' when implementing new technology and subsequently, rather than reevaluating or restructuring practices and procedures, educational managers have tended to simply place such technology over existing organisational structures.*
>
> (Henry and Rafferty, 1995, p.74)

Even after the high development costs of courseware have been met (few have been able to make it commercially viable) and copyright problems have been sorted out, there are a range of challenges for the successful implementation of educational technology. Apart from the 'not invented here syndrome' noted earlier, there are institutional infrastructure issues such as:

- The cost of providing enough up to date computers for students. In the UK the Nelson report recommended a target of one computer per five students by 1990 and the McDonough report recommended one computer per four students; few institutions are anywhere near reaching these targets (Reid, 1994). This ignores the need for students to have access to computers at home. Although home ownership of computers is rapidly rising it is still easy to disadvantage students who do not live on campus.
- The need for a physically different learning and teaching environment. Most computer rooms have serried ranks of computers designed for individual work but not for teaching, discussion or pair and group work. The question can now be asked 'why have large buildings when interactive learning can happen anywhere, at any time through the use of courseware and the Internet?'.
- Adequate and 'just in time' technical advice and support for teachers and students needs to be in place.
- Facilitative change agents need to be active in each department, faculty and institution.
- Teaching staff are currently a major challenge/barrier to the take up of educational technology solutions. Implementing technology based teaching requires teachers to rethink their methods, learn new skills and deal with the challenges above. There are few incentives or rewards to encourage teachers to undertake this formidable task. The rewards are much clearer if the time is rather spent on obtaining research grants or writing learned papers or books.
- Research as to the effectiveness of educational technology is still sketchy and as 'the new kid on the block' it has to prove itself more thoroughly than ever applied to lectures or seminars.

- The piecemeal approach to courseware development and implementation means there is a lack of integration into the curriculum and this results in marginalisation of this approach.

Reid (1994) outlines three modes of use of courseware similar to explanations of the use of computers in industry. In the first 'computers were used to do faster and more accurately the things we were already doing....'. In the second, ovelapping mode 'we started to realise more of the potential of the computer. In this mode we use computers to change how we do things, to change our methods of solving problems'. In the third mode 'computers enable us to change what we do, to allow questions to be asked which we could not even think of asking before'. Reid places higher education in the second mode with the third mode just beginning to emerge. It is clear within the first and second modes how computers can replace and enhance the teaching of established knowledge, hard facts, number manipulation. It is less clear how computers can support teaching and learning 'in a domain where knowledge is uncertain and conflicting principles often apply' (Flynn, 1986). Expert systems, knowledge based systems and artificial intelligence were seen as the way forward for dealing with 'soft' knowledge. However it is becoming clearer that we can develop useful educational technology applications that do not require the high technical expertise implicit in such systems. Reid (1994, p9) considers that computer based education will have a greater impact, and developments be more radical, in the humanities than the sciences: 'although both fields are concerned about teaching both facts and how to think critically, the latter is of greater concern to the humanities. Furthermore the third more radical or revolutionary impact of the computer is primarily to do with the social impact, the consequence for human systems, and so will more quickly be perceived and exploited by the humanities'. The same argument can be made for the discipline of social work but it will take creativity, persistence and money to achieve it well.

Revolution or evolution

So with all the difficulties why bother advocating the expansion of educational technology within social work education and training? In attempting to answer this question, a clear distinction needs to be made between teaching and learning the social work curricula **using** educational technology, and teaching and learning **about** the use of information technology in social work practice. Much of the writing on this subject in the social work technology literature has focused on the latter - what do students need to know to make them computer literate and how do we prepare students for practice in an information intensive industry which is fast expanding its use of IT. This less contentious area, not in terms of what should be taught, but that it needs to be taught, is discussed first. In 1986 DiLionardi wrote: 'Few, if any, schools of social work are preparing their students to integrate and adapt even current technology, let alone the cutting edge, or to consider the value implications of the necessary implementation decisions. This is their major need for the immediate future'.

The immediate future seems an ever extending horizon. Several social work schools began in the mid-80s to teach computer literacy basics to students. However this was often unassessed and taught by staff outside the social work faculty and therefore not properly contextualised into social work. There were and are excellent courses on the use of IT in social work practice, but where staff from within the faculty taught these skills it was usually in an adjunctival way. Teaching not integrated into the main curricula and the staff were often isolated and marginalised, as was the notion of anything to do with information technology. It is not as though the staff involved were unaware of a more extensive curriculum to be taught in this subject, but besides the kinds of challenges/problems outlined earlier, there were two additional issues.

Firstly it was and still is difficult to argue that other essential elements of an already over crowded curriculum should be dropped in favour of teaching IT. Secondly, teachers often did not have access to the source materials. It is relatively simple to teach students about flat databases. It is more complex to reproduce in the computer laboratory a realistic client information system *and* to devise exercises that motivate students to examine the data with critical awareness. In the United States Hudson developed a range of tools to support this sort of teaching, notably **CASS,** but these kinds of software tools are rarely transferable to other contexts and countries. The notion of an ethical value base underlying the use of IT in social work practice is still comparatively new outside the specialist literature. Teaching of this nature is seen as a 'bolt on' activity: 'the computer will not alter the fundamentals of social work education or violate its integrity; nor need one fear that the computer will radically reshape practice. The profession and its educators are, let us hope, too wise to allow that to happen' (Reid,1994).

Well perhaps they were wise, perhaps they were not, but the computer is radically affecting practice with new issues around information sharing, information accuracy and monitoring professional practice already well to the fore (Barnes, 1993, 1993). An alternative view was also presented by Geiss and Viswanathan (1986) 'significant shifts in social work practice will influence prevailing patterns or models of social work education, and vice versa.' They also noted that the developments in practice suggest the 'need to reexamine education program focus, content, methods and practice roles, and the professional stance on issues raised' (ibid).

There has not been so much a revolution as an evolution which has taken different forms. As the importance of delivering education to more and more students has reached the top of the agenda so the infrastructure is slowly being put into place for students to access the hardware. The software has improved as the supremacy of the 'C:\ prompt' has given way to the more user friendly graphical interface. Software authoring tools allow academics without programming skills to develop useful, if limited, courseware. As more social work agencies implement technology solutions to their information needs, employers expect students to be equipped to deal with IT.

Where there are national curricula, there is an expectation that students are taught about processing information through IT. Though it cannot be taken for granted, more students enter courses with basic computer literacy skills. Teachers also acquire basic word processing skills through research and administration. Model curricula are being developed - the building blocks are in place and work is progressing.

Teaching through information technology

Resnick was optimistic that we were about to enter the third mode of use:

> *I remain convinced that the financial resources, governmental, agency and university infrastructures; technology, and innovative people are now at hand to (a) radically shift our pedagogical model from one where faculty holds forth to a group of students; to one where they become more facilitators and integrators of information than information givers, and to (b) begin to change our field by adding to it electronic tools that have the capability to enhance our clinical, administrative and case management practice.* (1993, p384)

In 1994 this section would have focused on the use of courseware for teaching the main curricula subjects of social work education such as legislation and welfare benefits. The situation has changed and the agent for change, as is common with new technologies, has come from an unexpected quarter. It is not higher education management injunctions on efficiency that will succeed in shifting modes of teaching into new models, though they have been responsible for ensuring the infrastructure is in place, but it may well be the Internet. It is likely that the 'net' will change the world of education and training in ways that we can only start to imagine. The phenomenal rise in popularity of this invisible net is addressed elsewhere in this book. Here the emphasis is on the impact of the information technologies on teaching and learning social work. Specifically we are concerned with the Internet, computer assisted learning and information communication technologies (ICT).

The Internet and information communication technologies

There are no known surveys of social work educators with access to electronic mail but the numbers worldwide in 1996 must be in the thousands - a dramatic change from only a few years ago. Increasingly teachers and students have links to the 'net' and can send and receive electronic mail, join discussion lists and bulletin boards, and use browsers like **Netscape** to access the World Wide Web. They can reach information and join debates on a scale that was impossible even a year earlier. It is not just that the technology has changed so dramatically, though once set up it is much less daunting to use, but also change in the awareness and ability of teachers and students.

In 1994 the most interesting discussion groups were on commercial lists such as CompuServe which were not easily accessible. Those who could 'surfed the net' but found little of immediate relevance. As academic 'techies' discovered the pleasures and pains of HTML (Hypertext Mark Up Language), so a social work presence grew on the WWW and those venturing into the surf for the first time found easy to use and navigable ways of finding information that was of instant use in their teaching and research. These skills are now being discovered by students with introductory courses on IT now including an extra module on using the Internet. The path is now ready for imaginative and innovative ways of using the 'net' to support the learning process.

Meanwhile outside academia practitioners are going 'on-line'. Some agencies have had internal networks for some time but concerns around confidentiality and potential abuse of external links have made them cautious about joining the virtual world. This is changing as the advantages begin to outweigh the disadvantages and with progress in building secure systems (firewalls). Transparency in communication between academics and practitioners is an important development and opens up opportunities to bring theory and practice into closer alignment, for example for practice placements. Social work education is a partnership between academia and practice with students commonly spending up to 50% of courses on agency placements. Administering placements is often tricky as is managing communication between tutor, student and placement supervisor. Tutors may keep in touch through placement visits.

There are now a range of technologies which might help with these tasks. Electronic mail enables placements to be set up more speedily and tele and video-conferencing supports three way placement tutorials. The WWW would enable databases of placement opportunities to be visible to all regardless of geographical location. Lastly but by no means least, shortage of suitable placements could be ameliorated with the development of 'virtual' agency worlds. A student could explore and respond to cases, contact other support services and practise skills and knowledge without being let loose on real people. There are already examples of electronic mail and tele and video-conferencing support being used and placement databases exist - though not yet on the Web. The simulated agency has yet to be developed.

Computer Assisted Learning (CAL)

CAL often equates to courseware - which is usually defined as software for teaching and learning. This implies a packaged module of materials targeted at a particular curriculum area. Software for teaching and learning is much wider than this definition and below are some ways in which software is being used:

- delivering course timetables and assignments
- searching libraries on-line
- searching bibliographic databases on-line
- maintaining contact between tutor and students and between students

- exploring global information sources
- accessing legislation and policies
- supporting teaching the use of technology in practice
- supporting teaching the social work curricula
- learning from home or the office.

Courseware has not vanished because of the Internet, software for teaching and learning, particularly in the UK and the US has gradually increased. Standard interfaces for the Internet and for courseware means more consistent design and functionality, enabling students to be familiar with the technology and to get to grips with content. However there are problems. Schoech notes in the USA chapter that computer assisted learning 'has not seen the growth that many anticipated'. He cites inhibiting factors of higher specification hardware capacity in terms of sound, video and graphic resolutions than yet available in most computer laboratories and that there are currently few rewards for producing CAL. Schoech links this issue with distance learning and the questions that still surround this form of teaching.

In the UK multi-media courseware is given a high profile by the Higher Education Funding Councils who have invested £35 million in developing courseware across disciplines. Schoech's experience is reflected in the UK courseware developments for social work by the two main producers of courseware, SSRADU and ProCare. Both use Windows authoring tools but have not yet incorporated video or sound in order to avoid the higher specification hardware required. Another problem bedevilling the use of computers in higher education is cross platform compatibility. Software developed for the Apple Macintosh will not run on a PC and, without using an adapted Macintosh PowerPC, vice versa. Promises of each system being able to run each other's software have not materialised.

The CD-ROM is becoming the main delivery vehicle for courseware, partly because it is a protected medium that is difficult and expensive to copy but mainly through its capacity for storing vast quantities of text, graphics, sound or video. Yet CD-ROM is a closed media, you cannot add material to it, make links or write to it. As the Internet grows, specifically the WWW, cross platform compatibility and storage space become less of a problem. Materials mounted on a server, possibly using the HTML language, can be accessed whatever the system, as long as it is capable of running one of the WWW browsers.

Current debates on CAL focus on issues of implementation, learning effectiveness, types of interactivity, assessment and monitoring. They are in effect attempting to resolve challenges described earlier which apply to all methods of teaching and learning but which are crucially pinpointed within this medium. Courseware running on an institutional network is capable of a certain amount of interactivity, students can respond to questions, undertake exercises, take different routes through software, be advised of knowledge areas to revisit, discuss with other students. Teachers can monitor progress, provide on line tutorials and support. Gradually, as the use of the

WWW expands, this type of interactivity is mirrored on the web. Once this is in place it could transform learning. Why not take child protection learning from a local server and mental health study from an acknowledged expert in the US. Does it matter if you are a full time student attending a physical university environment, or a practitioner dipping into an updating course from the office or home? Nelson (1994) referring to his Project Xanadu argues: 'What we need is unbounded on-line media with compatible connections - for scholarship, controversy, anthologizing and understanding, the reworking of ideas and freedom. We need interconnection without boundaries and the ability to re-use in new contexts'.

Last but not least in this section an area debated less hotly is that of equity. Henry and Rafferty (1995) set out an agenda of action needed to ensure teaching and learning with technology does not leave many disenfranchised. They describe a process of 'equality proofing' to ensure that the implementation of innovations do not work to the detriment, intentionally, or unintentionally, of particular groups of people, or reinforce existing inequalities.

PROVISION OF SERVICES

From the first meeting between human services and information technology, now several decades ago, it has been a challenge to develop applications that not only supported service provision administratively, but also made professional activities more efficient and effective. Great expectations were raised in the early days with experiments such as ELIZA, a 'therapeutic' expert system, often quoted. ELIZA was developed in the early sixties to demonstrate the possibility of a computer conversing with humans in natural language. It raised the prospect and threat of replacing social workers and human interaction with computer therapy. Perhaps fortunately, there is a great distance between dreams and realities. Even today only a fragment of the aspirations and promises have been fulfilled. Conversely, innovations have occurred in areas never anticipated. At a more modest level, important applications have been developed and integrated into service provision processes. We can usefully distinguish between professional practice, information systems, managing services and finally using IT for social care policy. Historically however, applications emerged in a different order.

Professional practice

At the professional practice level, human services provision follows the sequence of assessment, care matching, care provision and evaluation. Each stage requires specific information, which means that use of IT varies with these needs. Assessment is the process of determining the nature and cause of a problem as well as the people and situations involved - the equivalent to diagnosis in medical care. While always the main activity during a first encounter between a professional and a client, assessment may be refined at any stage of service provision. Mattaini and Kirk (1991) describe different forms of assessment in social work, distinguishing between traditional, dimensional and contextual methods. Traditional methods involve gathering information and focusing on personal and social factors. Social casework stresses the importance of gathering information, making inferences and outlining a treatment plan. It uses techniques of semi-structured interviews with information on a nominal scale. The result of an assessment may be reduced to a label or a category from a classification scheme, either home devised or an established one within human services.

Computers may occasionally conduct assessment interviews. The main benefit proclaimed is not so much increased efficiency as that clients may be more candid and reliable when 'talking' to a computer than a person (Bloom, 1992; Nurius, 1990). Also, computers are more consistent than human interviewers and do not forget items. Many clients seem more motivated in computer interviews, partly because they see the computer as more earnest, more reliable and less judgemental. In one experiment, the language of the computer interview was varied from 'technical' to more 'humane'. Client feedback on the interview styles showed that the former yielded more honesty (Ferriter, 1993). At present, computer interviewing tends to be limited to structured interviews and questions with 'closed' answers. Developments using natural language may move computer interviewing beyond the current experimental state.

Dimensional approaches to assessment involve more structure and use scale techniques - item-based questionnaires that produce measurement scores. Results are shown not as a single category, but on one or more continua. Use of psychometrics is well established in psychology and psychiatry, but rather limited in social work. However there are substantial pressures from social policy makers on human services to increase the 'measurability' of different aspects of care provision. Rapid assessment scales have been developed to limit the time-taken by lengthy questionnaires. These typically involve no more than fifty items and can be completed quickly. As dimensional scales are more structured, they are easier to computerise. A good example is **Clinical Measurement Package** (CMP), from Walter Hudson (1996), with some twenty rapid assessment scales for completion on screen or on paper. The advantages of using software for this form of assessment are in more efficient collection and analysis of data and the ease of graphical presentation of repeat scores to chart client progress. Given social policy pressures that strongly favour measurement and use of scaling techniques, this type of software is likely to become more widespread.

Apart from traditional and dimensional approaches to assessment, Mattaini and Kirk (ibid) distinguish contextual approaches. These take into account the complexity of social or personal problems and seek to assess the interaction of multiple factors affecting a client's situation. For example ecosystem perspectives where the computer graphically displays data in the form of genograms and ecomaps to explore family relationships. These approaches also open possibilities of using expert systems which go beyond assessment and link to care matching. An important threshold in significant introduction of computers into assessment has been social workers' fears about reactions of clients towards the technology. Interaction shifts from client-professional to expand to client-professional-computer. However empirical evidence suggests that client acceptance of computers may be greater than professionals' acceptance.

While assessment provides the professional with information on the client's situation and problem, care matching links needs to care provision. This requires information not only on needs but also on possible services and their efficiency and effectiveness. Above all, information on these aspects must be combined and decisions made. Computer applications in this area are therefore labelled *decision support systems* (DSS) or *expert systems*. Most are based on knowledge elicited from experienced human service professionals and cemented into 'if-then' rules. The computer applies these rules and case information using artificial intelligence.

Although DSS attracted attention and research and development investment, few applications are used on a daily base outside the development site. Most development projects are technology-pushed, rather than application oriented. Those that succeeded are mainly oriented towards administrative and legal issues, such as eligibility assessment. There are a multitude of reasons and explanations why expert systems have not turned out to be a magic remedy. The first focuses on rules. Expert systems are rule based, hence working best in domains for which decision rules can be made explicit, however complex they might be. Most aspects of human service provision have been labelled as ill-structured domains - 'Practice in the human services or in any domain which is essentially ill-structured can never have an internally consistent rule-set in which correspondence between input-process-output has precise relationships' (Ravetz, 1996).

Not everyone might agree, but it provides a plausible explanation for problems of viable rule based expert systems. It also provides grounds for a different type of case-based DSS. A case-based system allows professionals to enter a case description in natural language and receive a series of 'most similar cases' including information on interventions used and outcomes. This data helps professionals to select appropriate interventions while retaining professional autonomy. Case-based reasoning is used in the **CASUS** system in the Netherlands and in work by Roy Carlson in Canada.

There is however a second explanation possible for the failure of rule-based expert systems. Rules may exist and be applied in daily practice, but be difficult to elicit. Although advances in design tools for expert systems are dramatic, eliciting knowledge remains problematic, invariably described as a 'bottleneck' (Benbenishty, 1992). Different techniques are available to elicit knowledge and experience, but are cumbersome and time-consuming. New technologies may however eliminate this bottleneck by bypassing it. Research and development on neural networks are gradually maturing this technology beyond the boundaries of laboratories (Steyaert, 1994). Neural networks can be used as the core of expert systems. They do not need to be constructed from rules, rather having the capacity to learn and build expertise from a library of cases. The quality of the data cases included is of course crucial. While neural networks are used in pattern recognition, their first significant application in human services has still to emerge.

There is another important, though technically less challenging, use of IT. As professionals need information on different forms of intervention, they can draw on their own or other's experience as well as on literature. Practitioner attitudes towards publications are ambiguous (as are author attitudes towards practice). However there are automated indexing and abstracting services such as **Social Work Abstracts** in the USA and **CareData**[2] in the UK. CD-ROMs bring the results of research and publication, if not the literature itself, closer to scholars and daily practice. More professionals can now use keyword searches to find short abstracts and assess the highlights.

Some information tools focus on specific areas of expertise such as the **Child Care Information System** (CCIS) developed by SSRADU (see UK chapter). CCIS focuses on research and legislation on child abuse and neglect. It enables practitioners to find information (references, abstracts and highlighted findings) in a variety of ways, including keywords or using a case template. We can now also see information on certain problem areas or interventions becoming available through the Internet and World Wide Web. Such developments increase the importance of assessing the quality of service provision and choosing the criteria for selecting interventions. Popularity or accessibility of information has to be a less important criterion than proven effectiveness.

Once a client's situation has been assessed and the most promising interventions selected, the process moves on to care provision. Involvement of computers in this stage of the care process has always been regarded with great fear. Experience of two decades of computer use in human services suggests that computers are unlikely to replace human care providers. What they can and will do is offer support in carrying out their professional tasks in a plethora of ways. Simple ways include directories of social agencies 'maps', or electronic information and referral systems that provide client and service provider with detailed information on care agencies and treatment packages. They come as easy to use yellow pages like **SokaFlits** or with intelligent interfaces that guide users to the right information, such as **DITO** (see Belgian chapter for both).

Another common example of computers supporting service provision are welfare benefit calculation systems (Dawson et al, 1990). Electronic advice systems are invaluable as social policy targets benefits more precisely. This leads to complex regulations and more errors and non-take up (see Glennerster, 1996; Morgan, 1996). The systems come in two varieties. Most assess eligibility for a particular welfare benefit and calculate how much a client would be entitled to under certain conditions. This type of system is highly useful, but presupposes knowledge of benefits to which one may to be entitled - ignorance of which is a main reason for non-take up. The second variety cover a wide range of benefits and assess likely eligibility. They not only calculate, but also advise and act as a guide through the benefits legislation. Good examples are **Ferret Maximiser** or **Lisson Grove** (see UK chapter). For a debate on the impact of welfare benefit calculation systems on non-take up of social security, see Morgan and van Oorschot (1996). Closely related are debt counselling programs which apply spreadsheets technology for data entry and management on incomes and expenses of individual clients or families.

More intrusive is provision of therapy by computers in clinical settings. It has often been a dream of developers that rarely went beyond wishful thinking or interesting experiment. The *New Scientist* reported on a computer program that relieved clients from light depression more effectively, both short and long term, than a human therapist. There are several programs that focus on learning and changing client behaviour for example in the area of alcohol and drug misuse, driving and sex education.

Once care has been provided and problems have been addressed through cycles of assessment, care matching and care provision, the client ends his or her career at the social service agency. The care process then progresses into evaluation. One needs to evaluate not so much an act of helping a specific client, as an act of using professional knowledge and assessing its quality. Evaluation of client intervention is a core ingredient of professionalism and the development of a thorough professional knowledge base. In most human services, case studies and supervision have been the main tools for communication and development of professional knowledge, but information technology offers new opportunities. The most obvious is statistical analysis of databases of clients, interventions and outcomes. The introduction of information technology has vastly increased the data available for secondary analysis and put the computational power needed within reach of small organisations and even individuals. Fortunately, computers not only facilitated statistical analyses, but have also brought qualitative research some of its deserved respect and status. Less fortunately, computers have not had a similar impact on the use statistics and the methodology of research.

Less obvious use of IT in evaluating human services includes electronic completion of questionnaires by clients as in the Dutch **SATER** program. The afore-mentioned CMP software also enables client-based evaluation by using single subject research. Finally, client information systems enable evaluation of service provision by statistical analysis or neural network technology, assuming that information on outcomes is part of the client file. Unfortunately, this is not often the case.

Whilst one can distinguish analytically between different stages of care provision, in reality they are highly interrelated. Not surprisingly, introduction of computers into this process has evolved from patchy applications towards systems that are more integrated. The latter do not focus on particular tasks or activities, but provide an array of information tools as well as administrative support for the professional care provider. Such systems are more complex in design and implementation and require a high level of hardware. Examples are the **GIRST** homecare project in the Netherlands, the **ADORA** general social work system in Belgium and **UCM** or **ACMS** in care management in the UK.

Information systems

Information systems gathering and processing data on clients are probably the most extensive IT application in human services. They are found in many organisations and formats and also provide the link between direct practice on the one hand and management and social care policy on the other. Information systems collect data on individual clients and process data for aggregated analysis. However obvious the application of IT in this area may seem, it is intriguing to notice how little progress has been made since the first client information systems were introduced. Literature and applications today are not significantly different from ten years ago, and the impact on professional practice is minimal. We seem unable to live up to the expectations of half a decade ago that IT would turn client information systems into some form of prospering monitoring instrument keeping close watch on the vital statistics of human services. Unfortunately, innovation is scarce and diffusion of existing experiments is problematic.

Only a few years ago, the introduction of a new paper based reporting system in a cluster of child abuse and neglect centres was welcomed because by providing carbon copy paper forms, it enabled practitioners to retain a copy for the client file. Surprisingly, Henry VIII considered this basic element when he issued an act in 1531 ordering local authorities to register names of aged, poor and important people in a bill or roll, of which one part was to remain with local authorities and the other to be used for centralised policy. Research in 1994 enables us to describe the baseline of client information systems. While the original data was from Flemish welfare agencies, the results have been validated internationally (Steyaert et al., 1995). They generate a gloomy picture.

Almost all human service agencies had some kind of client information system from individual client files to processing aggregated quantitative information. Their nature ranged from hand written loosely structured notes and tally tables to fully automated distributed databases combining structured data entry and free text. More importantly the data covered client characteristics, problem situations, interventions and assessments of outcome. Unfortunately these categories of data receive less attention, with clients details taking most of the energy and evaluation data seeming an endangered species. Analysis of data is often problematic through time delays (up to three years!) and lack of reference data. Lastly, use of information from client information systems is highly problematic, often relegated to footnotes or appendices in annual reports or used as a tool to increase funding. The term 'data-cemeteries' is apt.

These findings are not new. Ernst Burgess (1928) wrote: 'I find that many if not all of the more progressive and discerning social workers are dissatisfied with their present methods of record keeping for the purposes of social diagnosis and treatment'. Several decades later Jill Kagle (1983) reported on a social work records project: 'case recording is a long-standing problem for the profession. It is frequently a source of conflict between the direct-service worker and the manager'. A more recent article has the clear title *Data collection, are social workers reliable?* (O'Brien et al., 1992). Based on a survey among 244 social workers, the authors report the following findings: 'Three-fourths of the social workers questioned the accuracy of information recorded about clients' (p. 96) and 'social workers indicated dissatisfaction with the large amounts of perceived irrelevant information they are required to collect' (p. 97). This situation generates several problematic issues. A key concern is the reliability of data. The room for interpretation by practitioners in translating the reality into coded data is large and errors are possible. In a few experiments, fictitious case descriptions were given to practitioners and recorded results were compared. Reliability of data seemed to be related to the degree of face validity, but included several low reliability levels (Auslander and Cohen, 1996). Others compared data in client information systems with the client record, whether on paper or automated (Barnes, 1993). These showed a significant dissimilarity between client files and summary reports used for statistical analysis. Differences ranged from 0.7% for gender to 54.7% for the item 'living situation at the end of treatment'.

To our knowledge, no similar comparison has been done between client file data and client's real situations. Reliability levels would probably drop even further. Other problematic issues involve integrity (using data to mislead funders), lack of skills to use aggregated data, danger of privacy violations and the reality of symbolic use rather than substantial use. Moreover, the more data is used for symbolic purposes, the less reliability matters.

Information technology offers opportunities at three distinctive levels to alter this gloomy picture of how client information systems are used. First, statistical software can increase the efficiency and flexibility of data analysis. They can simplify and speed up data collection and analysis and improve presentation of the results, as well as enabling new forms of analysis. Earlier packages were complex and made human service organisations dependent on universities or data bureaux, but new versions with graphical user interfaces limit the dependency to statistical knowledge, rather than computer knowledge.

Secondly, computer programs were introduced to replace paper-based forms with on screen data-entry, mimicking the format of the form on screen. The practitioner no longer needs to fill out forms, but enters the same information on screen. Supplying clinical information as well as administrative information enabled the system to be used as a client database as well.

Finally, computer programs were introduced to replace complete client files with all the information those contained. These programs are more oriented towards practitioners' information needs than managerial needs. They integrate tasks such as assessment, care matching and treatment, as well as providing data for analysis.

Introduction of such programs is slowed by complex design and development issues, the high ratio of computers/practitioners required as well as fear of bureaucratisation of human service provision. However, some argue that the introduction of such systems is the only way to overcome the shortcomings previously outlined. Rami Benbenishty, author of an integrated information system for foster care, strongly argues this case: 'if you wish to harvest the fruits, you have to tend to the roots!' (Steyaert et al, 1995). Others fear that linking the future of policy or managerial information systems to those of clinical information systems is too complex. While reliability of information might improve, availability may become a bigger issue.

Managing services

It is not surprising that the use of IT has permeated furthest in management aspects of human services, for several reasons. For one, administrative and management tasks in human services largely resemble similar tasks in other sectors. Thus generic office automation products can be used for word processing, accounting and the like. Another reason is that managers control purse strings thus facilitating funding for IT in this area. Lastly, the enormous push towards accountability, efficiency and effectiveness in human services has led to more quantification and measurement. The answers to the question of what money is spent how, where, when and to what effect significantly influences future funding.

To be accountable, human services collect ever growing amounts of managerial data on their services, activities undertaken, money flows in the organisations and how staff time is spent. Management information systems are increasingly filled with useful data. Unfortunately, the data is not always used to its potential. Mintzberg (1975) has identified the myths of managers professionally floating on the waves of quantified information. His empirical study clearly indicates that managers spend nearly 80% of their time on verbal communication. Written reports hardly receive any attention and are looked at symbolically rather than substantially. According to Mintzberg, managers have a strong preference for 'soft', non-formalised information.

A humorous account, were it not for its realistic nature, of how client data finds its way into management reports is given by Rapp and Poertner (1986). They headline the basic characteristics as 'give them more', 'don't tell them how well they are doing', 'don't speak English' (to be understood as: don't use narratives), 'aggregate to the max' and 'never use graphs'. Presentation software provides opportunities to overcome the 'never use graphs' syndrome but their use in social welfare services has been minimal.

Social care policy

The use of information for social care policy has always been a difficult process. One not only has to take into account previously identified issues of reliability and privacy but also the precarious relationship between policy makers and human service organisations. The latter have always attempted to be fairly independent from policy makers and consider provision of information as a threat to their autonomy. This can be illustrated by remarks regularly made when researching the use of client information systems in social work organisations. They include : 'why does government bother?', 'If they pay, we'll do the caring', 'the government is only trying to control us by getting data on our work' and 'we are the professionals, we know how to do our business, we don't need an outsider to look over our shoulders'.

In the evolution of welfare states and the emergence of social policy, the relationship between state and human service organisations has often been shaped by the doctrine of subsidiarity. This concept, introduced by Pope Pius XI in his Quadragesima Anno in 1931, calls for a limited state influence and the organisation of state activities as close as possible to citizens. Applied to social policy, it calls for organisational, managerial and professional autonomy of the service provider. Welfare states based on subsidiarity include Ireland, Germany, the Netherlands and Belgium. The influence of such a system on information policy is substantial. Data on clients, interventions and outcomes is considered to belong to professionals and is no business of government. Government is often only supplied with enough data to legitimate subsidies. It is a situation comparable to a gas or electricity company having meters installed for billing but never asking what we do with the gas or electricity. Governments make do with annual reports on nearly always rising number of clients with no data on process or outcomes.

During the late seventies and early eighties, the welfare state went through a period of great doubt. Doubts about its effectiveness, but above all about its efficiency and the feasibility for any society to continue paying for ever growing social welfare infrastructure. These doubts led to the whole concept of the welfare state coming under close scrutiny, resulting not so much in abolishing the concept of subsidiarity as a guiding principle, but redefining its meaning and impact. Within this development, there are powerful neo-conservative influences in redefining the individual-state relation. These attempt to minimise state responsibilities for its members' welfare and place more stress on individual and family responsibility. Such influences are clearly visible in current developments in the UK and other countries, with developments such as community care and the mixed economy of welfare.

The relationship between service providers and the state is however also redefined. Rather than the service provider being the carer and the state the payer, the state is more and more looked upon as a purchaser of services, following market principles. This results in developments such as budget financing, more internal autonomy for the service provider but also considerably less external and professional autonomy. The effects of these developments on client information systems are a shift in content from client and problem data to information on interventions and outcomes, as well as greater importance in themselves as central to the existence of human service organisations. Information becomes a key ingredient of the accountability dish on the subsidies menu.

Having elaborated on the tense relation between human service organisations and government, the question remains of the extent to which data contributes to social care policy formulation. The answer remains elusive. Examples exist of data being sent to a ministry only to be dumped in cardboard boxes in obscure offices for several years. Where information is known or appears to be used, it may be only used symbolically to justify decisions taken for other reasons. Douglas Adams' novel *Dirk Gently's Holistic Detective Agency* describes a software package that starts from decisions and generates lists of arguments to support these decisions. A true decision support system. But how real are such scenarios? One can only wonder about the real impact of IT on policy. In the early sixties, use of statistics in policy processes was compared to the use of chicken entrails by shamans (Devons, 1961). Are computers the new format of chicken entrails?

Examples of IT use in social care policy is found in several of the country reports. Some are noteworthy. In Israel, the budget allocation among the over two hundred social service departments is guided by a large dataset and an automated decision support system. In Finland, care for the elderly is guided by **Evergreen** which enables policy makers to monitor and evaluate care policy, as well as simulate new or adapted care policies (Vaarama, 1996). Similar applications exist in other countries as well as more ad-hoc micro-simulations of different care policy scenarios. The availability of both powerful spreadsheet software and national statistical data in electronic format provides a platform for these applications. This increasingly also includes the use of geographical information systems to target social policy to the most needy regions of countries. However experiences with the Israeli system clearly demonstrate that technology and data alone are not enough to guarantee a smooth social policy process. If agreements on aims and models are not explicit before technology and data enter the policy process, politics become involved. A decision support system is not 'representing' an objective situation, and therefore is open to pressure of adjustment in a political/administrative process to mirror a 'reality' (Berman, 1992).

Another major trend is the development and implementation of coding and classification schemes in social welfare. For many years, client information systems were used in human services with little or no compatibility with similar systems. Diversity in the data generated comes from three sources. The first is historical diversity, data formats changed over time. Consequently data from client systems cannot be analysed over long periods. A second factor is the methodological one of organisations using different codes for the possible values of a variable. This kind of diversity is easily solved by data recoding. However the third source of diversity creates major problems. In countries with little central direction of service provision, few organisations use the same value range for the same variables. For example child protection centres may use completely different categories for recording types of abuse thus making their data incomparable.

In social welfare there are no parallels to the North American DSM psychiatric classification system or the ICD for health. However several projects to develop such a coding and classification system are emerging. Two countries have already implemented these systems - *Gemeenschappelijk Functioneel Ontwerp (GFO)* in the Netherlands and the *Standard Code and Keywords of Social Welfare* in Japan. Two other have started, the *Minimale WelzijnsGegevens* (MWG) in Belgium and the *Coding and Classification Project* in the UK. Each tries to establish uniformity in how human services record data to make data comparable at a national level. These systems mainly focus on provision of data for social policy purposes. Only one project targets clinical, professional information. This is the *PIE-project* from the American National Association of Social Workers (Karls and Wandrei, 1994). PIE is an acronym for Person In Environment. Unfortunately, with little or no international cooperation between these projects, the opportunity is missed to develop internationally comparative social welfare statistics (Steyaert et al., 1995).

Finally, we should take into account the influence that social policy has had for many years on how information and information technology is used in human services. Now however, the widespread availability of IT is beginning to influence social policy processes (Steyaert, 1996). This notion of 'business process redesign' is discussed further in the final chapter.

References

Auslander G and Cohen M. Reliability Issues in the Development of Computerised Information Systems. In: Rafferty J, Steyaert J and Colombi D (Eds.). *Human Services in the Information Age*. New York: Haworth Press. 1996.

Barnes C. Collecting Accurate Information about Child Abuse. In: Glastonbury B (Ed.). *Human Welfare and Technology*. Van Gorcum, Holland. 1993.

Benbenishty R. An Overview of Methods to Elicit and Model Expert Clinical Judgment and Decision Making. *Social Service Review,* 598-616. 1992.

Berman Y. A Decision Support System in Resource Allocation: the Political Process in Rational Decision Making. *New Technology in the Human Services* 6: 8-14. 1992.

Bloom B. Computer-assisted Psychological Intervention: A Review and Commentary. *Clinical Psychology Review,* 12: 169-197.1992.

Burgess E. What Social Case Records Should Contain to Be Useful for Sociological Interpretation. *Social Forces* 6: 524-531.1928.

Dawson P, Buckland S and Gilbert N. Expert Systems and the Public Provision of Welfare Benefit Advice. *Policy and Politics,* 18: 43-54. 1990.

Devons E. Statistics As A Basis for Policy. *Essays in Economics*. London: Allen and Unwin.1961.

DiLeonardi JW. Information Technology and Social Work Practice: A Second Look. In: *The Human Edge: Information Technology and Helping People.* p295, The Haworth Press, New York. 1986.

Ferriter M. Computer Aided Interviewing in Psychiatric Social Work. In: Leiderman M et al. (Eds.) *Technology in People Services.* New York: The Haworth Press. 1993.

Flynn M. Computer-Assisted Instruction and Experiential Learning. In: Geiss GR and Viswanathan N (|Eds.). *The Human Edge: Information Technology and Helping People*. P.295. The Haworth Press, New York. 1986.

Geiss GR and Viswanathan N (Eds.). *The Human Edge: Information Technology and Helping People*. The Haworth Press, 1986.

Glastonbury B and LaMendola W. *The Integrity of Intelligence: A Bill of Rights for the Information Age.* St Martin's Press. 1992.

Glennerster H. Future Funding Structures for Social Policy, Information Implications. In: Steyaert J (Ed.). *Information Technology and Human Services, More Than Computers?* Utrecht: NIZW. 1996.

Hammond N and Trapp A. Cal As A Trojan Horse for Educational Change: the Case of Psychology. *Computers and Education*, 19, 1/2. 1992.

Hančlová J. Unemployment in the Czech Republic and Development of an Expert System for Assessment of Unemployment Compensation. In: Rafferty, Steyaert and Colombi (Eds.). *Human Services in the Information Age*. New York: the Haworth Press. 1996

Henry MS and Rafferty J. Equality and CAL in Higher Education, *Journal of Computer Assisted Learning.* No.11. 1995.

Hudson W. Professional Practice for the 21st Century: Information Implications. In: Steyaert J (Ed.). *Information Technology and Human Services, More Than Computers?* Utrecht: NIZW. 1996.

Kagle J. The Contemporary Social Work Record. *Social Work*: 149-153. 1983.

Karls J and Wandrei K. *Person-In-Environment System, the PIE Classification System for Social Functioning Problems*. Washington: NASW. 1994.

Laurillard D. *Rethinking University Teaching.* Routledge, p.15.

Mattaini M and Kirk S. Assessing Assessment in Social Work. *Social Work* 36: 260-266. 1991.

Mintzberg H. The Profession of Manager, Myths and Facts. *Harvard Business Review.* July 1975.

Morgan G. Technology As An Under-hand Way of Supporting Clients. In: Steyaert J (Ed.). *Information Technology and Human Services, More Than Computers?* Utrecht: NIZW. 1996.

Morgan G and van Oorschot W. Do Welfare Benefit Calculation Systems Reduce Non-take Up, A Debate. *New Technology in the Human Services*, Vol. 9(1).1996.

Nelson TH. *Publishing in the Point-and-Click Universe,* Proceedings of the National Convergence Symposium. Sydney, Australia, 1994.

Nurius P. A Review of Automated Assessment. In: Reinhoel R. and Hanna T (Eds.). *Computer Literacy in Human Services.* New York: The Haworth Press. 1990.

O'Brien N, McClellan T and Alfs D. Data Collection: Are Social Workers Reliable? *Administration in Social Work,* 16: 89-99. 1992.

Orme J and Glastonbury B. *Care Management.* Basingstoke: Macmillan Press Ltd., p.188. 1993.

Rapp C. and Poertner J. The Design of Data-based Management Reports. *Computers in Human Services,* 10: 53-64. 1986.

Ravetz J. Limitations of Rule-base Measures of Professional Practice in the Human Services. In: Steyaert J (Ed.). *Information Technology and Human Services, More Than Computers?* Utrecht: NIZW. 1996.

Reid T. *Perspectives on Computers in Education: the Pomise, the Pain, the Prospect.* Active Learning No. 1, CTISS Publications, UK. 1994.

Schön D, *The Reflective Practitioner: How Professionals Think and Act.* Aldershot: Arena. 1991

Smith NJ. *Information is a Many Spendoured Thing!* CEDR, Department of Social Work Studies, University of Southampton. 1993.

Steyaert J. Soft Computing for Soft Technologies: Artificial Neural Networks and Fuzzy Set Theory for Human Services. *Computers in Human Services* 10: 55-67. 1994.

Steyaert J (Ed.). *Information Technology and Human Services, More Than Computers?* Utrecht: NIZW. 1996.

Steyaert J, Benbenishty R and Silon L. Developing Comparative Social Welfare Statistics. *EuroSocial Report.* Vienna: European Centre for Social Welfare. 1995.

Vaarama M. The Evergreen, Software for Planning Services for the Elderly. In: Rafferty J, Steyaert J and Colombi D (Eds.). *Human Services in the Information Age.* New York: the Haworth Press.1996.

Vargese J. Independence to the Blind and Handicapped in Asia Through Modern Assistive Devices. In: Rafferty, Steyaert and Colombi (Eds.). *Human Services in the Information Age.* New York: the Haworth Press.1996

Vygotsky L. Thought and Language. Cambridge, Massachusetts: MIT Press. Referenced in: Laurillard, D., *Rethinking University Teaching.* Routledge. 1993.

World Wide Web sites referred to in this chapter

1. Information Technology and Human Services: An International Perspective. Web site for this book with links to all web sites mentioned in the book.
http://www.fz.hse.nl/hsandit/

2. CareData bibliography database.
http://www.nisw.org.uk/

2 America (USA)

Dick Schoech

HUMAN SERVICES AND INFORMATION TECHNOLOGY

This chapter presents the current state of human services IT in the US. First, the human services delivery system in the US and its implications for IT developments are discussed. Next an overview of IT in selected areas is presented. Finally, the larger context and future of IT are explored. The chapter throughout is illustrated with typical, exemplary, or innovative applications. Sometimes the illustrative application was selected simply because it was familiar. An exhaustive search of relevant applications was not conducted.

To comprehend human services IT in the US requires an understanding of the US human services delivery system. However, understanding service delivery in a country as large and diverse as the US is difficult. Human services in the US are a complex patchwork of hundreds of federal, state, and local government programmes supplemented by for profit, not-for-profit, religious, and individual entrepreneurial sectors. It is not a service delivery system, but an overlapping and layering of services. Thus, community agencies often operate programmes funded buy a variety of private, church, federal, state, and local government sources as well as from agency fundraising. These programmes may not be coordinated with those from other agencies or with others within the agency. This lack of uniformity, coordination, and size have been a detriment to IT developments.

The government system

Services are often organised around Federal Government legislation and the corresponding government departments. Major Federal human service departments include the Departments of Education, Labor, Housing and Urban Development, Justice, Veterans Affairs, and Health and Human Services (DHHS). DHHS includes retirement, disability, and Medicare and Medicaid benefits. Medicare and Medicaid constitute the basic health care system for the poor and elderly in the US. Recent initiatives may move the Medicare and Medicaid responsibility and funding to individual states.

The federal government typically provides human services funds directly to states and local agencies. States may provide services directly or pass state and federal money to local service providers. State and local matching funds are typically required to receive federal funds and recipients are required to follow the federal mandates associated with funding. Some of these mandates involve collecting data about programmes. States often plan and coordinate services when passing federal funds to local service providers.

The voluntary system

The voluntary system consists of not-for-profits and religious service providing agencies that are guided by a citizen board or church. A major community fundraising entity for non-profits is the United Way. United Ways primarily fund services that in some countries are called personal social services. United Ways raise money from individuals through corporations and fund agencies based on United Ways' assessment of community needs. A United Way may fund a total agency or only a small programme of an agency.

Most United Ways maintain databases about citizen needs as well as about resources and services available in their community. Increasingly, these databases are computerised as part of the information and referral services that most United Ways provide. Fundraising is also largely computerised. However, United Ways are having difficulty combining IT with their role in the community. They typically do not have an integrated information system to support their diverse internal activities. They also have not been progressive in helping computerise the agencies they fund or networking these agencies.

Other coordinating entities at the local level are professional or interest groups. For example, most communities have Mental Health Associations and Associations for Retarded Citizens which advocate and plan for client services. These agencies typically have several small IT applications for accounting and information collection. Clients come to agencies with a multitude of problems, yet agencies are restricted by the source of their funding in the client problems they can address. As a result, most agencies are continually searching for novel ways to find the funds to provide all the services that clients need. Since human services are not comprehensive or coordinated at the community level, little community practice exists. Consequently, few community wide IT initiatives exist. Most services focus on the individual or family. This is especially true of services for individual and family dysfunction where an individual or family therapy approach dominates. The fact that the local human services are a non-system of competing agencies has relegated IT applications to agency information systems or specific applications, for example, billing or treatment planning.

The health care system

The US only has a national health system for the poor and aged. Everyone else must buy insurance through their employer, individually, or go without insurance. Since profit making companies sell most health insurance, recent approaches for managing and coordinating health care have been driven by cost containment. Without cost control efforts, unscrupulous agencies, especially for-profit providers, will deliver only services where a large profit can be made. This occurred in many states when private psychiatric hospitals were quickly established to provide services that maximise hospital profits rather than services that met individual or family need. Health care insurance companies that did not have strong cost control mechanisms quickly saw their expenditure on psychiatric coverage skyrocket.

Three cost control mechanisms in the health care field have important implications for IT. The first is the concept of a health maintenance organisation (HMO). An HMO is a health care organisation that contracts to provide all health care for individuals under its care. The concept behind an HMO is to change incentives. With a traditional fee-for-service health care system, providers make more money if more services are provided. However, an HMO makes more money when fewer services are provided. The incentive with an HMO is to minimise the use of services through prevention and cost controls. Thus, information systems are designed to track costs and minimise need. HMOs are just beginning to develop IT applications that focus on prevention.

The second important health care effort is referred to as DRGs (Diagnostic Related Groups). DRGs help classify a client's problem into diagnostic groups and then reimburses the service provider for the average cost for all clients in that diagnostic group. The DRG influence can be seen in the push towards classification, such as the DSM IV. Most software that helps manage inpatient or out-patient psychiatric services has a module that helps determine the client's DSM IV or medical classification.

The third and most recent health care effort is managed care. Managed care places a group of care managers into the system who are paid to reduce health care costs by a corporation, insurance company, or large care provider. These managers authorise services before they are performed, reducing costs by assuring that treatment received is needed and effective. Thus psychiatric management software often has a treatment plan generator that justifies and tracks client progress for each DSM IV classification.

The previous discussion presented various impacts of the human services delivery system on IT. As can be seen, due to size, complexity, and lack of a coordinated system of services, much of the basic information infrastructure for US human services has yet to be developed. The next sections will examine human services IT in several areas of major importance for this book.

INFORMATION FOR CITIZENS

Unfortunately, information technology has been underutilised to provide services and information directly to clients and to support citizen information networks. The reason can be seen in the previous discussion that pointed out that an entity is missing that is responsible for coordination, prevention, and advocating for client needs. However, the perspective of the centrality of informing the patient using technology is gaining acceptance. For example, the Behavior Healthcare Tomorrow Conference[1] will feature consumer informatics as a major theme in 1996. A discussion in several specific areas of citizen informatics follows.

Individual and community support

An area where IT has been used extensively has been in the self-help movement where BBSs and the Internet are used for self-help conferences and providing consumer information. Local BBSs, available in almost every city, offer self-help conferences on addictions, mental health, and disabilities. Network providers, such as CompuServe and America On-line, also offer self-help conferences and WWW resources[2].

Currently, several experimental projects in the health area provide information to citizens. One is the Comprehensive Health Enhancement Support System (Boberg et al., 1995). **CHESS** uses personal computers placed in users' homes and linked via modem to a central computer to provide information, referrals, decision support, and social support. Another IT project is the new town of Celebration, Florida which includes a joint venture between the Disney Development Corporation and Florida Hospital to create a 21st century health care system that will help make the town a healthier place to live partly by taking full advantage of the Internet (Bezold, 1995). Another noteworthy project, **Access Colorado**, connects every citizen of Colorado to the state libraries and to the Internet. Other initiatives involving agency and community networking have been funded by approximately $100 million awarded by the Telecommunications and Information Infrastructure Assistance Program of Department of Commerce[3]. One significant project coordinated by Tom Hanna of the Family Life Development Center at Cornell University uses various Internet tools to network over 5,000 people active in child abuse prevention[4].

Another outstanding community education project is the Playing to Win Network (**PWN**) whose founder, Antonia Stone, received the Norbert Wiener Award for Social and Professional Responsibility in 1994. Antonia opened a computer centre for the economically, socially, and geographically disadvantaged in a low income housing project in Harlem, New York. PWN seeks to establish a national community of neighbourhood technology access providers dedicated to universal technological enfranchisement. PWN now has over 45 affiliates in the US, Poland and Ireland.

Employment and training

The US suffers from the lack of an organised employment and training strategy for youth and adults. Industry is often left to provide whatever training is required once secondary education is completed. Private trade schools must rely on individual fees and government loan guarantees to provide training for youth and the unemployed. Technical training has not made extensive use of the WWW or distance learning techniques. Universities are beginning to experiment with distance learning and offering courses over the WWW. The World Lecture Hall contains links to courses using the WWW as a delivery mechanism[5]. For an example of a virtual campus, check out Diversity University[6] which hosted a virtual session of the 1995 Conference of the International Council on Distance Education.

Informal sector

Technology for advocacy has primarily centred around the management of mailing lists and fundraising. However, advocacy groups are beginning to use Internet tools such as e-mail, conferences, WWW sites, and chat sessions for mounting advocacy. An example was a National Electronic Open Meeting in May 1995 to develop an effective and efficient 'electronic government'. An interesting community IT project, developed at Case Western Reserve University in Cleveland OH, is **CAN DO** (Chow and Coulton, 1994). CAN DO[7] is an electronic network that makes a comprehensive databank on Cleveland neighbourhoods and surrounding suburban areas available to non-profit and government agencies. The databank contains over 10 years of detailed information on population; land and housing; health, education and social well-being; economic indicators; and organisations. The developers of CAN DO are currently exploring the power of geographic information systems (GIS) for displaying their data and performing spatial analysis.

Independent living

Technology for independent living is often referred to as assistive technology. The 1990 Americans for Disabilities Act requires accommodations to be made by employers and the service sector for persons with disabilities. This stimulated the movement of technology from the research laboratories to work and leisure settings. Currently, 20,000 assistive technology products are listed in the Disability and Adaptive Equipment Resource Library CD-ROM, (**ABLEDATA**[8]). One of the leading research institutions in the US is Trace R&D Center[9], University of Wisconsin. Trace is working with major hardware and software corporations in the US to make hardware and software accessible to people with disabilities. The belief behind this initiative is that very often small and inexpensive design modifications in hardware and software at the manufacturing stage can make technology much more accessible. Corporations have also found that making technology more accessible for people with disabilities makes it more usable for the average person, thus making products appeal to a wider audience.

CRERO is an organisation to help promote research in the area of rehabilitation engineering (including assistive technology, universal design and job site modification). From the CRERO web site[10], you can find information on sixteen specialty Rehabilitation Engineering Research Centers funded by the National Institute on Disability and Rehabilitation Research (NIDDR), US Department of Education. These cover such areas as house design, children, older people, lower back pain, prosthetics and orthotics, visual impairment, hearing enhancement, adaptive computers, and technology transfer.

VOCATIONAL EDUCATION AND TRAINING

Whether technology can be much more involved in imparting information, knowledge, and skills has yet to be proven, although initial research is promising (Reinoehl and Mueller, 1990; Resnick, 1995).

Integration into the curriculum

Ideally, IT would be integrated into the curriculum like other generic human service tools, for example, evaluation and interviewing. Currently, three approaches exist in US social work schools for integrating IT into the curriculum. The first and most common approach is to offer IT as an elective. The advantage is that it requires little curriculum and organisational change and is easy to implement. The disadvantage is that many students may not take the course, the IT content varies with the instructor, and content is not integrated with the rest of the curriculum. It is difficult to integrate IT into normal coursework until all students come with a certain level of IT competency or a course is offered to provide basic IT skills, thus taking several weeks of coursework away from the focus of the course.

The second approach is to require all students to take a basic ‘introduction to technology’ course. This course typically contains an introduction to generic and human services hardware, software, library technology, and networking. The advantage of having a required introduction to technology course is that all students have a basic level of IT proficiency upon which other courses can build. The disadvantages are the hardware, software, and instructional time required to teach students a new set of skills. A faculty member who is eager to teach the use of technology can quickly be turned into a computer lab manager who spends most non-teaching time keeping a lab operating and providing technical support. Also, it is difficult to sacrifice an existing educational course to make room for an IT course that some see as remedial and not human services related. Where a basic technology course is required, an advanced technology course might be offered. In the advanced course, students may conduct technology feasibility studies or program databases for school and agency projects.

The third, and less common approach, is to offer remedial work for students deficient in technology skills and to integrate technology into existing courses. An advantage is that it may be the most effective approach as technology is integrated with the other social work process that the technology supports. The disadvantage is that this approach is hard to implement, because it requires all faculty understand IT to the extent that they can integrate it into their course content.

Regardless of which approach is used, increasingly, the WWW is becoming a basic component of any technology course. Another commonly used tool in IT courses was **CASS** (Computer Assisted Social Services), a client information system that emphasises the management of client progress (Nurius and Hudson, 1993). CASS was replaced by **CMP** (Clinical Measurement Package) which focuses on client problem assessment, problem monitoring, treatment or service evaluation, quality assurance monitoring and management, and programme evaluation. A Windows version of CASS is however being developed for launch in 1996.

Educational support

Computer assisted instruction (CAL) has not seen the growth that many anticipated. One problem is that multi-media requires greater hardware capacity in terms of sound, video, and graphic resolutions than is available in most university computer labs. Another is that currently few rewards exist for producing CAL. A third problem is that substantial resources are needed to keep CAL products current with new research and new hardware and software.

Distance learning has received much more attention than CAL, but cost is still a prohibitive factor. One problem with using distance learning techniques in human service courses is that face-to-face class interaction and discussion is often seen as the essence of student learning. Instructors are fearful of the amount of learning and feedback that can be provided through distance learning, even using two-way video. The question is always asked: 'would you go to a counsellor or medical doctor who received a degree via distance learning?'. It will take time to determine what content can be effectively taught using distance learning and what is best taught in the classroom. Another issue is that distance learning requires careful course planning and different skills on the part of the instructor. A good classroom instructor may not make a good distance learning instructor.

PROVISION OF SERVICES

IT support for human services can occur at the practitioner, management and policy levels. These levels constitute artificial categories, because an information system that is primarily a management tool also might be used for practitioner or policy support.

The distinction between management support and practitioner support can be seen with information and referral software packages, such as **IRIS** (Battin, 1993). These packages are used independently by many agencies and by United Way agencies. They support the practitioner in providing I&R, but are primarily a tool for tracking and standardising the I&R process. While I&R software allows the unsophisticated I&R specialist to perform better, they are a burden to the sophisticated I&R specialist. They provide the sophisticated user little new information and require a lot more information to be formally collected.

Management is the best level at which to begin to discuss IT and personal human services, since IT for management has implications for practitioner and policy support. For a recent overview of IT applications, see Butterfield, 1995. For a list of software available for the human services check **COMPSYCH**[11], the nonprofit software index on the web[12] or the **CUSSNet** shareware/freeware/ demo Disk Copy Service [13].

Management support

Management support represents the majority of human services applications to date. One reason is that managers make decisions on what applications are developed. Managers understand their needs best and tend to meet them first. Another reason is that management information needs are more routine and easy to program than practitioner needs. Finally, management information needs are critical to agency survival, as agencies must have basic data to demonstrate progress to their funding sources.

After basic agency information systems are developed, management typically focuses on improving connectivity, for example, better internal networking and networking with other agencies. Other specialised advisory or performance support systems may also be developed, for example, systems that advise on worker safety needs or client eligibility. The experience with these advisory systems is not substantial. Often what seems as a good idea and a small development project becomes a major undertaking in terms of complexity, cost, training, and implementation.

The cost of maintenance and upgrading basic information systems is a large drain on agency resources. Many agencies have trouble keeping their current systems up-to-date with the most recent technology. They have little energy and resources to develop other systems. Large agencies especially have a problem, because replacing old technology may require total system redesign and major organisational restructuring.

Practitioner support

Practitioner support is primarily provided through agency information systems. Typically, support is in the form of helping the practitioner complete paperwork. A few agencies have experimented with decision support systems, such as those that help workers develop treatment plans. However, these systems mostly help structure a process or provide directions and advice about completing a process. Many of these decision support systems are little more than elaborate decision trees or expert coaches that insure that workers input data correctly. Most offer little support for clinical decisions. Support for clinical decisions using models or expert systems are rare (Gingerich, 1995).

Until the basic information system of an agency is developed, it is probably unrealistic to expect systems that support clinical decision making to be developed. Practitioner decision support systems (DSSs) are seen as luxuries that can be developed and supported after the basic information system is well developed. The few agencies that have developed practitioner DSSs have had difficulty using them. Two of the most researched clinical DSSs are not currently in use, even though they have proven their value (Miller, 1993; Schwab and Wilson, 1989). Miller developed a DSS that determines the best configuration of in-home support services given the agency's resources and the goal of maximising clients' stay in their home. Schwab and Wilson developed a DSS that recommended the best out of home residential placement for children.

One surprisingly lacking application is sophisticated analysis of the data currently collected by many agencies. For example, few manage care companies have sophisticated computer software that answers questions from their data such as 'what is the most effective therapy for a given DSM IV classification.' This analysis seems like a natural application, but few are using collected data to predict service outcomes. A promising technology for analysing existing case data is a neural network (Steyaert, 1994; Modai, Saban, Stoler, Valevski, and Saban, 1995), but little use has been made of neural nets to date in the human services. One notable effort to model existing data for practitioner support is the **WISDOM** project of the Texas Department of Protective and Regulatory Services. Models have been developed to predict staff burnout, staff turnover, whether an abuse/neglect case should be opened for treatment, and the priority assigned to an opened case. Other modelling efforts are planned in the future including predicting which children are at the highest risk for abuse/neglect recidivism.

Before concluding this section on practitioner support, it is important to mention the efforts of the Department of Veterans Affairs (VA)[14]. For many years, the VA has been developing and using assessment and testing software on a consistent basis.

Multi-agency and social care policy support

Social care policy support has been a neglected area for IT. Community human service information systems have been problematic due to the lack of a central agency to set up and manage the community network and the standardisation that many community networks required. Most community systems that currently exist are for exchanging client information in order to coordinate services and prevent abuse of services, such as food pantries and shelters. One problem with sharing agency information in a multi-agency information systems is data security and confidentiality. The US has few restrictions on database security and confidentiality. A BBS is often used for multi-agency networking but a BBS places a burden on the BBS operator, and they are not very secure. Multi-agency networking, however, may be changing as agencies become connected to the WWW. The Web offers the capacity for true distributed networking as every agency can set up its home page with links to other relevant agencies in the community. The WWW helps connect agencies using an existing inexpensive infrastructure and offers ways for the general public to obtain information about community agencies.

As indicated earlier, human service agencies rarely have the resources to pay for the computer expertise they need. Often the IT budget is spent on hardware and software with little remaining for training and expert consultation. One innovative project to remedy this problem is **CompuMentor**, which matches several hundred private sector volunteer mentors each year with non-profits. CompuMentor also collects used software and distributes it to non-profits. The power of this type of mentor program can be seen at **Dallas Helps**, a community coordination project. Dallas Helps received an industry volunteer who over the years has established a cooperative community information system for eighteen agencies providing substance abuse services to indigent clients. Dallas Helps assists agencies with hardware, software, maintenance, and support. At the agency level, the system provides for clinical management and billing. At the aggregate level, the system facilitates system-wide management, evaluation and planning. As the state and federal government moves into the complexities of a managed care environment for addiction services, Dallas Helps is providing the information technology and technical expertise that individual agencies need, but cannot develop on their own.

ANALYSIS OF THE CURRENT STATE IN THE US

One cannot get an adequate picture of the present just by looking at the past. Indeed, progress in human services IT has not been as revolutionary and as idealistic as many envisioned and the future will probably not be either. The big problem is that visionaries are good at seeing the potential, but not the struggle and time required to actualise the potential. While many of the visions have yet to be realised, dramatic changes have taken place in the last ten to fifteen years. Almost all agencies now have a basic computerised information system and most human service workers have access to a computer that they use for one or more human service applications. Human services IT seems to be ending one phase and entering another. One way to help envision the future phase is to look outward, that is, at the revolution occurring in non human services use of IT (Rockwell, Hardin and Loots, 1995).

The next section will present the current phase and allude to the future phase. The two phases will be discussed as if they are clearly distinct with crisp boundaries. This is useful for comparison and contrast purposes, but the reader must realise that these distinctions in phases have been exaggerated for analysis purposes.

Hardware and software

Current phase. The current phase is typified by agencies buying their first hardware and software, experimenting, and finally developing an agency wide IS. Agencies at the end of this phase are still perfecting the information system and finding better ways to incorporate computerised information into agency decision making. Practitioners in this phase have a personal computer on their desk that is key to their job. Moving from no computing through this phase has been a formidable task and continues to be for many agencies. System maintenance and enhancements and keeping technology current constitute large tasks, drain resources, and prevent thinking about the future. However, a few agencies are asking 'where do we go from here, now that our basic information systems have been developed?'. This question has yet to be answered and involves the future phase.

Future phase. In the future, existing technology will continue to support many IT tasks, but technology will be much faster and friendlier. However, a more important and fundamental change is beginning to occur, that is, the integration of telephone, television, stereo, and computers into a universal information device. This device will be as important for the information industry as the development of the model T car was for the automobile industry in the 1920s. The model T car was an integrated and inexpensive combination of mechanical technologies that allowed travel to become a basic part of business and pleasure for the average person in the US. This new device will be an integrated and inexpensive cluster of digital information technologies allowing information to be become a basic part of business and homes.

Impact on human services. Since the human services work with information almost exclusively, the impact of this inexpensive universal tool could be tremendous. Specific impacts will be discussed in the next sections.

Information forms

Current phase. Current information forms are print based (books, newspapers, magazines), picture based (television, film, video), and voice based (telephone, stereo). Currently, agencies view stored information as numbers and text because of the difficulties of storing, manipulating, and disseminating other forms. The oldest as well as today's most progressive human service information systems almost exclusively store and manipulate numbers and text. Even advanced technologies, such as expert systems and neural nets, use numbers and text combined in novel and powerful ways, for example, into rules, frames, and semantic nets. However, human services have always felt limited by systems that reduced the complexities of people's problems to records constructed of numbers and text.

Future phase. All forms of information, numbers, text, graphics, pictures, sound, animation, video, etc. are becoming digital. This means that it will be as easy to manipulate one form of information as another using IT tools. Not only can different forms of digital information be easily manipulated, old forms can be integrated into new forms, for example, multi-media. Also, new forms of information can be invented that offer great promise for the human services, for example, virtual reality.

Impact on human services. Human services have always been receptive to information in forms such as pictures, graphics, movies, and sound. If digital pictures are stored in a database with appropriate tools, much more powerful analysis can be conducted. For example, in child protective services, we could highlight a bruise on the picture of a child we are assessing using a mouse. Then, we could search the database to find pictures of children with similar bruises. New mediums also offer potential, for example, virtual reality has been used successfully to treat fear of heights (Lamson, 1995). Virtual reality could also be used to teach parenting. For example, parents could be placed inside a virtual room with a virtual child that exhibited problematic behaviours. A virtual therapist could guide and mentor as the parents improved their skills (select the fictitious futures option from the CUSSN web site[13]).

Interactivity

Current phase. Current users of information have little interactivity with the information they are examining or using. Information system outputs are printed or displayed as reports, treatment plans are developed and printed. Automated assessments yield printed outputs. Interactivity is typically possible only with an IT specialist or manager who is capable of manipulating the database. Typically, the end user perceives interactivity as something outside their purview, because simple data manipulations could take from hours to days to be requested and performed.

Future phase. Information is becoming interactive, that is, users manipulate, combine, and work with the information they are viewing. An example is the capture and use of a data field such as client address. When client address is just a text field in a database that is used on printed reports, it has limited value. However, geographic information systems allow the user to display clients addresses as points on a community map. When the user can interactively add other points to the community map, for example, income level or social service agencies, then client address becomes a more meaningful piece of information.

Impact on human services. When information users have the capacity to interactively control the information they are using, the value of information changes from that inherent to the information itself to that associated with its interactivity. An example is a treatment plan that greatly improves in utility when it changes from a periodic stand-alone report and becomes interactively integrated with agency and community information. When agency staff can visually view how treatment plans vary with other information, such as by type of diagnosis or address of the client, then the value of the treatment plan information greatly increases. An additional example is a program evaluation. When managers can visually view how selected changes in staffing patterns or workload impact program outcomes, then the program evaluation can become an important day-to-day decision making tool within the agency.

Connectivity

Current phase. Local and wide area networks (LANs and WANs), like other hardware and software, have gained in power and sophistication. Most agencies operate LANs and may be part of a WAN. Connectivity is primarily via e-mail, conferences, and file transfer. While networking inside one's agency is seen as a necessity, networking outside the agency is still seen as a luxury and personal need, not as an integral part of one's job. Connectivity technology has not changed substantially over the last ten years. For example, the 1984 Wye Plantation conference on Information Technology and Social Work Practice used the Delphi Network for e-mail and conferencing (Geiss and Viswanathan, 1986). The Delphi system was primitive, but essentially the same as today's networks. The Computer Use in Social Services Network (CUSSNet) began in 1986 with technology that is essentially the same as that used by CUSSNet today.

Future phase. The personal computer is moving from a stand-alone machine to one that is a part of the worldwide network of computers. Software will access computer programs on the Internet as simply as it accesses programs on the hard disk. This connectivity allows information to be a marketed item. This marketing of information requires an infrastructure to operate. Consequently, the infrastructure for the global village is being built. In the past people tracked down information. In the future, information will track down people. That is because less money is made by collecting information for a few to access at relatively high prices than by selling small pieces of information to millions of users at very small prices. This connectivity infrastructure will have a major impact on human services.

Impact on human services. Human services delivery is often viewed as the practitioner imparting information to the client. However, with global networking, everyone is an information producer and receiver. Clients will be able to prepare themselves for treatment by browsing local, national, and international resource sites. Those with specialised problems will be able to examine the latest statistics and research on their problem. They will also be able to examine the resources available and familiarise themselves with appropriate interventions before deciding to seek treatment. Self-help and home-bound treatment via networking will be an increasingly attractive option. Home-bound clients, such as those with agoraphobia, disabilities, and similar problems will find telecommunications to be a boon in receiving treatment and support for their problems in their homes.

While individual networking is important, the global village phenomenon will also impact the human services. Neighbourhood home pages will allow people in suburbs to experience some of the connectedness of traditional neighbourhoods.

Neighbourhood news and gossip will be exchanged via e-mail and electronic conferences. Electronic networking of neighbours will replace the face-to-face interaction that was popular when neighbours worked the same hours, attended the same social institutions, required only one breadwinner per family, and had no back yard fences. While suburbs will become more connected, people can easily become part of virtual communities anywhere in the universe (Rheingold, 1993).

Connectivity, especially the transmission of information throughout an organisation, has been flattening business bureaucracies and is beginning to do the same for government. Large government welfare bureaucracies, which have been the most difficult to automate, are beginning to feel this flattening as they develop basic information systems and networks. This flattening of the HSDS means citizens and clients will be more connected to the human service delivery system and clients, practitioners, and manager will function more as a team of equals.

Since electronic networking is creating virtual neighbourhoods, practitioners can again use the neighbourhood as part of the intervention strategy. For example, news and progress on illness and injury can be automatically posted on a neighbourhood home page as it is recorded in the hospital record. Networking provides the new tools, but the push to again involve the neighbourhood stems primarily from cost savings and philosophical reasons.

The path forward

The movement from one phase to the next calls for a paradigm shift that is difficult to make. Agencies that have successfully completed the current phase will be much more prepared to enter the future phase because they have begun many of the paradigm shifts required. The following views illustrate the paradigm shift required.

- Viewing practice as information based, that is, making day-to-day decisions about services only after examining processed information in its various forms.
- Viewing information as a commodity, for example, capturing and using information costs resources and failing to capture and use information costs opportunities because and less cost-effective services are provided.
- Viewing data acquisition, manipulation, and use as part of agency policies and procedures such that it is incorporated into new worker training, performance evaluations, etc.
- Viewing data as interactive and connected, that is, wanting to 'play with data' by applying predictive models to test hunches about a case, etc.
- Viewing practice as a partnership where client present technical information about their problem, practitioner apply the expertise of experience to this information, and communities provide help and support.

- Coming to grips with the privacy issues that IT raises. The US has been conspicuously absent of laws protecting client and citizen privacy and thus, most issues on privacy are settled in the courts.

Visionaries easily make paradigm shifts, but organisations and people with heavy workloads take longer to make paradigm shifts. More visionaries are needed to better develop this paradigm shift and help translate it to practitioners.

CONCLUSION

The current situation of human services IT is in many ways similar to the field in 1977. Then, there were many IT initiatives, however, almost no one knew about them. Connectivity mechanisms were needed. Newsletters quickly emerged that connected and informed people of the IT vision and attempts to implement that vision. Several of these newsletters were CASW (Computer Applications in Social Work), Computer Use in Social Services Network (CUSSN) Newsletter, MicroPsych Network, and Computers in Psychiatry/Psychology. The goal of all these newsletters was similar to the goal of CUSSN, that is, the linking of people, resources and ideas. As we approached the end of the current phase, all these newsletters have ceased publication.

We again have many IT initiatives that are know to only a few. To enter the new phase, new mechanisms are needed that will perform the functions that newsletters did for the current phase. Books, such as the one you are reading now, are an antiquated medium for presenting the current state of IT. This book imposes the limitations of the current phase on the vision about the new phase. The applications described in this book are missing the connectivity and interactivity of the future phase. With new mediums and tools, information on any application should be interactively available. For example, we should be able to quickly discover whether an application still exists, whether is was being used, whether the results were as expected, whether the developers advise others to follow their lead and if so, what problems could be avoided. The best way currently to get a glimpse of the future is by using multi-media and viewing the World Wide Web. Multi-media, such as the Myst CD-ROM, illustrates how information can be made interactive. The WWW illustrates how information can be linked. It is good for printed newsletters on IT and books such as this to die. However, mechanisms to take their place continually need to be developed. We need new visions to guide us, knowing that these visions will also underestimate the time and energy necessary to fulfill them.

References

Battin T. *Guide to Automating I&R systems*. CompuMentor, 89 Stillman Street, San Francisco, CA 94107 415/512-7784.1993.

Bezold C. Mental Health Services in the 21st Century: Challenges and Vision. *Behavioral Healthcare Tomorrow 4*(1), 86-88. 1995.

Boberg EW, Gustafson DH, Hawkins RP, Chan C, Bricker E, Pingree S and Berhe H. Development, Acceptance, and Use Patterns of A Computer-based Education and Social Support System for People Living with AIDS/HIV Infection. *Computers in Human Behavior*, 11(2), 289-311. 1995.

Butterfield B. Computer Utilization. *Encyclopedia of Social Work* (19th ed.). Washington DC: NASW, 594-613.1995.

Chow J and Coulton C. *Cleveland Area Network for Data and Organizing (Can Do) Project Summary*. Cleveland OH: Case Western Reserve University, Mandel School of Applied Social Sciences, Center for Urban Poverty and Social Change. 1994.

Geiss G and Viswanathan N. *The Human Edge: Information Technology and Helping People*. New York: Haworth Press. 1986

Gingerich WJ. Expert systems. *Encyclopedia of Social Work* (19th ed.). Washington DC: NASW, 917-25. 1995.

Lamson RJ. Virtual Therapy: the Treatment of Phobias in Cyberspace. *Behavioral Healthcare Tomorrow* 4(1), 51-53. 1995.

Leiderman M, Guzetta C, Struminger L and Monnickendam M (Eds.) *Technology in People Services*, New York: Haworth Press. 1993.

Miller LS. The Optimum Allocation of In-home Supportive-type Services in the Multipurpose Senior Services Program. *Computers and Human Services*, 9(1/2), 111-135. 1993.

Modai I, Saban NI, Stoler M, Valevski A and Saban N. Sensitivity Profile of 41 Psychiatric Parameters Determined by Neural Network in Relation to 8 Week Outcome. *Computers in Human Behavior*, 11(2), 181-90. 1995.

Nurius PS and Hudson Wh. *Human Services: Practice, Evaluation and Computers*. Pacific Grove, CA: Brooks/Cole. 1993.

Reinoehl RL and Mueller BJ. *Computer Literacy in Human Services Education*. New York: Haworth. 1990.

Resnick H (Ed.). *Electronic Tools for Social Work Practice and Education*. New York: Haworth. 1995.

Rheingold H. *The Virtual Community*. Reading MA: Addison Wesley. 1993

Rockwell RC, Hardin J and Loots MJ. Surviving the Three Revolutions in Social Science Computing. *Social Science Computer Review*, 13(2). 149-162. 1995.

Schwab JA and Wilson Ss. The Continuum of Care System: Decision Support for Practitioners. *Computers in Human Services*, 4(1/2), 123-140. 1989.

Siegel L. *Global Electronics Newsletter*, Pacific Studies Center, 222-B View Street, Mountain View, CA 94041 (this excerpt was edited). August 1993.

Steyaert J. Soft Computing for Soft Technologies: Artificial Neural Networks and Fuzzy Set Theory for Human Services. *Computers in Human Services*, 10(4), 55-67.1994.

World Wide Web sites referred to in this chapter

1. Behavior Healthcare Tomorrow, 1996.
http://www.ispot.com/CentraLink/education/bit.html

2. Self-help conferences and WWW resources.
http://www.colostate.edu/Depts/SocWork/webstuff.html

3. Telecommunications and Information Infrastructure Assistance Program of Department of Commerce.
http://www.ntia.doc.gov/www/otiahome/tiiap/tiiap.html

4. Family Life Development Center at Cornell University. Network of over 5,000 people active in child abuse prevention.
http://child.cornell.edu/

5. World Lecture Hall links to courses using the WWW as a delivery mechanism.
http://microlib.cc.utexas. edu/world/lecture/

6. Diversity University (hosted virtual session of the 1995 Conference of the International Council on Distance Education).
telnet moo.du.org 8888> or e-mail <moo@erau.db.erau.edu

7. CAN DO (has comprehensive databank on Cleveland neighbourhoods and surrounding suburban areas).
gopher://poverty.sass.cwru.edu:70/00/centers/c.pov/center.new

8. ABLEDATA - Disability and Adaptive Equipment Resource Library CD-ROM.
http://www.asel.udel.edu:80/at-online/assistive.html

9. Trace R&D Center, University of Wisconsin.
http://www.trace.wisc.edu/

10. CRERO (promotes research in rehabilitation engineering).
http://www.trace.wisc.edu/CRERO/

11. COMPSYCH.
gopher://baryon.hawk.plattsburgh.edu/1/.ftp/pub/compsych

12. Nonprofit software index.
http://www.shu.edu/~kleintwi/tnopsi.html#Editor

13. CUSSNet shareware/freeware demo Disk Copy Service.
http://www.uta.edu/cussn/cussn.html

14. Department of Veterans Affairs (VA).
http://www.va.gov/

Author details

Dick Schoech is a Professor in the School of Work at University of Texas at Arlington. He is editor of the Haworth Press journal Computers in Human Services *and founder of CUSSNet. His publications include* Human Services Computing *which was published by the Haworth Press in 1990. More recently he is developing multi-media in the areas of child protection and HIV/Aids.*

Contact: Professor Dick Schoech
University of Texas at Arlington
School of Social Work
Box 19129
Arlington
TX 76019-0129
USA

E-mail: Schoech@uta.edu.
WWW: http://www.uta.edu/cussn/cussn.html

3 Australia

Norman Smith

HUMAN SERVICES AND INFORMATION TECHNOLOGY

The title of a book, penned by one of Australia's leading historians, perhaps best describes the peculiar and anomalous factors at play within its society which influence the emergence and use of new technologies in the human services. In *The Tyranny of Distance* Geoffrey Blainey (1975) looks at the causes and effects of distance and isolation on the development of this small Westernised, democratic society. Australia, over 12,000 miles from Europe, with a coastline approximately 12,000 miles long, and a land mass which would swallow Europe and the British Isles, only has a population of about 18 million people. Distance and isolation are significant factors within the country since it is one of the most urbanised in the world. Eighty per cent of its population live in cities mostly centred on the Eastern coast and stretching over 4,000 miles. It is a new country as a European styled society, which displaced an indigenous peoples in just 200 years and only reached the federation of its sovereign states and territories in the past 95 years. These factors plus a basic entrepreneurial spirit, influence the use and development of information technology.

In effect, we are dealing with patterns of use which are essentially geographically based, since the states jealously guard their sovereignty even extending this to determining whether, if and when summertime saving begins and ends.

Although slow to capitalise on the mainframe computer stage, Australia is, according to one newspaper report, the second highest user of personal computers after the USA. The division of usage puts the government as lowest at 12%, followed by education 14%, business 35% and finally, home usage at 39%. This obviously does not include mainframe or network usage where government agencies would be the highest users.

The major human services under federal powers are principally concerned with social security; health provision through community grants and administrative control of medicare; the public health service; rehabilitation; employment and training and veterans' affairs. Professional social workers are employed in these agencies but it is the states who play a principal and differential role. Their major provision is aimed at the family and community - principally child welfare; juvenile justice; and support services for the disabled and the aged. In some states these are allied to psychiatric and general health services. Together, state and federal agencies employ the majority of social and other human service workers. Because of variation between states it is very difficult to draw a composite picture since much of the information is difficult to assemble. In addition, there are a lot of non-governmental agencies in the welfare area. Local government has not, up to now, been a major player in the provision of human services, although this is changing.

INFORMATION FOR CITIZENS

The use of micro based information services in public libraries emerged very early on following the arrival of personal computers. Quite recently it has been involved in supporting community projects and initiatives which have an information component. The aim of these programmes is to complement services and payments provided by the Federal Department of Social Security (DSS) and provide opportunities for people on low incomes to take action themselves to improve their living standards. Certain country areas were targeted in which community information networks were established and action research projects were instituted to test the effect of new innovative services on living standards. Where applicable, hardware as well as money support was provided. Some of the supported projects included databases to service barter clubs, develop skills banks, as well as information and guidance services.

There are now in existence national programmes such as that offered by the Department of Employment and Training which equate the level and kind of training required to particular jobs and occupations. Through a division of the Department of Employment Education and Training, the Technical and Further Education sector (TAFE) has been proactive in the provision of full time and short course computer familiarisation and advanced user courses.

The DSS now has a national database which enables it to track recipients of benefits. This is a task which proved extremely difficult without computer aid and with a transient population able to move large distances fairly quickly. The database is also accessible to social workers employed by Social Security who were able to be involved in the planning stages of the system.

In the field of disabilities it would seem that the educational, motor skill enhancement and coordination benefits of suitably designed software was recognised early on with the arrival of the PC. The picture of its use in rehabilitation follows that in other parts of the world and, I think, represents the value of professional rather than organisational contacts.

Despite the innovation in Australia of the Flying Doctor Services and particularly the School of the Air which both seized on the arrival of new communication technologies, nothing similar happened with the arrival of the PC. One of the forward thinkers of the day (Jones, 1982) drew attention to the implications of the technology facing Australia but it has taken nearly ten years for his message to be translated into visible action. In some states, Open Learning Centres are being established which aim to provide distance education and link ups for country and isolated communities using the whole range of information and communication technologies.

The biggest effect, however, has been the arrival of the Internet. This has received much attention and many people who would not otherwise think of using a PC are becoming active users.

VOCATIONAL EDUCATION AND TRAINING

Until about eight years ago, vocational education could be located in universities and Colleges of Advance Education (CAE) with some supportive courses offered by TAFEs. At that time social work education was located in universities and the preparation of social welfare officers in the CAEs. Then there were thirteen schools of social work. Following the federal government's forced amalgamation of universities and CAEs, plus the provision of new universities, there are now twenty schools of social work and about the same number of courses for welfare officers. Some courses are offered by 'distance education mode'. Each School of Social Work is an independent unit in terms of curriculum development but is subject to the accreditation of its course by the social work professional body, The Australian Association of Social Workers (AASW).

There is no requirement that social work or welfare courses provide students with instruction in the use of IT in their everyday practice. However, there is some evidence that they are exposed to the use of the technology indirectly through other courses they undertake, for example, psychology, economics and sometimes within the social work curricula itself. This is usually located within research methods courses and so is specialised, or as an introduction to word processing software. In a small study conducted by Smith (1991), of the fifteen schools of social work which were approached, nine said their students had exposure to some aspects of IT. This included learning how to use a computer, knowledge about computers and their use and a small number (three schools) examined the issues surrounding IT. There are grounds to believe that this has now improved both in number and also in more creative ways of using the technology as an aid and learning tool. With the arrival of the Internet and CD-ROMs in libraries there is more interest in technology. This is found particularly in postgraduate courses. Either specifically, or as part of research preparation, students are accessing the 'Net' and utilising overseas contacts as well as learning sophisticated search patterns when accessing CD-ROMs.

It is doubtful if there is any social work curriculum which was actively designed on the basis of information as a major concept in social work practice.

PROVISION OF SERVICES

To address this area would probably result in eight different pictures since states and territories are not only geographically and politically separate, but their welfare philosophy and service provisions also differ.

Generally, it would be fair to say that the utilisation of IT for the benefit of decision makers, as well as practitioners in the field, is a little behind that of Western countries. The arrival of the PC and networking has shortened the time lag and also enabled some of the problems encountered with mainframes to be avoided. Many of the small non-governmental organisations in the area of welfare introduced PCS primarily for their accounting and budgeting needs but then allowed practitioners to take advantage of the technology for their own needs. This was usually to develop client information systems either standing alone or coupled to the accounting or auditing needs of their organisations.

The major state providers using mainframes are more involved in client tracking and providing statistical data for planning purposes. The actual use of IT in social work practice appears to be limited to accessing client details. From information received from one state, no computerised client information system as yet exists.

With the increasing emphasis on quality control in the provision of human services and mandatory monitoring, more organisations are turning to IT as a means of establishing what money is spent, when and on what. Social workers are finding that the requirement to record and cost time for differential service provision is leading them to seek knowledge of information technology in order to comply with requirements.

It is perhaps in the area of hospital social work, however, that the earliest and more substantial use of information technology is to be found. In 1989, hospital social workers in Perth in Western Australia had developed and were using a common database. This allowed them to track their work and identify trends in time management and client problems. Because of the organisational and knowledge needs of the medical services in hospitals, the pressure for social workers to be part of use of information technology was earlier and greater.

There is a recognition by most practitioners of the value of using information technology, particularly in the area of policy and planning. However, they still lack the skills to use similar approaches for their own benefit. This may partly be an historical effect which will change with more computer literate practitioners joining practice and more user friendly hardware and software, particularly CD-ROM based information and the access to the World Wide Web.

CONCLUSION AND FUTURE DEVELOPMENTS

Despite the sophistication of IT with its potential for video conferencing, using the Internet or satellites, the tyranny of distance still seems to be a major obstacle in Australia. Cultures, laws and systems can change within one hour's air flight time yet we are still in the same country. In many ways it is easier to link up with overseas colleagues. There is an insularity within the country which seems to carry with it the assumption that personal contact is the only real way of identifying with others. This, in part, may be a characteristic carried over from the isolation of the early pioneers. Also Australia, as a sovereign country, has only been in existence a short while and identification with the 'state' as one's own locality is still evident.

There is no doubt that television has helped to shorten distance, but until fairly recently some parts of rural Australia were difficult to reach by telephone. IT has created some changes but will it be enough - either through its power singly to use the Internet or combined with video to lessen real and social distance? This remains to be seen and may only be solved politically between federal and state responsibilities.

In the area of professional social work and social work education the drive, which is present in other countries, to use IT as a learning and innovative teaching tool is not as strong here. Partly this is accounted for by the less legislated social welfare environment, compared to, for example, the UK, where social workers have had to develop information systems to satisfy specific administrative requirements. It is also the result of the professional ethos, partly transmitted by social work educators, which aligns technology with a specific mechanistic ideology.

Likely changes in the future are an increasing social work population who are computer literate but who do not contemplate major changes to harness IT to assist practice. There will probably be small groups of educators and practitioners who will experiment in the multi-media area in order to provide innovative ways of skills teaching.

References

Blainey G. *Tyranny of Distance: How Distance Shaped Australia's History.* Melbourne: MacMillan. 1975.

The PC Revolution. *The Weekend Australian.* Oct 28/29th 1995.

Jones B. *Sleepers Wake! Technology and the Future of Work.* Melbourne: Oxford University Press. 1982.

Smith NJ. *Technological Rationalism or Creative Humanism: Chicken or Egg Syndrome.* Paper presented at the 22nd National Conference of Australian Social Workers, Adelaide. 1991.

Author details

Norman Smith PhD, MA is Professor of Direct Practice in the Department of Social Work and Social Policy at the University of Queensland. He is also Dean of the Faculty of Social Work. Professor Smith's areas of interest are in disability and handicap, professional social work practice and the implications of information technology for welfare. He has published extensively.

Contact: Professor Norman Smith
Dean of Faculty of Social Work
University of Queensland
Australia

E-mail: Smith@social1.socialnet.uq.oz.au

4 Belgium

Jan Steyaert and Jos Mertens

HUMAN SERVICES AND INFORMATION TECHNOLOGY

The Belgian human services

Belgium is without doubt a 'welfare state'. This implies government regulates and finances the major part of the welfare services. Moreover, the state is committed to the existence and quality of social services. The welfare state is, as government itself, far from homogeneous, both at the policy level and in its institutional design. In this chapter we present an overview of the present development of information technology applications in Belgian human services. Use of IT in human services is no longer situated in the future, as human services increasingly introduce and use computers in their organisations.

In the eighties, the Belgian state organisation underwent a major transformation: the core of political decision making moved from federal government to the regional level. There is now a stratified system with federal and state governments as the highest authorities above provincial and local (municipal) governments. Each level has different responsibilities for different human services, which makes the Belgian welfare picture highly complex.

Organisation of services

The Belgian welfare services organisation can be divided into functional segments. These different segments can be distinguished, but not easily separated. A number of overlaps exist. The first functional segment is the **social security system**. This is a complex set of benefits to which entitlement is derived from contribution, with an underlying notion of redistribution. Social security covers various fields: retirement or pensions for widows, medical and disablement insurance, child allowance, employment policy and unemployment benefits. Industrial accidents and occupational diseases are chiefly a private matter for commercial insurance companies. Regulation and funding of social security is highly centralised under the authority of the federal government. Decentralisation of social security has become an important political issue since the deterioration of the solidarity between Flemish and Walloon parts of Belgium several years ago. Social security redistribution implies a transfer from Flanders to Walloon provinces. Although regulation and funding is centralised, administration of the social security system is by private organisations. Child allowance is the task of employers' organisations, unemployment benefits are handled by the unions, medical and disablement insurance is covered by sickness funds. These private organisations are responsible for these services within national financial and administrative regulations. They also form an important social partnership with government in policy development.

The second important functional segment of the Belgian welfare state is **health care**, with its own structure and ministry. The controlling body is not federal but state government, with differences encountered between health care in Flanders and Walloon. Health care services include the work of general practitioners, dental services and other specialists, pharmaceutical services and hospital services. **Social aid and assistance** are separately organised. They contain all personal social services, residential and non-residential, and are characterised by the personal relationship between the individual (the client) and the service provider. They include personal social services of local departments and of private agencies, child abuse and neglect centres, probation and after-care services, mental health agencies, geriatric help and many others. Services are decentralised under the responsibility of state government, either the Ministry of Family and Welfare or the Ministry of Health Care (mental health agencies). Some offenders services are an exception as a federal government responsibility (Ministry of Law), e.g. probation services and victim support services. Besides this functional division of social welfare, a typology based on different organisational approaches can be made, with four lines -

- **Zero-line care** or volunteer aid covers self-help, including family help, self-help groups and non-professional voluntary care. Services are close to individuals needing help and government intervention is non-existent or negligible. This zero-line is often neglected as it is not organised or professionalised and makes little impact on government funding. It is still an important part of social services. Flanders has almost 1,000 self-help groups, including some 200 Alcoholics Anonymous (AA) groups. Others are for physical illness or social problems (including handicaps and divorces).
- **First-line care** consists of a range of formally organised general social services, including general aid and assistance for the public. These first-line organisations keep the access threshold as low as possible. The most important examples are the Public Centres for Social Well-being, responsible for securing the right of each inhabitant of a municipality to a basic minimum income. They are organised by

the local government with substantial government intervention through subsidies and regulation.

- **Second-line care** consists of a range of specialised services, with a higher threshold and working with a specific target group. Again with significant government regulation and funding, but the initiative lies almost exclusively with private organisations. The subsidiarity principle applies: government does not organise itself that which can be organised by 'lower' organisations.
- **Third-line care** consists of specialised residential aid and assistance, with an even higher threshold, again involving government regulation and funding.

The organisational landscape of social aid and assistance in Belgium is not completed by these functional segments and organisational lines. Three more characteristics are relevant. The first is that there are a multitude of somewhat rigid initiatives lacking the flexibility to adjust to new realities and new problems. The consequence is a proliferation of organisations which are difficult to coordinate. Ideological segregation makes for duplication of services, each claiming and obtaining public financing under the rule of pluralism and according to the strength of the respective 'social pillar'.

Secondly, there are a large number of small scale service organisations with low numbers of staff. This has severe implications for innovation in services. In 1990 a new law aimed to improve the coherence of social service provision by reducing the number of agencies through merging different services into locally oriented 'social centres'. This should provide more flexible and less fragmented service provision as well as reducing administration and housing costs. Unfortunately, reality teaches that these aims are not easy to achieve. An opportunity has been created to organise social services in a more efficient way, but ideological boundaries are hard to cross. In at least two cities in Belgium, two schools of social work are situated less than one kilometre from each other, divided by the ideological boundary of being Catholic or non-Catholic. Similar examples exist at the level of practice provision.

Lastly, the numerous private human service organisations are organised in several 'federations', each covering agencies with similar services. These federations are organised in two superstructures, Catholic and non-Catholic, both publishing regular journals. Organisational support for IT is a function of the federations and super-structures, but the quality of support and focus varies according to the interest of people involved.

Information technology in Belgian human services

Social services have had a poor IT infrastructure for many years. Up to the end of the eighties, only large organisations had access to IT, together with a few advanced centres. With lower hardware prices and emergence of de facto standards for commercial software, social services started buying personal computers from 1989 onwards. About two thirds of all agencies now have at least one PC, usually relative new types as agencies started buying recently. The government is also providing certain agencies with computers, as part of a larger project to introduce IT in government administration. This is not always welcomed by social services, as it is part of process involving more administrative work and more control. Recent statistics on the availability of hardware and software in human services are not available. The most recent survey on this dates from 1992 and is outdated. It is the authors' impression that currently the vicious circle between 'no available hardware and therefore no available software and therefore no available hardware and ....' has been broken with the introduction of some cheap but useful programs for human services, such as the social map **SOKAflits** and the calculation program **BerTa**. Also the general introduction of computers in society and ever cheaper prices support a more general penetration of information technology in human services. However, the available technology is not state of the art. Specifically the availability of Windows based environments cannot be taken for granted, and a few Windows programs recently developed for human services have been faced with an extremely limited market.

The application of information technology in the human services received increased attention after the successful HUSITA 3 conference in Maastricht in 1993 and the ENITH and Causa 5 conference in Eindhoven in 1995. Both had a significant number of participants from Belgium. In order to stimulate these applications further, a number of government initiatives have been planned, some of them in cooperation with the Netherlands. Also, an overview of literature and publications on this topic is available electronically on the World Wide Web[1].

Ethical and legal framework

Belgium has been one of the last Western countries without elaborate legislation on privacy. There were three separate legal acts but no coordinating one. These covered National Registration, the Databank for Credit Purchases and the civil servants databank. Additional regulation covered professional secrecy (highly approved of in the medical sector) and establishment and regulation of a 'cross-roads' databank for social security which includes clauses to protect privacy. Development of a new privacy law gained momentum with the Schengen agreement between some European countries in police matters. The first proposal for a coordinating regulation was presented to parliament as long ago as 1976. In 1992 a modified text was accepted and became law in March 1993. This new regulation is based on six principles:

- The obligation to provide a clear description of purpose when setting up a databank (whether automated or not). Data may only be used within the framework of this purpose.
- Definition of a range of sensitive data (race, ethnic origins, philosophy of life, political ideology, etc.) which may only be processed when the purpose of the databank is established by law.

- Assignation of rights to all those concerned. It must be brought to a person's attention that data is gathered about them. People have access to their data and the right to ask for its removal if not relevant to the purpose of the databank.
- Obligations on the keeper of the databank to provide information and to protect the data physically.
- Prohibition on data exchange between different databanks and on trans-national exchange of data. The government can make exceptions.
- Finally, a commission was founded to supervise implementation of the legislation. Each databank must register with the commission with a description of its purpose.

The implementation of the privacy law has been cumbersome. Some of the practical issues such as the registration of the databases have caused substantial administrative problems. More importantly, the law has been developed with a business environment in mind and some of the regulations are unsustainable in a human service environment. As a consequence, many human service agencies are now violating the privacy law, not so much with their automated systems as with the paper-based client files.

INFORMATION FOR CITIZENS

Individual and community support technology

Flanders has several different automated public information systems. First are **information pillars** which are independent units with a screen and keyboard, sometimes integrated by video. Anyone can use them without charge.,Many local authorities use this technology for their own administrative services. Information in the social field is limited as most is aimed at tourists. An exception is Antwerp where the Public Centre for Social Wellbeing is experimenting with information pillars to provide information and facilitate administrative services to their clients. It is surprising that information providers do not make more use of this technology as observation indicates that many people use information pillars to browse through the available information. Unfortunately, the information offered is often very limited and seldom up to date.

Secondly, there is **Teletext**, where text screens can be consulted on television sets, but it is mostly associated with television or radio programmes. A very similar system is called **Videotex** and can be consulted using a personal computer with a modem. It is similar to the French Minitel, including an electronic telephone directory. Videotex is mainly used by firms to create a mailbox system between branches. Shortly Videotex services will also be available on an experimental basis through interactive television, but it is too early to evaluate.

A few years ago, the City of Antwerp started a **speaking database** that could be consulted through telephones, giving information on tourism, culture and city administration. The information was provided in Dutch, but the aim was to make it available in French, English, German and Spanish, and also Turkish and Arabic for immigrants. It contained social welfare information about doctors, dentists and social services and the only cost for users was the telephone call. The system was sponsored by commercial organisations, such as a local newspaper and a local free radio station. Several local municipalities adopted this idea although Antwerp itself ended it for reasons that are unclear. Public libraries have experimental **community information systems** which include the very broad and heterogeneous information that people need in their daily environment. The experiment has been undertaken by the Department for Information Sciences of the University of Antwerp. The electronic part of the system is based upon CDS/ISIS, a shareware program developed by UNESCO. The experiments have already shown that quality software need not be expensive.

While these experiments continue, reality however surpasses the expectations. With the emergence of the Internet and the World Wide Web, a much better technical multi-media platform with wider coverage becomes available. The experiments however clearly indicate that the critical success factor in a community information system is not the technology, but the network of information providers. It is much easier to write software and install computers in public libraries than it is to get local authorities to make information available.

Finally, the application of the Internet is gaining popularity and has by now surpassed the results of combined efforts of the previously mentioned technologies. Information availability on the Internet is largely from commercial organisations, but also from central government, some local authorities (digital cities such as Antwerp[2] and some small villages) and tourist information[3]. Information from human services is very scarce but the new minister of social welfare has substantial plans in this area. The Flemish government also committed itself in establishing a new broad-band network in co-operation with cable television companies and publishers.

While government and cable companies are eager to go ahead with Telenet Vlaanderen, publishers seem to be a bit more wary as the main focus tends to be on telephone rather than multi-media applications. This network will bring value added network services such as video-on-demand and the Internet into every household. As one of the partners in this project, the Flemish government is currently also stimulating projects offering information and services through this kind of network. At a more modest level, the Internet is made accessible to a broad audience by the introduction of ‘cyber-cafes’, not only in pubs but also in public libraries. Those bigger libraries already offering this service are overwhelmed by the success. Plans are being made at a ministerial level to expand this service to all public libraries and to transform public libraries into public information centres.

Employment and training

In the area of employment, the Flemish agency for labour (*arbeidsbemiddeling*) and vocational training (VDAB) has recently launched a number of projects involving information technology. A number of years ago, it already used **SIMONA**, an automated client files project which was used by professional labour consultants in their work of matching unemployed persons with job vacancies. This SIMONA system is now being replaced by a Windows program, but the conversion created tremendous difficulties. The SIMONA project has now also been complemented by the highly popular **WIS** system. WIS is an acronym for *Werk Informatie Systeem* or labour information system. It consists of information pillars that can be used by citizens and contains information on many job vacancies in Flanders. The information pillars are found in all agencies of the VDAB, and also in public places such as institutions for higher professional education or public libraries. More recently it has also become available on the Internet[4]. It is an extremely successful information system, and unemployed people have to queue to browse the available information.

Within Belgium, hundreds of large and small organisations organise vocational training packages to help match the profiles of unemployed persons to the needs of the job market. Very few involve training in information technology, although some specifically do such as **ATEC** in Antwerp (focused on one of the poorest areas of the city) and some agencies provide courses for disabled persons. Within the Antwerp and Boom region an electronic social map has been created to structure the information on all the available vocational training projects within the region. **DITO** is a hypertext text based program and guides the practitioner through a series of questions in order to suggest a relevant training that is available for a particular client.

The informal sector

As the name suggests, the informal sector is mostly organised in an informal and unstructured way with few standard information processes. The use of IT is therefore largely absent. There is however a small but significant part of the informal sector that is organised. With the 1994 Flemish law on organised voluntary work, this part of the informal sector is also receiving more attention. For Flanders, it is organised and coordinated by one central agency in Antwerp. The core task of this agency is to gather information on the supply and demand for volunteers and try to match these at an individual level as well as an aggregated level. For some years, the organisation has used **ELVVIS**, a computer program initially developed by similar Dutch organisations. The program allows data management on organisations and vacancies as well as on candidates for voluntary work. Users can retrieve information by search queries, or can express their preferences and have the program match them to a sample of volunteer vacancies. Again, this application demonstrates that data gathering and data entry prove to be more critical to the overall success of the project than the actual technology.

Independent living

There are only a few initiatives for training support systems for social welfare clients, although some centres organise computer literacy courses for disadvantaged people.

These aim to enhance people's level of general education and their employment skills, and are analogous to the ITEC centres in the United Kingdom. At present three centres are working: **Computergalerij** in Ieper, **FOYER** in Brussels (mostly immigrants), and **BOM** in Antwerp. There is specialist training to educate handicapped people in informatics within the fourteen centres for general education officially recognised (eleven for mentally disabled persons and three for physically disabled people). It is only recently that integrated informatics courses for physically disabled people have been developed, offering courses leading to a qualification in computer science, with options for administrative or technical applications. There is also a small tele-training experiment for severally disabled persons which involves installing hardware in clients' homes including two phones (one for data and one for voice). Tele-training is very intensive with the minimum of an hour per day. The specific nature of this remote training implies the need for a counselling service, so an instructor visits every trainee at home on a regular basis. Another organisation aims to provide work opportunities for those who have completed the course.

Concerning employment of disabled people, several initiatives can be identified. The software company **CIL** (Commercial Independent Living), was started by someone who is confined to a wheelchair, and is based on a network of physically disabled software developers. The company provides the training, hardware (PC, modem, etc.), the integration of the modules produced and the external contacts with software clients. The initiative is entirely commercial. Another small organisation concentrates on stimulation of the employment of physically disabled persons through tele-work by liaising with employers to provide work opportunities. A similar organisation in Walloon, **Différences**, offers a range of special services including tele-labour, but also tele-teaching, electronic mail and other facilities to improve the integration of disabled persons in society.

As a direct result of the first HUSITA conference and following a visit to the Centre for Special Needs Technology in Birmingham UK, a similar centre has started up in Flanders (**MODEM**, Antwerp). This centre applies PC technology, related communication systems, custom software and peripheral equipment to help disabled people. Consultations are held, advice given, documentation provided and opportunities offered to test hardware and software. Experience shows that often it is not exactly as expected or completely applicable. The Centre is mainly concerned with mental disability and prefers to work with individuals not linked to an organisation. This choice of target group is deliberate because they are ignored in other initiatives. The Centre explicitly does not aim to be a change agent for other organisations. Moreover, policy is determined by a technology led demarcation.

This is different from an earlier initiative (**VLICHT**, Leuven) which collects and distributes information about all kinds of appliances for disabled people. In this organisation, there are work groups for motor disabled people, for visually disabled people and for those with hearing or speech impediments. It pays no special attention to mental or learning disabilities and is structured according to its target groups not by technology. The main activities are the distribution of information and setting up a communication network between experts. Distribution of information has taken concrete form in construction of the **VLIBANK** database which expects to become a part of the HANDYNET databank.

VOCATIONAL EDUCATION AND TRAINING

In Flemish welfare organisations a wide variety of professionals are employed: social nurses, social workers, remedial educationalists, psychologists, educationalists, doctors and researchers. The biggest group are social workers, who receive their education in 'social schools'. There are twelve such schools in Flanders (for a population of six million) providing higher education of a non-university type. Training takes three years and in all schools there is a choice between personnel management, social/cultural work and social work, with two schools offering an extra union work option. In the standard first year, an initiation course in informatics is part of the curriculum. This aims to reduce the fear of computers, to learn the 'turbo language' of informatics, and notions of word processing and data management. In some schools informatics are included in the second and third year, within the specific options. Course contents vary with the option: in personnel management they include spreadsheet work and in socio/cultural courses work with Desk Top Publishing (DTP). Not one school has an extensive informatics course for the social work option. At best, a visit is made to a welfare organisation using computers or an introduction to data management is given.

After years of diversity in choices of software packages, a number of de facto standards had emerged, but with the introduction of Windows, these have ceased to exist. During 1991 teachers of informatics at the different social schools met on several occasions following a seminar organised by ENITH at which information on curriculum development for the social schools in the Netherlands was presented. Similar curriculum development took place in the academic year 1992/3 in Flanders, on basic technical informatics for social workers as well as the broader scope of information in social work and social work organisations. This resulted in a manifesto developed by teachers of informatics at different schools setting out the proposed policy and plan of action.

The focus is no longer on technology (students know how the basic principles of how to work with computers) but on how information is used in practice and for policy. This document has been used in the most recent curriculum changes. The trend has continued and been strengthened by a series of seminars where teachers of informatics invited colleagues to focus attention on using information technology in their classes, rather than refer anything to do with technology to the informatics classes.

The issue currently highest on the agenda of vocational education is gaining access to the Internet and teaching social workers the ins and outs of cyberspace. Currently, schools of higher education can only gain access to the Internet through commercial

Internet service providers, which is costly. The aim is to be on a par with universities who have structural access based on organisational size rather than on use.

PROVISION OF SERVICES

Practice level

Human services practice is supported by information technology in a number of ways including electronic social maps, welfare benefits calculation systems and software to manage client files. The areas of practice that are not, or only marginally, supported by information technology include assessment, direct practice provision and evaluation.

Flemish human services have been jealous of US, Canadian and German human services for their 'information and referral systems'. These offer a tool to know who is providing services, where, for whom, when and how. These offer, in its most modest form, a human service map (*sociale kaart*) used by service providers to find their way around. In the first European edition of this book, we noted that different organisations had started developing information and referral systems for the human services. Separate experiments existed for mental health agencies, unemployment projects, human services in Antwerp and probation and after-care services. Not one had been distributed as an electronic information system but two years later, the situation has changed. Commercial firms that considered publishing a 'social map' waited too long. A small new company started developing one, which has recently been taken over by the Antwerp school of social work. Developed on a low budget and sold at low cost, **SOKAflits** contains addresses, names, telephone numbers and descriptions of over 13,000 human services.

Although SOKAflits is the most detailed electronic social map, it is not the only one. Its main competitor is a major publishing company, marketing an electronic social map with half the addresses at the same price. Also, the welfare council of Kortrijk in Flanders has published a similar social map for their region with over 700 addresses. An organisation in Gent has published a social map with specific information and referral details for unemployment services. Antwerp organisations have developed the same 'unemployment map' for their region under the name **DITO**. The agencies for school social work (career and education officers) have an 'educational map' that provides students with information on where and what to study, for how long and on what conditions. In fact, four different programs and databases are available, one for each official languages (Flemish and French, not available for German) and one for each of the main ideological pillars (Catholic and pluralist).

Finally, special mention needs to be given to **HOME**, an 'intelligent' electronic social map for residential care for elderly people. It has been developed and is run by the national association of socialist social insurers. It goes beyond the traditional data provision such as address, telephone, capacity, infrastructure etc by also offering quality assessment. A substantial survey is completed by practitioners of the socialist social insurers on each residential care situation, and a score on several functions such as hospital and hotel function is computed. These scores form the basis for a total quality assessment score that is used in HOME to help elderly people find the most suitable residential care. For organisational reasons (autonomy of service providers), HOME does not contain information on free capacity of service organisations. Thus, it is possible that HOME suggests five best residential care settings, but all may have a waiting list of several months.

All these examples concern social maps in Flanders although an equivalent one was developed in the Walloon part of Belgium by the Youth Information Bureaux or 'Infor Jeunes'. It contains not only data on organisations, but also on social services in the French community, on youth movements and holiday facilities. It also includes references to documentation material available.

Whereas SOKAflits and other existing social maps only contain addresses, the new **SOKAbib** program offers social service providers immediate access to a library of social information. SOKAbib has been developed in a hypertext environment, allowing associative links between otherwise logically structured texts. The program is integrated with the SOKAflits social map. The many items include - occupational health, - divorce - basic minimum income - marriage - nationality - dying - psychiatry - unemployment. A similar aim is attempted by the **Delta** project of the youth advisory organisations, however with limited success.

Welfare benefits

At present, three main programs are available for calculation of welfare benefits. Development of these systems is complicated: the financial compensation system is fragmentary and the legislation is complex and subject to many changes. Of the three systems, one is based on the work of the law department of a Flemish university, which started research in the mid 1980s on possibilities of representing legal rules in a system of decision rules. The main objective was to investigate how and the extent to which informatics can be applied in law and law research. In this context advisory systems were a spin-off. As an example, the **Handipak** advisory system for financial compensation for disabled people is available for people and institutions directly involved in services for disabled people. It can also be used as a reliable source for individual advice. It is not explicitly intended for independent use by disabled persons, but rather to give support to the social worker in his or her advisory function.

ProSoc, the second application in this area also builds on the research activities of this law department and involves an advisory system for payment of basic minimum income. It covers both Flanders and Walloon, as regulation of basic minimal income is a federal government responsibility. This system has been developed by a ministry and is freely distributed to all public centres for social well-being.

A third and final application is for study allowances. Non-take up in this domain is substantial to the extent that the government advertised in newspapers with the catchy phrase 'pile of money is looking for student'. The calculation program for study allowances became necessary when the criteria to benefit not only included income from work, but all other income as well. The program is called **BerTa**, is distributed at low cost and used on a substantial scale - by nearly all services of school social work.

Client information

A major trend over the past few years has been the introduction of more sophisticated software to handle client files. The aim is to surpass client registration software by going beyond quantitative summary information and become more integrated with care provision. In the probation sector, one program has been tested in five pilot projects. The evaluation was positive, and a budget for the distribution and implementation of this program is available for the eighty four probation services. The program includes case management and follow-up of current cases (an average of a 100 per probation officer) together with periodic planning of the work to be done. It also has general administrative applications such as standard letters and general data management such as literature and addresses. The selection procedure, by which cases are selected for review, is strongly formalised which made automation possible. A similar case management system is being developed for the private social services working with offenders. This system includes elaborate information gathering during intake, aid and assistance provided and extensive follow-up.

Finally, the network of general social work agencies of the Catholic social insurance organisation is using **ADORA**, Windows software that provides an automated platform for all administrative activities on client files. ADORA is an acronym for *geAutomatiseerde DOssier-Registratie en Administratie* or automated file-registration and administration. It starts from the information needs of the practitioner and builds data-entry, processing and output options around those needs. While the concept emerged in one regional district, it has now been developed by the national agency and been implemented in all districts. This implies that currently about 300 social workers use this system, the majority on a laptop to enable use during home visits. As a further step in the development of this system, aggregation and analysis of data facilities are now being developed. It is interesting that these are only now coming into the picture as traditionally these needs are precisely the rationale for development of this kind of information system.

Information systems

With the fragmentation of Flemish welfare organisations, no uniform registration scheme yet exists. Registration in welfare work started in 1976 in the 53 centres for social work on a voluntary basis. In 1983 registration became a condition of receiving subsidies, though later lapsing in practice. In 1980 the OCMWs started registering, later encouraged by a financial incentive and from 1989 there was a compulsory uniform registration scheme for these centres. In other sectors we can also note this tendency towards uniform registration schemes. Sometimes uniformity arose as a consequence of a subsidy rule explicitly based on the number of clients. As a result accurate standard registration has an immediate impact on the revenues of organisations.

Several social service agencies use software to maintain information on their clients. However, no off-the-shelf systems are available, as for example in the Netherlands. Software is either tailor-made for the agency or an agency cluster, or in standard software as Dbase or Excel. Data gathering, and therefore the involvement of software, is mostly restricted to quantitative information on clients and their problems. Information on treatment activities or outcomes is not systematically gathered, nor is software used on a large scale to structure client files.

Social care policy

The main development regarding the use of information technology in social care policy concerns implementation of the **ISP** or *Informatie Stimulerlings Plan*. This plan aims to introduce IT at all levels of the Flemish ministry, including its department of social care. Within this plan, all administrative files for funding and other activities are automated, enabling not only more efficient processing of data, but also the use and analysis of aggregated data. At present, the data set emerging from the automated funding files is balanced with data from the different human service funding agencies. This process will provide the ministry with a valuable data set on human service agencies, their finances, staff, clients and treatments. Efficiency and effectiveness measures will be deduced from these data. The implementation in 1996 will enable a complete first year data set to be available is 1997.

CONCLUSION AND FUTURE DEVELOPMENTS

A few conclusions can be formulated from overviewing this state of affairs of information technology in the Belgian human services and comparing it with a similar overview three years ago (Colombi, Rafferty, Steyaert, 1993). A first conclusion is that information technology applications have moved into the human services, and within that sector, have moved from the back office (administration, bookkeeping, ...) to the front office (counselling, care provision). This is due not only to ever decreasing prices of hardware and software, but also due to a number of effective applications such as SOKAflits, BerTa, WIS and ADORA.

Secondly, it is surprising that none of the major innovations in this area over the last five years has been caused by technology innovations. The hardware and software platforms being used in today's applications have been around for several years, though not at current prices and reliability. None of the applications really makes use of the front line technologies of which one expected so much, such as hand held computers (Newton) or neural networks.

Regarding the future, two major developments are likely to have a significant effect. The most apparent of these is of course the introduction of the Internet. Popular with young and old, obviously useful for the serious and less serious users, it is the current buzz word with those working with information or information technology. Applications in the human services reflect the average application on the Internet, such as e-mail and the World Wide Web.

Finally, for the first time, a coherent information policy for the human services may become available during 1996. If and when this happens, it will have a major impact on the relation between Belgian human services and information technology applications.

Reference

Colombi D, Rafferty J and Steyaert J. *Human Services and Information Technology: A European Perspective*. ENITH.1993

World Wide Web sites referred to in this chapter

1. Overview of literature and publications on IT in the human services.
http://www.fz.hse.nl/nl/zw_intro.htm

2. Antwerp digital city.
http://www.dma.be/

3. Tourist information central address.
http://www.online.be/online/

4. WIS - Werk Informatie Systeeem
http://www.vdab.be/

Author details

Jan Steyaert is senior lecturer at Causa, Faculty of Health care and Social Work at Eindhoven in the Netherlands. He is also secretary of ENITH (European Network for Information Technology in the Human Services) and co-editor of the international journal New Technology in the Human Services. He has published extensively on client information systems in social work and social policy and recently edited Information Technology and Human Services, More than Computer? (1996)

Jos Mertens is a psychologist who lectures in the Social Work Department of the Karel de Grote-Hogeschool, Antwerp. He also coordinates SokaData, a non profit organisation that develops and publishes software programs for human services.

Contact: Jan Steyaert
Hogeschool Eindhoven
Causa
Postbus 347
5600 AH Eindhoven
The Netherlands

Telephone: +31 40 2605940
Fax: +31 40 2435274
E-mail: j.steyaert@fz.hse.nl
WWW: http://www.fz.hse.nl/ca/causa.htm

5 Canada

Robert MacFadden, Raymond Carlson, Oscar Firbank and Jack Sieppert

HUMAN SERVICES AND INFORMATION TECHNOLOGY

Canada is the second largest country in the world, bordered by three oceans and extending 5,187 km east to west and 4,627 km north to south. The estimated 1995 population of Canada is 28.5 million with a density of three persons per square kilometre. About 75% of Canada's population lives within 150 km from the southern border with the United States. Approximately 23% or 2.4 million Canadian households have at least one personal computer (Maclean's, January 17, 1994, p.41).

Given this vast size and diversity, its impossible to provide a representative sampling of what is occurring in information technology (IT) in human services within this country. Consequently, this presentation will describe various trends and applications from across Canada within these three topical areas: information for citizens; vocational education and training, and personal social services. The chapter begins with the Canadian context to human services and concludes with some comments on future directions of IT in human services in Canada.

As a federation of ten provinces and two territories, Canada has divided responsibilities based on the British North America Act (1867) and incorporated into the Canadian Constitution. The provinces have primary jurisdiction over social welfare, although the federal government has authority over social welfare concerns such as unemployment insurance, old age pensions, supplementary benefits and penitentiaries. Political changes and accumulating provincial and federal debts have placed considerable pressure on human service agencies.

Human service organisations within Canada vary greatly in terms of structure, funding and services. Some provinces have a centralised structure for certain government services while others reflect more decentralised models. Agencies range from being totally government funded to privately funded organisations supported by donations and fees. It is not unusual for a social agency to report to several funders including a municipal government, the United Way, and the provincial government, as examples. In terms of education, most social work education occurs at community college or university levels and is funded mostly from provincial education grants and other sources such as tuition and fundraising.

INFORMATION FOR CITIZENS

Canada is a world leader in telecommunications. Canadian telephone, cable and video recorder penetration rates are among the highest in the world. The quality of the telecommunication networks in terms of fibre optics and digitalisation is second to none and Canada has the largest volume of information supply per person in the world (Stentor, 1993). Nationally, the Canadian National Research Council (NRC) has funded **CANARIE** (the Canadian Network for the Advancement of Research, Industry and Education) which has launched a 10 million dollar (Canadian) upgrading of **CA*net** as part of a two year, 115 million dollar program to expand and improve Canada's electronic infrastructure (Maclean's, January 17, 1994, p.43). CA*net is a collaboration between IBM Canada and the University of Toronto, and links provincial computer networks across the country acting as the Canadian segment of the Internet.

One common experience for most provinces within Canada is the growth and use of the Internet. New sites are emerging each day. Many universities have Front-Pages on the World Wide Web (WWW) and some libraries offer access to their catalogues via the Web. Social agencies are starting to appear. Recently, **Child Cyber Search** Canada was initiated on the Web in conjunction with the Royal Canadian Mounted Police[1], to provide information on missing children in Canada. Many of the examples throughout this chapter refer to specific applications which use the Internet and the WWW.

In 1995 the Canadian government announced the elimination of 5,000 jobs at employment centres and the closing of 150 employment offices. As a replacement, 400 electronic kiosks with self-service terminals will be installed within libraries, community centres and shopping malls across Canada. The kiosks will offer job information, applications and information on programs, including unemployment insurance, Canada Pension Plan and Old Age Security benefits (*Toronto Star*, August 3, 1995).

In Eastern Canada, consumer self-assessment applications are being explored by the New Brunswick Department of Community Services. A feasibility study is being conducted of computer-based self-assessment intended to help potential applicants determine their eligibility for various support services. The intent is to help those who are not eligible avoid the long waits that can be part of the application process.

Such self-assessment currently requires that the consumer go to the service provider's office. The development of low cost Internet access has been viewed as a likely way for consumers to acquire more information and even self-assessments without such travel. At this point, the **Chebucto Community Net**[2] in Halifax, Nova

Scotia has been particularly successful in allowing individuals who are not university-based to have low-cost access. Some organisations such as the Halifax Police Department[3] have demonstrated that the Internet can be used to provide useful information to consumers.

In Quebec, the government has already opened a WWW site[4] in the Internet, and it is expected that agencies in the human service field will examine the provision of information on services of various types. The government has in fact established a special fund (the *Fond de l'autoroute de l'information du Québec*) to sponsor specific projects related to the information highway - some of them connected to human services (*Le Devoir,* July 14, 1995).

A second trend that seems to be unfolding in Quebec, is involvement of the private sector in the area. One project under development known as **UBI** (Universality-Biodirectionality-Interactivity), sponsored by a private consortium of cable companies and private corporations, hopes to create an infrastructure to provide services using cable TV. Most of the services relate to consumer transactions, but some public agencies, such as the Ministry of Income Security (MSR), are considering the possibility of buying space in the system to provide information to people on services and programs. A **FreeNet,** to be inaugurated toward the end of 1995 in Montreal, is an initiative of government and a computer association, and is expected to include information from almost all public service agencies in Quebec (Dutrisac, 1995).

From an Ontario perspective, **Online Ontario** was established in 1987 as an electronic network of community information and referral centres designed to provide information on a range of community and government resources and services to the people of Ontario (MacFadden et al., 1990). The electronic network, currently with seventy members, was created by the Association of Community Information Centres in Ontario (ACICO) in a distributed manner so that each community information centre (CIC) would be responsible for local information and share information at the regional, provincial and federal levels. Thus information travels up and down the network and is maintained at different levels. A common data dictionary, shared standards and quality assurance strategies ensure up-to-date and high quality information that is used by the information counsellors within the CICs and other sources who have their software and database. Contracts with other agencies have been negotiated to share the database and system. Currently the database contains over 60,000 records and the ACICO and its member agencies have been successful in marketing various features of Online Ontario, to government ministries and programs, including the database, software and database structure.

The Ontario Prevention Clearinghouse in Toronto has been co-ordinating a Better Beginnings/Better Futures project which networks eleven sites each in Alberta and Ontario. The purpose is to promote prevention programmes and activities related to children and families. Participants include both grassroots and formal organisations such as community and native groups, social planning councils and social agencies. E-mail, conferencing and information are available on the network. The Ontario

Prevention Clearinghouse has also been engaged in providing IT training to unemployed people through a **Transitions** program. With over 150 corporate partners, the program includes IT training and apprenticeship and has been successful in securing employment for participants.

In Western Canada, information sharing and networking technology are expanding rapidly. One of the best examples of this trend is **HumanServe**. HumanServe is a bulletin board system operated by the Association of Human Services in Alberta. It is designed as an electronic meeting place and information library for human service organisations, practitioners, government, and private citizens. Users connect to one of several sites throughout the province via computer and modem. Once connected they have access to: electronic mail; both open and private electronic conferencing capabilities; an on-line library containing recent materials on legislation, policy, research, event calendars, and current medial releases; databases of organisations and funding sources; a job board for the posting of vacancies and résumés; and gateways to other BBSs and networks. In short, HumanServe promises to provide users with fast and easy access to information that in the past they might have waited weeks for.

The Internet is also serving as a popular information-sharing tool for the human services. In Saskatchewan, on the **Saskatoon Free-Net**, many community agencies have created information pages on the Internet. By using commonly available Internet browsers users can discover the mission and services offered by the Alzheimer Association of Saskatchewan[5], and connect with a provincial library of Alzheimer-related materials. Or they can access a page that profiles the Saskatchewan Adoptive Parents Association[6], and then link to a range of related adoption, foetal alcohol syndrome, infertility, attention deficit disorder, learning disability and parenting support groups. This list of Internet information sources in Saskatchewan grows daily. Recent additions include the Schizophrenia Society of Saskatchewan[7], the Saskatchewan Head Injury Association, the Saskatchewan Institute on Prevention of Handicaps[8], and Saskatoon Public Health Services[9]. Just as importantly, this growth of Internet information about the human services is mirrored in all of Western Canada's provinces.

Another innovative, but very different application of technology to direct human service provision is found in the city of Vancouver, in the province of British Columbia. A non-profit organisation called the Neil Squire Foundation is striving to enhance the independence of individuals who have severe physical disabilities. One of the ways that the Foundation achieves this goal is by developing hardware and software technologies which supplement a disabled individual's abilities at home and work.

For example, a device called the Jouse (Joystick Mouse and Keyboard Emulator) has been developed which allows users to sip and puff on a breath controlled device that substitutes for the standard keyboard, mouse, and joystick. The sip and puff is used for keyboard emulation through Morse code, and the joystick is used for computer mouse operations. The Foundation has also developed a **Home Automation Control System** that can control most functional aspects of the user's home. This system is based on a portable remote audio/video terminal that is mounted on a wheelchair. The terminal can be activated by voice, and offers a menu system to the user. Users select commands from the menu, using their voice, thereby sending instructions to a central control unit. This unit in turn manipulates appliances and other amenities in the home. One last application developed by the Foundation is **SARAW** (Speech Assisted Reading and Writing). SARAW is a talking computer program designed to help teach basic reading and writing skills to adults with severe physical disabilities. Among other features it offers a talking word processor that speaks as the student types, thereby providing immediate feedback about the word just typed.

VOCATIONAL EDUCATION AND TRAINING

Professional education in Canada also shows increasing use of information technology. Word processing is the most common focus, but an increasing number of students take advantage of computerised literature searches and exploring the Internet. Some professional schools such as medicine and law have focused significant resources on developing computer-based educational materials. The Medical School at Dalhousie University has a professional staff unit devoted to locating, promoting and developing such materials. That effort has stimulated discussion among other professional schools, but the carryover is limited. For example, one course on statistics in the School of Social Work at Dalhousie is built around computer-assisted learning, but, in general, schools of social work in this region do not offer special courses on information technology.

Computer-assisted learning materials seem to be more common among distance education projects in Eastern Canada. For example, the Continuing Care Program at Saint Francis Xavier University has commissioned an interactive, multi-media CD-ROM covering the content for its first nursing course. Individuals living in small communities have consistently advocated for distance education as a means to access professional education. The challenge has been cost. Information technology offers an inexpensive form of communication and content delivery that is not dependent on the number of students at any location.

The expansion of distance education seems focused on programmes with a higher job potential such as business, education, nursing and social work. Several use the Internet or conferencing software for communication. A surprising fact is that normally competitive universities are tending to cooperate in working on information technology-based distance education. An example is the World Wide Web site produced at the University of New Brunswick[10]. This site is dedicated to collecting information for those developing and offering courses over the Web.

IT within Schools of Social Work in Ontario varies related to its extensiveness and initiatives. Many offer computer resources through their university computing resources and some have their own computer labs. Most applications are word processing, spreadsheet and some statistical applications. The use of CD-ROM based research databases (e.g., PsychLit) are becoming common as is the use of Internet for e-mail, research and collegial collaboration. The Faculty of Social Work, at the University of Toronto, maintains its own computer lab and has been teaching courses on information technology and social work for most of the last ten years. Courses in computer-mediated communication, developing computer-assisted instructional programs, and courses which explore the range of applications of IT in social work are examples of some offerings.

In Western Canada, many schools of social work use common hardware and software as a tool in existing research courses. At the University of Northern British Columbia, for example, a research course introduces students to a range of statistical, spreadsheet, and graphics packages. Using these packages the students explore a wide variety of databases, such as Census data, the Aboriginal People's Survey and the Violence Against Women Survey. By exploring these data sets students are better able to develop community profiles, present briefs and engage in advocacy.

Social work students at the University of Manitoba can work through a multi-media, interactive presentation of basic statistical concepts as part of their research courses. Based on the MacIntosh computer, the application offers a graphically-based tour of concepts such as descriptive statistics, normal distributions, correlation and regression. Students can review these concepts at any time they choose, at their own pace.

Similar efforts are underway in the Faculty of Social Work, at the University of Calgary. All students have access to tools such as CD-ROM, optical scanners, laser and colour printers, e-mail, and the Internet. In addition to the usual training on traditional software, promising students are encouraged to explore software development. Recent examples of prototype software developed by social work students at the University of Calgary include a statistics tutoring package, an application that provides information about Alzheimers to clients, and a volunteer management system.

PROVISION OF SERVICES

Eastern Canada has experienced a strong interest in accountability and acquiring information on service outcomes. A variety of data collection methods have been tried, but disappointment in the results contributed to developing a centre to seek useful outcome information for mental health services. This project is currently relying on computer-assisted telephone interviewing to facilitate use of complex interviews. Consumer response to these surveys has been very positive.

In Quebec, currently 32 information technology related projects are in progress in the health and social services institutional network (Gouvernement du Québec, 1993). Many of these projects, however, are still at an experimental stage, and some that have been concluded, have not yet been implemented on a large scale.

Of particular note is the **Accès-DI** which focuses on the provision of services for the mentally handicapped. Sponsored by the MSSS and the District Council of the

Laurentides region, the project's main objective is to facilitate the planning and management of a wide spectrum of services for the mentally impaired so as to meet their needs and enable them to remain in the community (Larose, 1994). The first stage of the project, concluded in 1989, involved the creation of a software package to support and facilitate the activities of social practitioners and administrators; a second stage, currently under way, will finalise the application and test it in a number of sites. The project prioritises an individual case management approach. It seeks to both co-ordinate interventions among professionals and across services and facilitate the active participation of the clients themselves (or their representatives) in the decision-making process.

Accès-DI intends to simplify the process of identification and appraisal of community services by providing access to the system via a single entry door. After initial contact with the Local Community Service Center and an assessment of needs, a regional committee of several professionals and the client decide on the specific package of services needed and the course of action to be taken.

From a managerial standpoint, the data collected through Accès-DI would allow administrators to know, at any time, how many beneficiaries are registered in a waiting list for a given service, whether accessibility is an issue, and whether an expansion or a reform of existing services is actually needed. Practitioners would be more easily able to monitor the client's progress and make more informed decisions on the adequacy and appropriateness of services through comparisons of data on individuals afflicted by similar conditions.

Another population in Quebec to have been targeted by IT innovations is children and youth. Following the 1991 reform of the Quebec health and social services institutional network, services in this area have been largely centralised at Centers for the Protection of Children and Youth (CPEJ). Besides the protection of children and youth, their activities focus, in large part, on the supervision of youths (aged 12 to 17) convicted of an offence under the federal Young Offenders Act. They also provide services in relation to child adoption, family placements and family mediation. As CPEJs frequently act in consultation with other agencies and institutions, the availability of current, centralised information is crucial.

Prior to the 1991 reform, the Local Community Service Centers had already implanted a number of computerised information management applications (Baril, 1994). The youth protection system, also known as the **LPJ** system, was developed toward the end of the 1980s and consists of a software package and a data base that collects information on individuals covered by the provincial Youth Protection Act. The system assists managers and practitioners in their decision-making and evaluation activities. A second example of IT utilisation for youth relates to the implementation of a 'monitoring system'. This system is designed to help in monitoring the effectiveness of placement services for young offenders and generates updated financial information on the cost of interventions per client. Its main objective is administrative in that the system will help in determining the budgetary allocation required by Centers for this type of services.

A third population affected by IT innovations is the elderly (Beaulieu, 1994). The most important experience in this area is the construction of a system of information for clients of long-term and residential care institutions called **SICHELD**. The system, created in 1986 under the auspice of the Regional District Council of Saguenay-Lac-Saint-Jean, involves the integration and co-ordination of information on services from several hundred institutions. SICHELD's main objective is to support clinical rather than administrative activities. It is composed of three major sub-systems: a first one, called *Client and Program*, which identifies the client and his/her environment; a second one, called *Biopsychosocial Profile*, which establishes a profile of the client based on personal data, health status and degree of functional independence; a third one, called *Management of Interventions*, serves to identify and manage the services needed by each individual client. The SICHELD project collects information on elderly individuals who are either registered in or have been admitted to one of the institutions concerned, are part of an intermediate program associated to one such institution, or are admitted to an intensive rehabilitation program.

A research project conducted at the Sainte-Justine hospital lead to the creation of a software package to assist paediatricians in their practice by establishing a 'social profile' of patients afflicted with a chronic condition. The data on the patient's clinical situation can also be used by social practitioners who might at one point participate in the intervention (Turgeon-Krawczuk, 1993).

Finally, a project worth mentioning is the development by the Quebec Health Insurance Fund (RAMQ) of a health card featuring a microprocessor to collect information on the holder's clinical history (Trahan, 1994). The card, whose information is to support the activities of professionals in the medical field as well as social practitioners, is still in its experimental stage. Following the evaluation of a test conducted at the Regional District Council of Rimouski, a plan to generalise its use at a larger scale is being considered.

In terms of personal human services in Ontario, the child welfare network in Ontario represents a human services sector that is investing in information technology and presents several interesting illustrations of applications. **CASNet** is an electronic network of children's aid societies in Ontario designed to promote communication and innovative applications of IT within the network. (MacFadden and Pieterson, 1993). Co-ordinated by the Ontario Association of Children's Aid Societies (OACAS), the network has been in operation for two years and has moved from using an outside BBS service to more local control through locating the server and network within the Association.

Many of the child welfare agencies are moving towards increased networking at a LAN and WAN level. This involves exploring workgroup technologies and document processing to identify cost-efficient, safe ways of storing large amounts of data and ensuring secure network access. Hardware and software are being upgraded to move towards more graphical user interface technology and open architecture and systems are becoming more the norm. Information system development has occurred both through third party vendors and in-house or collaborative ventures. Distributed processing through small systems rather than mainframes is common now.

The Child Welfare Network is recognising the necessity of collaboration, supported by a strong OACAS, and is looking to developing some common data elements and information that can be shared and used provincially for social reporting and advocacy purposes. Most major projects of the OACAS have an IT component attached. The recent development of an eligibility framework for child protective services (*The Intervention Spectrum*) has been computerised into existing agency information systems permitting the social worker to reference specific Reasons For Service and severity classifications and enter this decision into the information system. The system also identifies the minimum intervention level within each category which signals those cases which should be opened.

In Western Canada, one of the most noteworthy endeavours to introduce information technology into direct service provision can be found in Saskatchewan, with a program called **Casework Coplanar**. This application was originally developed in the College of Education at the University of Saskatchewan. It was designed to support the instructional planning and service delivery of teachers of children with special needs. Now it is being tested by the provincial department of Family Services as a tool to assist teams of caseworkers in working with clients. The program uses portable computers and modems to enhance communication between caseworkers, systematic planning, maintaining accessible service records, and reporting client progress. These goals are accomplished through a variety of software functions: an e-mail system; two-dimensional electronic worksheets to facilitate consensus building among team members; a forms generator capable of creating rating scales, checklists, and other assessment tools; storage and cataloguing of client records; cross-indexing of client information and assessment tools; and an interactive facility for report planning. Perhaps most importantly, caseworkers can access all client information, assessment tools, and other professionals at any time, any place in the province.

CONCLUSION AND FUTURE DEVELOPMENTS

The most immediate and serious challenge for human service agencies in Canada will be in adapting to the increasingly restrictive financial situation as all levels of government attempt to reduce deficits. Project and grant monies for IT initiatives which have funded many previous innovations will not be as available and base funding will likely be frozen or reduced for many agencies. IT may be used to offset some of the consequences of these cutbacks through greater efficiencies or innovative approaches to service and management.

This fiscal situation may encourage more collaboration at all levels and foster partnerships, including more with private enterprise. The movement towards increased connectivity (i.e., networking) will enhance this collaboration through expanding agency boundaries and increasing knowledge, supports and partnerships.

Another significant trend having implications for the future is the increasing use of IT by front-line professionals within human services. Historically, front-line workers have been disenfranchised in the development and use of IT in human services. Although it was often acknowledged that front-line workers should have significant input into the design and operation of information systems, this has rarely occurred in practice.

More recent developments have incorporated their input. A doctoral study at the University of Toronto, Faculty of Social Work, is focused on assessing the information needs of front-line social workers. Information systems are becoming more attractive and easy to use. Context-sensitive help, Just-in-Time Training, point and click selection, bar coding input are examples of more recent IT features designed to assist front-line workers. Other examples include look-up tables for addresses, postal codes, eliminating redundant data entry through automatic insertion of common data into appropriate fields, and development of specialised databases.

The notion of IT providing actual decision-support is becoming a reality. With front-line workers becoming significant users of IT and representing the largest bulk of human service workers, the centre of gravity for IT within agencies will shift increasingly towards the front-line worker needs. This should promote applications which are user-oriented and task directed.

In summary, the future of IT in human services in Canada promises to be varied and significant. Given the rapid pace of technological evolution and expansion, it is expected that significant ethical issues will continue to arise. Currently there is much discussion of the availability of child pornography on the Internet and how and whether to police this network. Increased networking raises the issue of who has access to the information, which can create new classes of people 'the haves' and 'the have nots'. There is also increasing concern about the effect of computerisation on increasing depersonalisation within our society. As Quebec parliamentarian Francine Lalonde, MP, notes in reaction to the introduction of the electronic employment kiosks described above (*Toronto Star*, August 3, 1995, p.A13): 'People need individual help and counselling when they are out of work or in dealing with the system. All the computers in the world will not give you that'.

Finally, connectivity or networking is emerging as the brightest star in the universe of IT applications. Given the enormous expanse of Canada and its range of diversities, IT offers the potential to break down many barriers and promote knowledge, awareness, tolerance and communication within the country. As the introduction of the great transcontinental railroads opened up this vast country, the new information superhighways like the Internet promise to add substantially to our connectedness at all levels, as we move to become truly citizens of the world.

References

Baril G. Les Centres Jeunesse du Québec: Le Défi de l'Intégration. *Le Réseau Informatique,* 6(3):5-15. 1994.

Béaulieu G. SICHELD: Les Soins de Longue Durée à l'Haure de l'Informatique. *Le Réseau Informatique*, 7(1):5-12. 1994.

Dutrisac R. Le Libertel de Montréal a des Grandes Ambitions. *Le Devoir*. June 25, 1995.

Gouvernement du Québec. *État d'Avancement des Principaux Projets d'Informatisation du Réseau Sociosanitaire*. Quebec: Comité de Concertation et de Coordination sur les Systèmes et les Technologies de l'Information du Réseau Sociosanitaire (COSTI). 1993.

Larose Y. Mécanismes d'Accès aux Services en Déficience Intellectuelle: Une Première dans le Réseau Sociosanitaire. *Le Réseau Informatique,* 6(3): 8. 1994

MacFadden R, Carson D and Jackson M. Electronic Community: Developing An Automated Network of Information and Referral Services'. *Information and Referral*, Vol.12, No. 1-2, Summer-Winter, 32-51. 1990.

MacFadden R and Pieterson C. Casnet: Linking Child Protection Agencies Electronically. *Computers in Human Services*. Vol. 10, No. 1: 51-53. 1993.

Stentor. *The Information Highway: Canada's Road to Economic and Social Renewal*. Ottawa, ON: Stentor Telecom Policy, Inc. October 1993.

Trahan L. *La Carte Santé (Carte à Microprocesseur ou Carte à Puce)*. Québec: Document de Travail Préparé pour le Groupe de Travail sur l'Utilisation des Médicaments chez les Personnes Âgées; MSSS. 1994.

Turgeon-Krawczuk F. *Un Logiciel Interactif en Service Social: Effets sur les Parents d'Enfants Atteints d'une Maladie Chronique*. Sainte-Foy: École de Service Social, Université Laval. 1993.

World Wide Web sites referred to in this chapter

1. Royal Canadian Mounted Police.
http:/www.maracomm.com/ccsc/

2. Chebucto Community Net, Halifax, Novia Scotia.
http://www.ccn.cs.dal.ca/home.html

3. Halifax Police Department.
http://www.atcon.com/HPD/Hpd.htm

4. Quebec government.
http:/www.gouv.qc.ca

5. Alzheimer Association of Saskatchewan.
http://www.sfn.saskatoon.sk.ca/health/alzheimer/index.html

6. Saskatchewan Adoptive Parents Association.
http://www.sfn.saskatoon.sk.ca/health/sapa/index.html

7. Schizophrenia Society of Saskatchewan
http://www.sfn.saskatoon.sk.ca/health/ssos/index.html

8. Saskatchewan Institute on Prevention of Handicaps.
http://www.sfn.saskatoon.sk.ca/health/siph/index.html

9. Saskatoon Public Health Services
http://www.sfn.saskatoon.sk.ca/health/health/index.html

10. University of New Brunswick. Information for those developing and offering courses over the Web.
http://www.unb.ca/web/wwwdev/

Author details

Robert J. MacFadden, PhD. (Senior Author), is Associate Professor in the Faculty of Social Work at the University of Toronto.

Raymond Carlson, PhD., is a Professor in the School of Social Work at Dalhousie University, Halifax, Nova Scotia.

Oscar Firbank, Dr. Soc., is an Assistant Professsor in the School of Social Work at the Université de Montréal.

Jack Sieppert, Ph.D., is Assistant Professor in the Faculty of Social Work at the University of Calgary.

Contact: Robert J. MacFadden, PhD
Associate Professor
Faculty of Social Work
University of Toronto
700 Bay Street
Toronto
Ontario M5G 1Z6
Canada
E-mail: robert.macfadden@utoronto.ca

6 Denmark

Morten Lindström

HUMAN SERVICES AND INFORMATION TECHNOLOGY

Denmark has a population of five million and an unemployment rate of about 10% (more than 300,000 people). The economy is improving, the trade balance is healthy and high taxes remain the norm. Social and unemployment benefits and pensions circulate through the tax system to those that are eligible for them. There is a tendency for a move more towards the insurance principle, though Denmark remains a welfare state. Compared to other European countries Denmark still has a fairly high level of public service.

Organisation of public services

The state, county councils and local councils are the three main bodies providing public services. The state's role is mainly social legislation, control and refunding expenses to the councils. Some expenses, for example, pensions are 100% state-funded. Others, mostly social benefits, are 50% state and 50% council funded. All guidance work is paid for by the local council.

The role of the fourteen county councils, in the social services is mainly related to severe disability and children/family-guidance, finding foster homes, rehabilitation, running institutions and guidance for local counselling.

The local councils, of which there are 275, vary in size. The smallest council has 6,000 inhabitants and the larger ones have up to 100,000. Two councils break this pattern, Aarhus which has 250,000 inhabitants and Copenhagen which is even larger. The local councils are responsible for culture (education and arts), local infrastructure (roads, buildings, pollution), and social services. They also have their own tax departments. The local councils administer social legislation in general. Any social problem is dealt with and all councils have counselling as a central part of the service.

In Denmark, social workers are a small group of 7,000, of whom 50% are employed by local councils. Residential work is undertaken by other qualified groups, who are trained in a separate school, and called social pedagogues.

In the social service departments of the local councils, approximately 80% of the people employed have access to a personal computer and/or terminal. The rate of investing in both on-line solutions and personal computers is increasing. Computers are used by all councils to calculate and pay benefits. The legislation relating to social benefits was simplified in 1989 and benefits are now paid according to the size of household, rent and few other expenses. This has made it a lot easier for computers to calculate and pay out benefits.

Private organised services

The private human service sector is not a very large part of the social services. The various private organisations deal with people with a specific illness, mental or physical disability, alcohol or other social problems. The organisations mainly support individuals (and/or the family) and function as pressure groups on government and councils. Very few have sufficient funding to support or pay any benefits to the individual. Many have counselling as a main function that is undertaken both by professional staff and volunteers. The government stresses the importance of private organisations taking over responsibility for social services. In Denmark there is no great history of charity and privately sponsored aid, apart from one or two organisations like the Cancer Organisation.

Electronic society

In general, use of technology is increasing across Denmark. Every third household has a personal computer and it is believed that, in a few years time, it will be every second household. Public services are based on computers to a very large extent and the holding of computerised personal information by public services is both accepted and expected by the population. The Central Personal Registration number (CPR) on which the allocation of public services is based is an example of this. Every Dane, or foreigner for that matter, who registers with an address at the local 'people's registration office' (the local council), will have a unique CPR. This consists of the individual's date of birth expressed as six numbers, plus four numbers, where the last number will be even for females and odd for males. The change of attitude from distrust to acceptance of public registration has taken place over the past ten years. Conflict now is not so much between the individual and the services, but rather a matter of what parliament will permit through legislative controls.

Information Society - Year 2000

A new strategy for the Danish society *Information Society - Year 2000* has been proposed. In summary it suggests that:

- Denmark should lead developments to achieve an information society.
- A Danish model will be developed, building on values like, openness, democracy and responsibility for the weakest in Denmark.
- The public sector shall work actively together with the private.

These aims will be achieved by connecting all public bodies in an electronic net. The aim is that once a citizen has given information to a public body, he or she should never have to give the same information again. All public bodies would be able to draw the information from each other's databases. Individuals, public bodies and private firms, would also have the opportunity to communicate electronically, if they so wished. Slowly the strategy might show itself to be a self-fulfilling prophecy like many other strategies from the IT world: in other words it will happen with or without a strategy. Other ways of achieving the 'information society' might be:

- All citizens to be offered an electronic card with PIN-code and picture.
- All public bodies to establish an electronic mail (e-mail) address.
- Some services to be offered as self-services, which can be reached from home-computers or as telephone services.
- The Danish Parliament to publish laws electronically.
- The communication between public services and private firms to be organised via a registration of all firms, like the CPR register.
- Public administration to abandon paper-based ways of working. Paper documents in the future would be scanned and kept in an electronic form.

What then are the implications for human services of this future society? Confidentiality in public services might appear to be lost in a society where information floats freely. Rules and regulations about who shall have access to what, have not yet been established. The European Union states only necessary information should be gathered and kept about citizens and some information should not be gathered at all. Human rights are very much the central discussion here. In Denmark, councils want to combine databases to ensure that citizens do not get more benefits than they should. 'Big-brother-society' is clearly here, but how are we going to handle it?

In human services, the only solution seems to be to establish some ethical rules, about what to register and what not to register about the individual. Ethics are difficult to handle in practice and cannot solve problems before they are known. This is a vital point because information technology has its own way of focusing attention on very important questions, such as how work is organised and how different professionals work. If such matters have not been dealt with before, then information technology forces decisions to be taken. If this is not done, then the problems will be exacerbated at a later stage. We see this much more clearly now that the information-society is moving closer. How are we going to organise human services in the future? How are hospitals going to cooperate with councils? How are social workers going to register files in the future and who shall have access? Some ethical rules for human services could be suggested:

- Do not enter into a computer anything which you do not want to see on someone else's screen.
- Make sure information is correct before any action is taken.
- Information about who has looked at files and when, must be recorded and given both to the citizen and the professional.
- The citizen should always give his or her permission when information is gathered from other sources.
- The professional should never take any action without the client's knowledge.

This list is not complete, but the idea of using ethical rules to regulate professionals' behaviour seems the only way to deal with an information society in the future.

INFORMATION FOR CITIZENS

As outlined above, public services in Denmark are mostly publicly funded and organised at three levels although there are also some private organisations. The information strategy for citizens has been developed mainly by local councils through a council-owned national company called Kommunedata. Some of the advantages of information systems are:

- Fast and correct information.
- Citizens can get access to relevant information about themselves, their rights and obligations.
- The public administration can serve a larger number of cases, when services are provided with computer-assistance.

Self-service

Self-service information, where citizens access information via telephones or computers, is very much in evidence in taxation in Denmark. People who have simple tax forms, only have to sign that all the information required is there. They can also call the telephone service (with their own PIN-code) and accept or alter the tax form. There is a strong movement towards more information being provided by computers thus the personal contact between the public services and the citizen will lessen. Some groups, like the elderly or handicapped, have difficulties using the systems. Special services are offered to meet their needs but the result is they cannot use the services in the same way as the rest of the population. Once again there are fears that these groups will miss opportunities open to others.

The self-service strategy has been fairly successful with the telephone as the media but so far it has not been as successful with computers. Various experiments using computers have been carried out but it was found that people stopped using the computers after a while. This might, however, change in the future when access to many services, like travel, shopping and so on might be gained by using computers. Home banking has been taken up, but so far only by a few banks. On-line services are being offered and it seems that people will use systems, if they can get relevant information, and are able to handle the technology. User-friendly technology is therefore the key. As more and more daily business can be dealt with from home, the use of the systems will increase but for many years we shall still see electronically based services alongside staff based services.

Quick counters and background workers in local councils

Local councils have organised their services with front staff on a ‘quick counter’. These staff will either deal with citizens’ questions or refer them to other services or guidance. This front line service is crucial to how the individual’s problem is dealt with. Computer supported guidance is offered and appointments are handled. Only if citizens have a problem which cannot be dealt with over the counter, will they be referred to specialist background staff such as social workers who take care of, for example, children, the family, the unemployed and elderly people.

The organisation of local councils differ, but the main tendency is to organise services by age-groups. Services for children consist of daycare, kindergarten and schools. Adult services are focused on people with disabilities; people who are unemployed; rehabilitation services; and, for the elderly, home help and homes for old people. Computers are integral to the services as they provide data for the professionals on which they can register and handle information and pay out financial benefits. Documentation then moves from the local archives to countrywide mainframe computers.

Social work and computer use

In most councils, social workers do all the administrative work such as paying out money and writing files and documents themselves using a computer. In the near future they will also use electronic mail. This means that clients meet both a social worker and a screen. Already complaints have been heard from both clients and social workers that the screen takes attention and time away from the clients. However, the social worker doing the administrative part of the work while the client is there, can be a good thing. Agreements are handled on the spot and things happen here and now. Importantly, clients do have an opportunity to control the information on screen but in some cases they may not understand what is presented on the screen. If people are not used to having information presented in this way, then they may easily be confused. In addition, the design of screens is not all that user-friendly, and with the possibility of a lot of windows of information on screen at any one time, a skilled reader is needed to keep track of it all.

Community information

Access to general information about the community can be reached through libraries and many have links to databases or give CD-ROM access locally. These services are rapidly increasing. Some councils offer citizens direct access to administrative information, agendas and information about the economy. Systems such as these are being developed and experiments carried out. However a general model for development has not yet been found.

Unemployment

Employment is dealt with by both the local councils and the state funded employment offices. Citizens can walk into the offices and look up information, either printed or on screen (in both cases information comes from computers). Job matching is the major concern and has been in action for many years. Now that the unemployment rate is going down, it has become much more important as there is a lack of available workers in some areas. Labour cannot always be retrained to meet the needs of industry quickly enough. Much effort is put into this area and hopefully we shall see less people in the future without relevant work experience.

VOCATIONAL EDUCATION AND TRAINING

Social work education is changing and so is the information technology that is taught. In 1994/95 social work education was evaluated and practitioners, employers, students and teachers all gave their views. One of the points which was stressed, was that the teaching of information technology needs to be strengthened. When a social worker is employed in councils, it is expected that he or she can handle computer assisted tasks such as: report writing, paying out money and administration. Files must be kept up to date and general information for management must be produced and processed. This situation demands an ability to handle both counselling and computing, often at the same time. A small survey revealed a social worker in one week had looked at nearly 1000 different screens as part of his work. Often secretaries have been transferred to other tasks.

Social work practice is putting pressure on schools of social work to educate students to be able to cope with the technology found in practice. The schools are putting more effort into this, but lack of trained staff/teachers who can actually teach this subject is a major barrier. Younger teachers with technology skills are slowly moving into the schools, but older teachers still predominate. The schools offer courses in word processing and tools for statistical purposes are taught. One program to handle law and regulations is well developed, and is taught integrated with law subjects. The next part of the curriculum to be developed will be on ethics in information technology and this will be a key feature of future teaching, again integrated with other subjects. A special course in information technology with examinations is not a part of the plan. The technology will be used as a part of social work itself, and therefore closely linked to relevant, or perhaps all, subjects once more software is developed.

The software used by the councils is often developed within each council. Each has its own standards and their systems differ in functionality which gives new employees problems. In some places staff have had a lot of influence on the development of the programs to be used for administrative purposes and feel good about them. However, when new staff arrive they often cannot identify with the programs and may even find them difficult to use. This situation presents schools with the problem of what to teach. Additionally there are issues such as confidentiality: students cannot work with real family data but have to set up test data. In this way they are only working with a model of reality. For training reasons this might be acceptable, but it gives the impression to the students that they are playing rather than working with real life situations. Though this same pedagogical problem is also found in other subjects, it becomes much more a key issue in information technology. One of the problems is that most of the systems in use run on large mainframes which the schools cannot access.

The tools for practice are improving - screens are better and the on-line social legislation relevant for supporting advice-giving are very good now. One company, Schultz, has the largest market share with their program **Lovguide.** Other big companies tried to compete, spent a lot of money and, more or less, went out of business. Even the biggest company Kommunedata, gave up the development of their law support system. Denmark is probably too small a market for more than one company in this field. The schools do use Lovguide with their students.

In the near future, the schools will have to face new technology in order to prepare students to work as social workers beyond the year 2000. As the information-society moves closer, as files are being shipped between councils and information floats more freely between public and private bodies, social work has to be aware of the problems and possibilities. It is likely that all councils will get Internet links in the future. Kommunedata runs the largest network in Denmark at present, with all the councils linked to their mainframes. The idea is to link this to the Internet. Some councils already offer WWW home pages, an extension of information systems which will be very important in the future.

PROVISION OF SERVICES

There are as many different information systems as there are councils. A few systems are countrywide but no-one has a total overview of what is used and to what extent. Nonetheless some general comments are offered. Local councils are responsible for counselling and paying out money. To fulfill these tasks, the systems used are the CPR-database, the benefit calculation system, employment possibilities and records of files. Systems like these are used by all councils with the aim to register money and progress in counselling, as well as to control staff and finance. Denmark has had very few cases where staff have shifted money to their own bank accounts and systems are designed so that it should be very difficult or impossible to do this.

The development of managerial tools are of great importance. Well presented data generated from other systems are very useful for management. These data will often have importance at the political level as well and are, to some extent, integrated into systems being developed for politicians. Electronic mail and remote access, enables local politicians to work from home and gather information at any time of the day. Agendas and files are being transferred. Whether this is a useful development or not, remains to be seen. Experiences are limited but one belief is that information can kill all initiative. So much information can be received that there is a problem with sorting it out and deciding what to read.

Hospitals are a part of the responsibility of county councils. The aim is for files to be transferred electronically to and from other hospitals and private GPs. This is ambitious given the many different ways in which professionals work. This has not yet occurred but the development is towards the generic electronic file. This means all staff in the sector have to agree on how the file should look, what information is needed and for what purpose. Doctors will look at their special needs of registration, as will others such as nurses, physiotherapists and social workers. There is also the problem that various professionals will differ in their views about what information is important. To create a general, more or less global information system seems to be a very difficult task, even though many developers believe it can be done. One point to be made here is that social work has a multiplicity of methods which are adapted to the problem to be solved. Computers tend to use one methodology and if the system also has to be used by other professionals, some clear boundaries and common fields need to be defined. Fast and up-to-date information will benefit services and patients, but the use of limited resources must be questioned in relation to other needs.

CONCLUSION AND FUTURE DEVELOPMENTS

Some of the future developments are described earlier in this chapter, specifically self-service developments and remote access to information systems. They encompass some of the key issues which human services will be faced with in the near future:

- When systems are developed for a certain professional group, the professionals have to be very clear about their methods. For example, when social workers in the hospital sector define how the screens of their file system will look, they need to agree on one method to keep files and how and what to register about the citizens. This cannot be done without some compromises. The alternative is not to define categories of problems and methods but the screen will then have a lot of free text and with less possibility of drawing out general information about the client group. Management will consequently have less statistical information and therefore less control of workers and policy.
- Can professionals agree to a single recording method? Such a system might restrict the use of other methods or future developments. Systems are normally very difficult to alter, once they are running. Thus social workers have to compromise on methods because of computer systems and supply general information by other means. On the other hand, general information about the work, can be very useful in supervision or just to give feedback to the social worker on the state of the art. The future will show how this problem is dealt with, but it is hoped that professionals will be aware of the traps once development and implementation begin in earnest.
- Until recently, software was not been able to meet expectations and to some extent this is still the case. Social workers have been disappointed many times when introduced to new systems. The promises have been high but the reality once the systems are implemented is very different. The user interface has been frustrating, for instance when working on mainframes the user has to log in and out when using different systems. Many special commands have to be remembered and, in the beginning, large manuals took up work space. Better tools for developers and improved computers are slowly changing the situation. Social workers and other professionals will use systems to a much greater extent when the interface problem has been overcome. Windows seems to be the answer.
- Simply introducing more information technology is not the answer to professional questions and IT should only be used as a tool for professionals in their other tasks. IT appears to have the nature of being the answer, without anyone knowing the question. This trap demands that professionals must be very clear about what to use and why. Clarification of professional aims and methods are key words here.

Citizen information is a means to greater influence over one's own situation and is basic to the feeling of power and being enabled to make changes. The more information the citizen has, the better he or she is able to act. In critical situations the self-service systems should offer counselling for the citizen to help them to decide what to do. Therefore a major task is to look into what types of information should also include the offer of counselling. If somebody wants to know how far down the waiting list for daycare they are, this information should be given, with no further advice. If a question of how you get a divorce is asked, one might consider offering counselling along with the information. Automation in human services means citizens themselves diagnose the problem. Often this is straightforward, but sometimes the diagnosis is not clear. When this occurs, the citizen will have difficulties about which questions to ask.

Author details

Morten Lindström trained as a social worker and is the head of department at the School of Social Work in Aarhus. He led a research-project on the impact of computers on public services, focusing on social service departments and computers used directly by the public. He is a member of the ENITH executive committee and serves on various Danish committees on use of information technology.

Contact: Morten Lindström
Head of Department
School of Social Work
Aarhus
Stenvej 4
8270 Hojbjerg
Denmark

Telephone: + 86 27 66 22
Fax: + 86 27 74 76
E-mail: mortenl@inet.uni-c.dk

7 Finland

Sirpa Kuusisto-Niemi and Victor Savtschenko

HUMAN SERVICES AND INFORMATION TECHNOLOGY

Finland has about five million inhabitants of whom more than three million live in cities and less than two million in the countryside. The country is divided into 450 municipalities which vary in size from 140 inhabitants to 500,000.

Social policy is a living and changing entity in Finland. Within social policy are included social security and labour, health, housing, alcohol and education policy. The arena is frequently divided into social welfare and social insurance, representing different types of funding and welfare organisation. For its part, social security includes preventive social welfare and health care; social welfare and health services and income security. Social welfare services include social work, income benefit (income security assistance), home help services, housing services, child day care and institutional care. The functions of social welfare services change over time and now also include the care of refugees. Social insurance is based on both statutory and voluntary insurance. From a citizen's point of view, municipalities and the Social Insurance Institution (SII) are the most important players in the field; both basic and special social care are mainly provided from here. Furthermore, the role of the informal sector in these services has been relatively small, even though they are now expanding.

As a result of the large degree of autonomy with elected councils and taxation rights, municipalities shoulder the main responsibility for providing welfare services and guaranteeing subsistence for people without means. Municipalities also provide the most basic services to citizens, mostly their own inhabitants, including elementary and high schools, technical services like water and waste supply as well as cultural services such as libraries, museums, and sports and recreation services. Each municipality produces its own services or, in cooperation with other municipalities, purchases them on the private market. Municipalities are subsidised by the government to cover their expenses in proportion to their population. At present, over 100,000 people are employed in different aspects of social welfare services with another 100,000 employed in municipal health services.

The other main player, the SII, is a national insurance agency under parliamentary supervision. Its activities are funded mainly through insurance contributions from insured people and employers. Its functions include National Pension Insurance, National Sickness Insurance and National Basic Unemployment Allowance. The SII also has various additional functions, for example, child allowances and maternity allowances, which are not based on social insurance but funded through taxation. Use of advanced computer technology is a cornerstone of SII's operations, with a huge computer centre, large mainframes and customised software.

Nationwide development and planning activities take place in the Ministry of Social Affairs and Health. The Ministry sets overall guidelines and the main development areas in the five year plan, renewed yearly, by Parliament. Control of the municipalities has diminished since 1993, when the Act of State led to renewed subsidies to municipalities to respond to their growing demands to practice more independent and locally adaptable policies. During 1994, the Ministry took an active role in evaluating information technology development, preparing for the National Strategy for Social and Health Care in this area.

The Ministry for Social Affairs and Health has several agencies executing its tasks. One of interest here is the National Research and Development Centre for Welfare and Health (STAKES). By agreement with the Ministry it is concerned with matters which include IT development in the field.

State policy is put into effect through provincial administration. Twelve Provincial Boards have Departments of Social Affairs and Health, which direct and supervise implementation of welfare and health policy of the municipalities in the province territory. The Provincial Boards started extensive use of information technology in the 1980s and a computer network was established between them which has been further developed. The status and role of the Provincial Boards are under discussion because Finland's joining of the European Union in early 1995 raised questions concerning subsidiarity. A new provincial institution, Provincial Administrative Councils (Maakuntahallinto), which is based on economic and other aspects has been founded. It is also a part of state administration, but has not (yet) been given any social or health care activities.

The future of the welfare infrastructure is now in flux. Finland has experienced a grave economic recession from the early 1990s which has raised unemployment rates to a high level. As a consequence, public expenditure - including welfare funds - has been severely cut. The widely accepted idea of Finland as a welfare state has been challenged in the public debate that has taken place. The desire for municipal sovereignty has also raised discussion on the type and level of services municipalities are to provide to their inhabitants with demands to open regulated social and health care markets to the market economy. Planning welfare development can now be considered to be under scrutiny more than ever before.

Ethical aspects

There are two key ethical questions in the ongoing discussion. Firstly, there is a fear that the nation will divide economically and socially into two, with those who do well under self-help in one group and those on low incomes or living on allowances (which have been lowered to an absolute minimum) in the other. Secondly, questions concerning confidentiality in IT and the collecting of sensitive information about customers and service producers have been acute. It is this second issue that concerns us here.

Administration in Finland is based on the principle of openness. Information in documents can be divided into public, discretionary and secret information. In social security and social welfare services, however, confidentiality is the main principle. The rules are stipulated in sector legislation and in the general Data Protection Act concerning personal information and other legislation.

The Bureau of Data Ombudsman and the Union of Finnish Municipalities have published in cooperation a data protection document concerning municipal administration. Special interest has been paid to social and health care matters, with examples of everyday situations, since issues of privacy are found mostly in this area. There is a simultaneous process in the Ministry of Social Affairs and Health to prepare the law on customers' rights in social services. The goal is to define equal rights for social and health care customers, the latter having already been defined in 1993. There are still many questions, some due to the different nature of social and health care services. Nevertheless, this is seen as a means to put right present short-comings in privacy protection legislation in this sector.

Difficulties in solving actual data protection problems in IT in social services include the questions of uniting databases for different social and health care services produced in cooperation between sectors; transferring personal information inside and between service providers and using data for other than customer service functions, such as statistics. The amount of information collected from one person is huge even for minor services, due to the lack of a standard dataset for customer services. In addition, it has also seemed quite difficult for both IT companies and IT users to solve the conflict between collecting data only for specific purposes and the general administrative requirement to collect all possible data for future purposes.

Finland is participating in the European discussion on data protection which, so far, has concentrated on health care. From the Finnish point of view, the discussion of gene technology is of special interest because patients' rights to privacy might relate to the discussion of the rights of social service customers, especially when compulsory administrative decisions are to be made.

The following example illustrates the present discussion on data confidentiality. There is a customer database jointly used by different sub-applications in social welfare applications. The best way to create a customer database for municipal welfare work is by automatic direct access into the population register covering all local inhabitants.

This avoids typing in each welfare client's personal data. Identification of an individual client can be performed efficiently and accurately by use of the statutory identity number. As welfare work develops towards a comprehensive system, this enables extensive and flexible management of the user's situation. To protect confidentiality, applications normally restrict access by each employee to information needed specifically for accomplishing their duties. The question is, who decides who is to have access to the information already collected?

INFORMATION FOR CITIZENS

The use of IT in the municipalities actually started in the 1960s. This rapid development did not initially produce any direct services for citizens, even though there were some ambitious experiments to bring basic service information to all. These ideas, however, have survived, and since the beginning of the 1990s there has been a new wave of such ideas. They are examined in this chapter.

At the national level, the present government of Prime Minister Paavo Lipponen has published its program called *Developing a Finnish Information Society.* Social care and health are being discussed generally and the development of a welfare cluster as a part of the industrial strategy has been raised as a crucial point. The aim is for faster and more flexible service availability and better functioning services for social welfare and health. Services, such as, telemedicine, use of multimedia, electronic transactions and security services, which help citizens in their homes have been raised in status.

Individual and community support technology - citizens and IT

In recent years there have been several serious attempts to develop an arena for citizens to find information about services. One of the most ambitious was a large Neighbourhood Office Project, which followed the Danish example, in cooperation with Finnish municipalities and State administration. The activities continued after the project finished in 1994 and now about thirty municipalities, many in cooperation with state authorities like State Post, have this technology in everyday use. The Neighbourhood Offices offer an opportunity to fill in applications, make reservations for municipal services and get advice from 'general officers' who guide the customer to a 'special officer' if expert help is needed.

Another interesting example is in a provincial library located in Jyvaskyla City. There a neighbourhood office called **PALLAS** Service Forum has been implemented for applicants. The office has a micro-computer connected to a network offering multi-media and hyper-media systems. The user can obtain information and request services by means of a touch screen. The basic directory models a human life cycle with potential fields of difficulty and services needed, including childhood, youth, old age, personal crisis and economic distress. The hypertext features enable the user to dip into the points of his or her interest. The system includes the opportunity to fill in application forms for services (such as day care), which are automatically transmitted electronically to the appropriate system. It is also possible to perform allowance calculations and net income simulations.

Another interesting program is being presented by Perlacon Oy, a small-size IT company, which has specialised in maintaining and delivering the **KOTO** program, a three-level model of calculating household income and subsidies in relation to each other. It can be used at a citizen level, an individual giving income details and then shown different alternatives of state and municipal subsidies. It can also be used by government officials in their everyday work of managing a client's finances, and at the planning and development level of administration to evaluate the effects of changes to subsidies or taxation. The Ministry of Social Affairs and Health is cooperating with the company and updating the information included.

In the general information network in Finland there has been a telecommunication project called **TELMO** (Integrated Teleservices) which started in 1988. The initial development phase ended in 1992 and TELMO is now the overall name for the interactive information network medium - for enterprises and the public sector as well as for ordinary citizens. TELMO is competing with other information delivery channels, such as radio, television and newspaper and its use is expected to rise. Applications most used include the banking system, electronic mail and messaging systems and directory services. Information services and entertainment applications are also widely used and there are opportunities to link to international networks from TELMO.

Linked to TELMO the Ministry of Social Affairs and Health started a sub-project in 1991, called Social Security in Public Telecommunication Network. Today this application, available also through the Internet as Web pages, provides information for recipients and service providers about social security and social and health services in Finland. Responsibility for recording and updating this application rests with government and municipal authorities, the Social Insurance Institution, public and private foundations and organisations providing services.

It has been estimated, that at the beginning of 1995 there were over a million micro computers in households and organisations in Finland. This development, together with the reduction of employees in municipalities, may cause problems for citizens not capable of using IT or with no access to it. The possible consequences have not yet been discussed widely.

Municipalities and information technology

In Finland it is difficult to talk about social welfare IT development without mentioning municipalities. The 1980s saw a rapid expansion of the use of IT. Today even the smallest rural municipalities possess, at a minimum, a microcomputer. In social services, the most widely used applications are those for home help services, children's daycare and financial administration for institutional care. A close runner-up seems to be an application for social workers to evaluate work by themselves or together with the customer (and his or her family).

Social welfare has always been an integral part of municipal administration. This creates demands for hardware and software. It is important to pass payment transfers to clients' bank accounts and to organise salary payments for social welfare staff, and this happens through municipal IT equipment. A side-effect has been that applications have not been developed further. By far, the greatest use of IT in municipalities is in administration. This is now saturated however and in recent years the biggest rise in IT investment has been social and health care. It seems set to continue further.

The applications markets have also stabilised during the last two to three years and there are two serious suppliers in the social welfare field: KT-Tietokeskus (jointly owned by communes) and a subsidiary of the State Computer Centre, VTKK Kuntajarjestelmat Oy. Several smaller suppliers are selling applications for different social welfare tasks, but they do not form a comprehensive system for the whole field.

Employment and training

Professional training for disabled people is given in fifteen specialised educational establishments with about 2,000 pupil places in all. IT has a role either as an auxiliary system supporting training, or as a part of the curriculum. Worth mentioning in this respect are the Training Centre of the National Association of the Disabled, and the ARLA Institute which trains people with visual disabilities. The former is for people with physically disabilities. It has one branch for commercial training, another for other professions, with training for two to three years for about 500 pupils. IT occupies a crucial position both as a technological base supporting teaching and as a part of the curriculum. A microcomputer equipped with specially designed support devices may be the sole means for a person who is severely disabled to participate in training. The Centre has experimented with multi-media training, and informatics are also an important part of the teaching. Disabled pupils receiving training for commerce are taught the use of IT in financial management and operational accounting. Pupils trained for office work receive instruction on the use of informatics in office automation.

This Training Centre also organises evening and weekend classes for people with disabilities. Distance education is arranged for some twenty severely people with disabilities who are unable to participate in classes. They are enabled to study at home using micro-computers equipped with auxiliary devices, provided by the Social Insurance Institution. Course materials and written exercises are exchanged by electronic mail.

The ARLA Institute is a state vocational training establishment for people with visual disabilities, but includes some pupils with hearing disabilities and even some deaf-blind pupils. There are about 160 pupils. IT is a supplementary facility used in all teaching. Each pupil receives practical instruction at some level of micro-computer use. Those unable to use an ordinary micro-computer use specially designed programs and equipment such as enlarged display texts and braille display. Blind pupils unable to learn braille use a speech synthesizer. Computer aided instruction is also used in teaching languages. The Institute also educates pupils as computer professionals by teaching software programming and design. Courses in installation of micro-computers have also been arranged and the Institution has developed a braille display of its own.

Informal sector

The informal sector can be divided in two in matters of information technology use. Established organisations like the Finnish Red Cross, the Central Union for the Welfare of the Aged and the Finnish Federation for Social Welfare, which have been active for decades, are trained to use IT on a large scale. Registration of members, internal administrative actions and customer services which are liable to charges, like home helps, are supported by IT. Earlier small information systems, usually for specialist groups, were available through the public telecommunication network, maintained by the Finnish Telecom. The *RULLATEN Association* maintains a database for people with disabilities in the public telecommunication network. This consists of twenty items, including the Act on Services and Assistance for the Disabled and guidance on the application of the Act. It also enables interactive communication, with a bulletin board for discussion and creation of ideas. **FIMNET**, the information system for physicians maintained by the Finnish Medical Association includes use of e-mail and contacts with medical databases.

A new experiment in this field is **JELLI**, an information network for citizens from the Finnish Federation for Social Welfare together with City of Joensuu in Eastern Finland. The aim of this experiment is to offer local social and health care service information in a welfare-mix context and at the same time advise on effective IT use.

New informal organisations have not necessarily been organised in a traditional sense, and it is usually a question of finance as to whether they have significant IT development. However, there is a promising start of this kind. The *Citizen Forum* (Kansalaisareena) is an open forum for everyone who wants to cooperate on questions like: voluntary work and voluntary centres, self-help groups, alternative ways of employment and citizen actions in local communities. It is now expanding its activities by planning a register of self-help groups who are willing to cooperate, and providing its information services to all who want access. This project has financial support from the Finnish Slot Machine Association to start a service station, which also includes database registers.

Independent living

Information technology is also applied in several specialised fields. These include rehabilitation of disabled or elderly people and promotion of their independent living, information, communications, and planning welfare development. Research and development work has been undertaken by government boards, by associations for disabled people and by private companies. In developing systems for disabled people, a major contribution has made by the state-owned Technical Research Centre of Finland (VTT) and its Medical Engineering Laboratory.

Use of computers in rehabilitation and training of people with disabilities, and as auxiliary devices supporting their independent living, has greatly increased over the last few years. Finland has several centres, in central hospitals and institutes, that examine need for supportive devices and procure equipment. A pioneer in this field is the Finnish Association on Mental Retardation which maintains experimentation and research activity on rehabilitation and training. It also maintains the Centre for Teaching Materials, a databank and a resource centre. Another active organisation is the National Association for the Hard of Hearing. Through its research and development activities, several types of IT-based supportive devices and services have been produced.

Kaikuharju School (in Lahti City, Southern Finland) has, for over ten years, been developing IT-based teaching methods tailored to the needs of children with impaired hearing or with logopedic disturbances. Connected with this school, is a standing exhibition and we may safely state that Kaikuharju School represents the very top in its field worldwide. An important contribution in the development and application of information technologies for support devices has also been made by the Central Association of Visually Handicapped. This has been particularly in developing a library (largely IT operated) maintained by the Association available for visually disabled people nationwide. There is also a long-term experiment communicating newspapers to visually disabled people using IT.

A person who is severely disabled can apply for an allowance from the Social Insurance Institution to purchase auxiliary devices that enable participation in working life. An allowance presupposes there is a prospective job or that the applicant is receiving professional training. In the latter case, the device must be essential for the training. About 250 allowances are granted each year, mainly to people with sensory handicaps, usually for micro-computers with accessories.

It is difficult to estimate how many disabled people depend on IT to work. Employers have very limited access to subsidies to provide employment to disabled persons. The explosive increase in unemployment from the early 1990s further reduced employment of disabled people. Finland, like most countries, has some well-known, severely disabled experts, entrepreneurs and even politicians whose activities are only possible through use of auxiliary equipment based on IT. Some employers are also applying telework and there is even an association called Finnish Flexiwork Forum to support the program started by the Ministry of Labour. However, none of these address problems of integrating people with disabilities into working life.

Supply does not, however, match the need and we are far from each person with disabilities having at his/her disposal an IT-based supportive device for rehabilitation, study or needs of everyday living or participation in working life.

European integration of policies for people who are disabled and elderly makes international cooperation important. The Nordic countries have a tradition of cooperation between themselves. The National Institutes for Technical Aids, for instance are highly involved in European IT development programmes.

As in other Nordic countries, organisations of people with disabilities play an important role in the development and implementation of aids - along with rehabilitation and education organisations, and the business world as a professional partner. Access to information about technical aids is a cornerstone for development and implementation of these products. Nordic cooperation functions directly between the institutions concerned and is also disseminated via common Nordic bodies. One is the Nordic Committee on Disability (NNH), an institution under the Nordic Council of Ministers. Many Nordic initiatives originate from the NNH which has initiated joint Nordic resource centres such as the Nordic Development Centre for Rehabilitation Engineering (NUH) in Tampere, Finland. The NUH promotes Nordic development of high technology technical aids and coordinates and finances projects. These include computer based hardware and software for disabled people, with the main areas being telematics, access to computers and communication.

There is also the Nordic Forum for Telecommunications and Disability (NFTH) which coordinates and exchanges experience of work in telecommunications. This ensures, for example, shared work in the European Standardisation body for Telecommunications (ETSI) and in the other European standardisation bodies. Disability groups have established an umbrella organisation, the Nordic Council of Disabled Persons Organisations (HNR) which coordinates and ensures exchange of information between the different organisations and represents disabled people.

VOCATIONAL EDUCATION AND TRAINING

IT integrated in the curriculum

Social welfare workers are educated in universities, taking a higher academic degree in this field. Finland has six universities in which social welfare education is available. In addition to these academic professions, the welfare sector has several other vocations. Education for these posts is available in over twenty educational establishments of intermediate grade. Normally, the length of this type of education is two to four years. Instruction in IT, at least at some level, is today available in all universities and intermediate grade educational establishments. However, this is mainly composed of basic courses in informatics (for example, text processing and spreadsheet use). IT applications needed in their future professions as social service providers are not normally taught in these classes. Specialised informatics training is usually given in work situations. Suppliers of computers arrange training in the use of newly purchased hardware and software. When required, employers arrange extra training for their employees.

The Outokumpu Vocational Institute in the small town of Outokumpu, Eastern Finland, provides education in social welfare, in addition to other subjects. This education is an experiment for a new type of intermediate grade educational establishment where an academic degree in social welfare can be taken. The degree in question includes a compulsory course in social technology, which can be taken alternatively as a brief (nine study weeks) or an extensive (twenty weeks) course. Social technology is divided in three subgroups: technology in relation to living environments - technology supporting independent living - technology used by social welfare workers. The scope of social technology is naturally wider than that of information technology. However, the latter has a prominent role.

Since the beginning of 1992, the University of Lapland has been using the aforementioned PALLAS application in education. The idea is to evaluate functioning of technical systems in social work. The University is working to find out how IT can direct social work practice.

PROVISION OF SERVICES

The first aspects is that of developments at a practice level. Applications used by social welfare authorities are administrative, planning and development or welfare service production tools. Software is mainly available for welfare fields in which activities are based on clear calculation formulae or on established traditions (child daycare and homecare systems). The available software does not necessarily support new activities developed by the municipalities and is of limited help in developing the substance and implementation of welfare policy.

The main applications today of IT for communal welfare activities are home service and care systems, child daycare systems, maintenance allowance (income security assistance) systems, service invoicing, client information systems and family maintenance systems. The latter includes several applications for different tasks in the field, like child welfare, maintenance allowances and work with intoxicant abusers.

Information systems

Client, community care and management information systems are mostly based on quantitative information about clients and service provision. Monitoring of quality and effectiveness aspects are still, in general, waiting to come. There are, however, some interesting recent innovations, like applications including service planning items or evaluating the progress in clients' situations. In these applications the social worker plans future work or evaluates work done, either alone or, in more developed versions, together with the customer. Of great importance in these applications is the fact that the final users have been active in the IT development process. An example is the decision making system in childminding in Helsinki City. Another is in Jyvaskyla City, concentrating on social work effectiveness and evaluation.

An application, including planning and developing items to applications, has been developed by Tieto-konserni during the last few years. The **Care and Service Plan** application includes elementary information about services used by a customer and about his or her housing, social situation, physical and mental situation, medication and daily managing. This application is used in cooperation with all social and health care professionals involved in an individual's daily care at home, service houses and homes for the elderly as well as in primary care. All social welfare decisions made in municipal administration are subject to a formal complaints procedure which customers can follow. This procedure has transferred well to computer applications.

Managing services

The standardisation of social welfare terminology is poorly developed and this has caused problems, for example, for data transfer from communal to state statistical databases. On the other hand, standardisation of basic customer information is well organised. Client information systems enable data transfer from the population register database, maintained by the State Population Registration Centre, to the respective client database in a communal computer fairly well nowadays. The population register has personal data on all people living permanently in Finland.

Social welfare departments use both administrative applications of the municipality and office automation systems of word processing, spreadsheet and electronic mail. There are several companies offering applications for managing personnel and administrative data in use. Recent studies on municipal IT use show that the coverage of accounting, budget and wages applications is up to 100 per cent in IT user municipalities.

One telematic application, called **SANTRA**, has to be mentioned here, due to its modest price and the effective use of existing telecommunications network. It has been developed for use in home help units and other similar contexts where staff move around and see customers in their homes. It is difficult for the staff to reach their manager, for instructions or for changes in customer information because distances, especially in rural areas, are quite large. Using a normal telephone, a home help worker can dial a personal identification sign to get tape-recorded instructions or leave messages for a manager. This application is used in several units, especially in those municipalities, where home help work is delivered by modern, independent work-groups.

Policy level

Four different tools for policy level applications are presented here.

- **Evergreen** is an application, which includes the whole continuum of care for the elderly in the welfare and health sectors. It consists of three modules: the main file with one hundred variables; the basic analysis module for socio-economic monitoring and evaluation; and the modelling module for systematisation of alternative models. Evergreen enables processes for analysis and evaluation of the care system, and modelling care policy and its consequences in terms of the number of clients and resources required for the services. The resources include personnel, funds and premises, as well as total and per capita expenditures. The application includes three fixed models: a trend-extrapolation model and two optimisation models. The modelling facilities will be further developed to improve the cost-efficiency of elderly care policy. The end users of Evergreen are the local authorities responsible for welfare and health services and researchers interested in socio-economic policy research in the field. The first version was developed during 1989/90 in STAKES where development work continues.

- Making use of data coming from client and administrative information systems is the basis for STAKES preparing and updating the national **SOTKA** database of social and health care indicators, based on yearly statistics from the municipalities. Statistics will be gathered from various sources, for example, statistics and registers of STAKES, Statistics Finland and the SII. Statistics include both client and economic data. There are some 2,700 variables in the database, of which about 1,700 are raw data and the rest, ready-calculated variables. SOTKA is designed to be the main source of welfare and health statistics for municipalities. Technically, the user needs the SOTKA software for a PC and Internet-type of access to general information networks.
- On a commercial basis, the municipalities are creating, defining and updating their own **VERTTI**-benchmarking database tool for comparisons in and between municipalities. A database has been developed for technical sectors in municipalities and is now expanding to social and health care indicators in child day care, care for the elderly, social work and municipal primary health care. The emphasis in defining parameters is on economical aspects, productivity and effectiveness. The coordinator of this project is Efektia Service Ltd, a consultant company owned by The Association of Finnish Municipalities.
- **Quality Profile Estimation** is a more comprehensive application, uniting different demands for resource use at local administration levels. It was developed initially for use in social planning, but has also been tested for use in service planning for people who are elderly or disabled. The aim is to gather users/customers and their organisations, society planners, authorities and politicians to discuss targets, to evaluate common goals and to value different environmental factors. As a result this application produces graphical quality profiles. Profiles are turned into alternative development strategies with the help of experts. The model can be tailored to the requirements of the customer. Having started at the end of the 1980s at a government level, it has now been developed further privately.

There is one more aspect at a policy level to be mentioned. A large working group was appointed to prepare a research programme for social technology and this was accomplished in 1991. As a result of this work, STAKES has adopted the role of promoting development of social technology, requiring good cooperation all round. The Social Technology Research Programme examines technology from three viewpoints, these are: living environments, independent living and technology needed by personnel. This policy has been put in practice through numerous projects - some international (COST, TIDE), others are purely national. Some projects originate from the research programme, others are older or otherwise independent.

CONCLUSIONS AND FUTURE DEVELOPMENTS

Some development processes can be seen as necessary at this stage of information technology use in Finland. There is an urgent need for research and development in the IT industry countrywide instead of concentrating on tailoring applications which, in practice, means wasting resources. As a result, there is an unavoidable need to standardise the structures and terms used in social welfare work and IT practices. This work has been started in STAKES with a small-scale terminology study of basic terms needed in a standard dataset base for customer service, and preparation of the revised archives regulations for social and health care documents both in authority and private care. This task will be finished during 1996. Still, it is the beginning of standardisation work needed in the field.

The demand for the development of data protection in applications seems unavoidable. This is also connected to standardisation issues because if a database has not been standardised, it is impossible to define exact units for user access.

Coordination of the legal basis of customer service in human services depends on the stage of development of legislation. Customer rights cannot be defined in applications without the appropriate regulation (which is not yet in place but is under preparation). To verify customers' rights, they should be strengthened with obligatory cooperative stages. Without the customer signing for the plan or report at certain stages, it would not be possible to continue documentation of the case.

A widening of views about information systems at a national level is also needed. The narrow view is to see systems as useful only in order to utilise statistics for state purposes not for client services. This has a harmful effects on the quality of the statistics which, at the client serving level, are seen only as a nuisance and not as any kind of help for future work development.

Author details

Sirpa Kuusisto-Niemi is Chief in Social Service Informatics at STAKES, the National Research and Development Centre for Welfare and Health in Finland. She specialises in Social Care Informatics both planning social care forms for nationwide use, and planning and development of an information framework for social and health care services in municipalities and NGOs. Sirpa Kuusisto-Niemi is also a consultant for functioning and quality for municipal social care, and she coordinates social and health care data development and evaluation at a national level.

Victor Savtschenko is the senior planning officer for STAKES. He specialises in development projects applying information technology in human services and is Secretary General of the bureau responsible for the HUSITA 4 conference in Lapland in June 1996.

Contact: Sirpa Kuusisto-Niemi
Chief in Social Service Informatics
Stakes/Tilre
P.O. Box 220
FIN-00531
Helsinki
Finland

E-mail: Sirpa.Kuusisto-Niemi@stakes.stakes.stakes.elisa.fi

8 Germany

Bernd Kolleck and Berndt Kirchlechner

HUMAN SERVICES AND INFORMATION TECHNOLOGY

The human services in the Federal Republic of Germany have grown historically from their roots in Bismarck's social reforms in the last century. After the first world war, the Weimar Republic extended them significantly. However, the decisive change to a modern social system took place after the Nazi dictatorship and the second world war. Social welfare is part of the constitutionally prescribed and fundamental goals of the state. The development of human services was possible because of almost continuous economic growth over the past decades. This, too, led to broad agreement of the idea of a social welfare state. Its social and political aims are fundamentally accepted although controversies exist about contents and the extent of social security.

The question as to what extent social aims have been achieved is of major importance in the discussion on growing poverty and the definition of poverty. Another issue is the cost of social services, especially during economic recession and public housing shortages. This is a crucial concern given the manifold additional demands in the process of German unification. Discussion on targets and practice of social services has taken place, notably in the sixties and seventies. Some central critiques, which influenced reforms, were:

- the low capability of social administration to react to complex and multi-dimensional problems. This led to the extension of individualised social services in contrast to the predominance of financial transfers;
- the critique of purely financial help also led to strengthening self-help groups and alternative projects;
- the efficiency of the whole system, which had the second highest cost in the European Community. This supported consideration and initiatives for reducing bureaucracy and promoting privatisation of social services.

A central result of the debate was that, at the start of the eighties, more room was given to small and local help and self-help groups, which were supported to a greater extent. However, their part in the system must not be over-estimated, often they are of limited development and do not offer a complete service structure. Costs were not diminished, but raised. From year to year, social benefit costs grew more rapidly than income. This may also reflect a continuous shift of income from the poor to the middle and higher classes. A great deal of money is spent on the care of the frail and the elderly, fostering intense discussion about care insurance.

Organisation of human services

Social insurances covering health, accidents, pensions and unemployment are financed by equal contributions from employers and employees. Taking part in them presupposes membership of an institution. These 'social insurances' are independent corporations under public law. Dependent employees (blue and white collar workers) and their families are obliged to be insured, independent of their consent. For health insurance this obligation holds only below a certain income level.

Public assistance is regulated by law and paid by the government. Recipients were people who made certain sacrifices to the state or to society or who became victims. Initially these were primarily victims of war, but nowadays public assistance is received mainly by families or parents with children, by people on low incomes and by victims of violence. Examples include *Kindergeld*, paid to each parent and *Wohngeld*, paid as a contribution for rent payments.

Welfare is a vast complex of social help and services, regulated by special laws. Their principle is subsidiarity in respect to insurances and public assistance. They can be subdivided into social benefits, health services and child welfare. The system is conceived as a social 'net without holes', mainly because social benefits, as the lowest level, are intended to fill the gaps left by social insurances. At about 5% of total social expenses, social benefits are comparatively small but nonetheless important for the security of the system as a whole. Social expenses are about 30% of the gross national income.

Public social services are organised on three levels of federal government (*Bund*), federal state (*Laender* like Saxony, Bavaria etc.) and communities (*Gemeinden*). Alongside public services there are private welfare services who choose their activities according to their moral, ideological or religious aims, but who are not excluded from legislation. Their contributions, rights and duties are explicitly fixed in corresponding laws, thus giving their activities a legal basis. Institutions of private welfare organisations form six unions:

- *Diakonisches Werk* (Evangelical Church)
- *Caritas Verband* (Catholic Church)

- *Deutscher Paritaetischer Wohlfahrtsverband* (ideologically neutral, and represents most middle and small independent social service agencies)
- *Deutsches Rotes Kreuz* (Red Cross)
- *Arbeiterwohlfahrt* (came into being with the labour movement)
- *Zentralwohlfahrtstelle der Juden in Deutschland* (Social Service of the Jewish people)

They are active in nearly all fields of human services, sharing tasks with the public services according to the principle of subsidiarity. This means, that public institutions are founded only if private institutions are not able to perform the corresponding tasks. Central tasks of the unions are to counsel their member organisations doing practice work and to train their staff. They also represent their members in relation to the government and legislation, coordinate their work and develop professional standards. Typical services from private social welfare organisations and many also offered by communities, are: hospitals; homes for young people, elderly people and people with disabilities; kindergarten; social welfare services for young people; counselling and therapy; home care service, home help for elderly people and people with disabilities and vocational training for human service professionals.

Public social services

Unemployment/employment services are organised by the Federal Labour Authority (*Bundesanstalt fuer Arbeit*) in Nuernberg, with employment/unemployment offices in all greater communities. The Federal Labour Party Authority is centralised and responsible for information about jobs (mainly for young people), mediation of jobs, retraining, and vocational rehabilitation. It also pays unemployment insurance and other benefits in this sector, as well as child allowances. The service researches the development of jobs, careers, employment and unemployment and the labour market. It is highly computerised with a nationwide telecommunication network on a mainframe system. It also develops counselling systems for vocational guidance (for young people) and other counselling systems. Insurance aid for unemployment is only paid for a limited time (about a year, but for elderly people a bit longer). After the end of the payment period there will be a reduced 'help for workless people', financed by the government.

Social benefits, including rent rebates, are calculated and paid by local authorities. The nationwide regulations are modified by each federal state (*Bundesland*) and by each community. Some routine work is supported by mainframe computers. Personal computers and adapted systems are increasingly used to calculate social benefits, like **PROSOZ** (see below). The federal state is responsible for some social benefits, such as for disability and placement of young people and psychiatric patients. Responsibility for war victims, army victims and conscientious objectors against military service and some other groups also rests with the federal government. Help for youth is organised at community and federal state level.

Medical and vocational rehabilitation services are organised by many, mainly semi-governmental, institutions. They depend on the cause of the disability, relevant insurance and the level of income. Services are supplied by:

- *Bundesanstalt fuer Arbeit* (federal labour authority)
- *Bundesversicherungsanstalt fuer Angestellte* (social insurance pension for white collar workers)
- *Landesversicherungsanstalten fuer Arbeiter* (social insurance pension for blue collar workers)
- *Gesetzliche Krankenkasse* (obligatory health insurance)
- *Sozialhilfetraeger* (social welfare authority, local and federal state, with very different names, for people with no insurance and no means).

The local authorities mainly process financial transfers, caring for populations of up to 300,000. Offices are run by clerks and not social workers who are predominantly employed in child-welfare and health offices. This separation of administration and social work produces problems in practice, including separation of responsibilities, complicated decisions, lack of efficiency and poor contacts with citizens. Another consequence is that computer technology is introduced mainly for administrative tasks while social work stays apart.

The East German system, however, was quite different, based on high employment linked to comparatively low levels of productivity. While health care and pensions were central tasks of the state, the trade unions cared for holiday centres. Public employers, factories and unions supplied kindergartens, and the socialist party organised volunteer social work and health care (*people's solidarity*). With the new economic system, introduced through the unification process, the social infrastructure has had to be rebuilt. Essentially, the Western system, legislation and structures have taken over. Unemployment has risen tremendously, especially among women (who also stay unemployed longer than men) and the supply of placements in kindergartens has essentially diminished. The major part of monetary transactions from the federal government is for unemployment insurance and not investment.

Human services and information technology

Information technology has been used widely since the early sixties by nearly all welfare institutions with large numbers of clients, members and routine operations. They include the semi-public social insurances, community social benefits, youth aid offices and the federal labour authority. Small communities, which could not afford mainframe computer centres, built joint centres with neighbouring communities and their uses were administrative, financial and statistical. Data processing often meant decentralised data collection, transport on magnetic tapes or data cards, central batch processing with standardised routines and returning results to local bureaux.

With the introduction of personal computers, centralised programs were modernised or rewritten to allow local processing, often combined with central data storage and program service. With the development of data processing in the seventies, computing gained considerable respect. Sometimes this was a type of euphoric belief that planning could be more efficient, just and democratic. For public and social services, this led to projects like citizens offices (*Buergeramt*), and *Prosoz* (see below). The former combine tasks such as registration, social benefits, dog taxation and fishing licences to make services more convenient and accepted by the public.

Data protection and privacy

Quite early on, public opinion was concerned about the increase in power of central, public and private institutions with large data files. The first laws on data protection were passed by the parliament in Hessen in the early seventies. This was followed by a federal act, twice renewed since then, which provides a framework for federal state legislation. The acts regulate data collection, editing, storage, processing, transfer and use. Everyone has the right to see data stored about themselves and to demand deletion of data which are inaccurate, illegal or unnecessary. Exceptions have to be justified by specific laws. Data protection commissioners, who are responsible for supervising personalised data files in public administrations, are nominated by the federal and state parliaments. Any file containing personal data must be declared to the commissioners, who must be consulted on how data protection is organised. Commissioners have no right to give orders or prosecute violations of the law, but instead to report to parliament or inform the press. However, data protection commissioners have proven to be a powerful institution, gaining considerable public respect. A special, voluminous act regulates data protection in social agencies, be they private or public. Its general principals are:

- discrimination of internal and external use of data with greater freedom within agencies, but restricted transfer to external agencies;
- data collection and storage is limited to declared purposes;
- data must be necessary to achieve the declared purpose;
- transfer to security services, courts, financial and other services is restricted by precise regulations as to the sort of data that can be transferred, as well as necessary steps to obtain authority.

Public discussion on data protection culminated in debate on the Census Law of 1983. The problem was that the law mixed statistical purposes with updating local inhabitants' registration files. The Law was examined by the constitutional court and declared unconstitutional in a famous 'census sentence' which, at the same time, outlined the principle of fundamental information rights. The *sentence* has constitutional status, so that 'information self determination' has become a fundamental right.

Protection of young people

There are several laws for the protection of children and young people concerning movies, videos and print media. Public and private institutions observe the market and their primary concern is the presentation of violence. In 1994 the first institution for interactive media was opened for 'independent self control' and is a collaboration between youth workers, producers and retailers of video games. The main aims of the institution are to approve the games, to testify their appropriateness for children in relation to their age and to inform the public about youth protection problems in interactive media.

INFORMATION FOR CITIZENS

Individual and community support

Some local labour offices supply their clients with computerised job information. At a time of high unemployment this was an immediate success, for example, in Berlin. A user friendly interface allows direct access to job information in different branches. Employers also discovered the medium as an efficient tool for very fast mediation of jobs and the only drawback is the long queues at offices where the terminals are placed. Several cities provide automated information facilities, mainly on tourist and cultural events, but also for social work activities and resources. Terminals are placed at central locations around cities, mainly airports, railway stations and other traffic nodes. Some social information is provided by the German videotext system (BTX now called T-Online).

Many communities have books and automated registers on social service institutions, some available as PC-based retrieval systems. There are several computerised information systems of social institutions in Berlin. One of them, called **CISS**, was developed by the School of Social Work and used by institutions for information and counselling. The system will also be used in other federal states. Another system, **Stattbuch,** was developed as a frequently updated book and is now available on compact disk. A generic software program called **Prosedis** was designed to be applicable in all cities and communities. It is now available as a demonstration version with Berlin data. Another information system called **BICO**, developed by the School of Social Work in Frankfurt, informs people with disabilities, especially the young, about their social rights. A third system focuses on remedies and resources for disabled people (developed by FH Darmstadt and CeBeeF Darmstadt). The **Handynet** and **Handiaid** European Union projects should produce detailed information and communication facilities for people with disabilities.

There are also other information systems which are not widely published and not as well known to the authors of this chapter. **DWA,** for homeless people, was developed by the federal co-ordination for the homeless, and contains mainly information on shelters and advisory boards. **EBIS** is a similar system for social service institutions working with drug abusers. Both systems are designed to store and retrieve data in agencies working directly with the clients and anonymous data will be collected nationwide and evaluated.

Telecommunication

Some telehouses have been opened in communities, following the Scandinavian model and giving telecommunication access for personal or business affairs. The telehouses also offer information on community politics, cultural events, allow the use of remote data bases and organise assemblies and cultural activities.

Several other networks exist for local or national use, for example, **DISA** for social work mailboxing in Hildesheim has several nodes across the country. The mailbox **Kommhelp**, is provided in Berlin for use by people with disabilities. **Spinnennetz** is operated by youth workers to help young people to link up and allow them to address politicians like the Senator for Family and Youth by directly asking them questions.

Individual support

Soldi (*Soziale Leistungen im Dialog*, social benefit in dialogue) is a counselling program for social security benefits. It may be used by social workers or clients without any previous knowledge of computers and social benefit regulations. SOLDI advises on local benefits which may be claimed and calculates their total value. It needs detailed personal information to calculate benefits, but does not retain this after calculation. SOLDI may be used to train people in benefit calculation. **The Konstanzer Wohngeld Program** (developed at the University of Konstanz) is similar to SOLDI, but advises people on their eligibility for financial help to pay for housing and rent. There are also **Cadas** and **Suzec** for advice on debts. These perform calculations, advise on the legality of interest rates and suggest how debts can be paid under the financial conditions involved. They can only be used by professionals as part of wider advice and help. Finally in this section, the Federal Labour Authority has a counselling system, **coBer**, for vocational guidance.

Employment and training

The Federal Labour Authority performs all routine work on a nationwide mainframe system with terminals in all local employment offices, called **Cosima** (Computer

System in the Labour Office). It contains three sections: computer assisted mediation of jobs (**coArb**); computer assisted mediation of apprenticeship (**Compas**) and computer assisted calculation of unemployment pay (**coLei**). Vocational training and retraining for the long term unemployed, people with disabilities (rehabilitation) and job changes are paid by the labour office from unemployment insurance. There are special courses for young jobless people and deprived people. For example, a successful private initiative trained young Turkish people on computers, some of whom went on to obtain jobs through the knowledge gained. In many professions and in many schools - except social work until recently, training is supported by computer assisted learning (CAL) programs, mainly used for technical, science and language training.

Independent living

Some agencies provide computer courses for people with disabilities, leading to vocational training or just self help and self esteem. Some have severe handicaps with little ability to move. Special tools, not necessarily using a keyboard, are developed sometimes in co-operation with private agencies for the handicapped. There are systems for people who are blind or with very low visual faculty - PCs with Braille output, voice in- and output, magnification of visual output on a screen, or transformation of text into voice output. Transforming graphic symbols into voice output is being developed. As a training aid for speech or hearing impaired people, voice is transformed into coloured pictures to produce a visual comparison with the correct speech sound and to help pronunciation. The **PC-Bliss** program allows users to work with symbols on the computer screen. For mobility disabled persons there are keyboard simulation programs - **Bypass**, **Simula** and **2StepX.** Computer based systems help manage switches to open doors or to use a telephone, TV or radio. For people with learning disabilities there are programs which encourage concentration or correct spelling (**Verbos**). **Cokos**, a spelling game, was developed at Freie Universitaet Berlin. A research centre (IPN) for computer applications at schools for disabled children and children with learning disabilities, exists at Universitaet Kiel. New media are developed there, evaluated, tested and published in a series called **Compass**. Further important institutions in this context are:

- *Paedagogische Hochschule Stuttgart* (learning software, spelling aids)
- *Bundeswehrhochschule Muenchen* (tests and develops tools for disabled)
- *Stiftung Rehabilitation Heidelberg* (software developments, help for mobility disablement, publications)

There are several databases on tools for disabled people at Stiftung Rehabilitation Heidelberg, at Dortmunder Institut fuer Arbeitsphysiologie, at Fachhochschule Frankfurt Abt. Sozialpaedagogik and at Universitaet Hamburg, Institut fuer Soziologie, Abt. Rehabilitation, which participates in the European Union HANDICAP II project.

VOCATIONAL EDUCATION AND TRAINING

For IT in Social Work Education, curriculum development is handled at the level of Schools. Most curricula comprise basic informatics and more specialised aspects. A working group on computers in social work - National Union of Schools of Social Work - has met regularly since 1984. This group monitors developments of programs and equipment and supports the development of computer teaching. It has also published papers on fundamental issues, such as curriculum development. The main argument in this paper was against standardising the curriculum while departments are so different with regard to staffing, software and hardware, as well as in organisational and financial capacities. In the meanwhile, however, a group gathered for the purpose of promoting curriculum development in co-operation with CAUSA in the Netherlands.

Computers are used as a tool for word processing, desk-top publishing, calculation and statistics and as a medium through which students are taught about computer use in social services. No use of self-contained courseware and examination is known. There will be training about electronic mail and data exchange when **Sonett** is installed (see below). Standard commercial software is used for word processing, desk top publishing, painting, business graphics and calculation. Special software, such as **CISS, Prosoz, Soldi, Suzec**, **Klient** (see below) and some US software products (eg. **CASS**) are demonstrated and used. Recently, a development was initiated on graphics data processing for vocational training. Video records on practical treatment situations are stored on CD-ROM. A 'teachware' program provides a frame for a user dialogue and displays the filmed sequences on the screen when demanded by the user.

Sonett is the name of a telecommunication network between ten social work departments of the Fachhochschulen (polytechnics). Sonett is supported by the Ministry of Research and uses the research network (**WIN**), a high speed high efficiency network for scientific purposes. A medium size unix-computer for SONETT is located at the School of Social Work in Berlin as a basis for communication and information systems, as a support for users inside and outside the country and as a national and European communication centre.

Research uses tools which are developed mainly in connection with empirical social research methodology. These are usually statistical or other data analysis programs, databases and programs for the management and evaluation of open interview transcriptions.

PROVISION OF SERVICES

At a practice level, local authorities have, since 1972, run mainframe programs such as the widespread **HES-SIAS** (Hessian Social Benefits Information and Calculation System) a 'heavy' or large scale off-line system. Since 1984 there has been decentralisation towards PC calculations programs. PROSOZ (Programierte Sozialhilfe) was developed and implemented in several cities and communities including Bremen and Berlin. Implementation into the social benefit system in Bremen was supported by the federal Ministry of Research. It had the rapt attention of the expert public, not only on the program itself but also on the ambitious aims of participation and democratisation in offices. The project was well documented in all its successful and problematic aspects.

Information systems

Several information systems are for the use of professionals. **Solex** informs on selected social laws. Special paragraphs or contexts can be retrieved by a keyword list and it can also be used to support the learning of social laws. Large databases on social legislation and court sentences are kept in the **Juris** system, an on-line accessible, commercial database. Founded by the federal government, Juris, like many other scientific databases, was privatised when economically successful. It is used more by lawyers and courts than by social workers due, in part, to access difficulties and comparatively high retrieval fees. However, with a regular service of parts of the data on CD-ROMs, JURIS becomes more interesting for less wealthy institutions.

A well used large database on social work literature is kept in Berlin on a mainframe computer by a public institute for social issues. This is a major source for students, scientists and also social workers, telecommunication access has been opened recently. Other interesting large databases in the general computer network are **Dimdi** containing literature on medicine, **Solis** on sociology and **Foris** with reports on research projects. Information on social and census data are accessible via telecommunication, being held by the federal and states offices of statistics. Municipal offices hold databases with social variables for planning purposes, sometimes well evaluated and printed as maps. A database on poverty, unemployment and social benefit spending in Germany is kept in Braunschweig and published in graphical form as social maps. Finally, the Ministry for Labour and Social Affairs, the Federal Labour Authority, the Federal and State Social Insurance Boards all have databases with information on the social welfare system. There is no direct access for the public.

Managing services

Federal and community authorities have developed information and book-keeping programs for financial, statistical and planning affairs, often using a mainframe computer in an IT centre. Only small communities use personal computers but financial operations is the task of administrators, seldom of social workers. Client information is included in the benefit calculation systems, also run by administrators. The database is an integrated part of the system and is used for supervision as well as for statistical and other management information. This applies to all other large scale systems supplying financial help. For small, private organisations giving non-material help, several accounting and information systems are now available, e.g. **Klient** but not yet well established.

Even the systems of the six big private social unions appears to be unsatisfactory. However with money shortages, problems of justifying costs of several areas of social work and in view of basic needs to be met following unification, assessment systems promise to be a tool for social services assessment as a whole. Special administrative software is available for:

- homes for young and old people;
- out-patient treatment;
- ambulatory services (such as meals for old or people with disabilities);
- transport services;
- book-keeping for special tasks (fund-raising, donations, welfare stamps).

For some of these tasks, a variety of different programs exist. An overview of these and the other software programs can be obtained in a book on collected software (EDV-Handbuch Sozialwesen von H.Kreidenweis).

Client assessment and treatment

A broad development has taken place in the health services, where sophisticated equipment on PC and mainframe computers exists for hospitals and clinics. This comprises assessment systems for physical or mental illness. Although health care is traditionally quite separate from social work in Germany, social workers may be using some of these systems. However, they are not yet discussed as specific tools for social work. A number of treatment and therapy supporting programs have been developed for rehabilitation centres. Such programs treat problems of reaction, identification of objects, correct spelling and other aspects.

CONCLUSION AND FUTURE DEVELOPMENTS

The future will bring a greater independence of IT development from the Universities and Schools of Social Work, which have been dominant in the past. This is because the software industry has discovered its interest in the special social work market. Probably, telecommunications and information centres will be of greater importance and may well become a self understood daily tool in the offices. First attempts appear to be promising. The Schools will integrate information technology into the normal syllabus. No longer will IT teaching be separate from the essential contents of the training because IT methods will become more easily accessible and young teachers, as well as students, will be acquainted with the technology. IT will be the task of a special service department which cares for computers, networks and programs, not of specialised social work teachers. CAL will be an additional tool to transport knowledge in addition to other media such as videos, acoustic tapes and literature.

References

Kreidenweis, Helmut. *EDV-Handbuch Sozialwesen. Eine Markt-Uebersicht mit Praxistips.* Freiburg: Lambertus (with disk, Software-Datenbank). 1993

Author Details

Bernd Kolleck is professor of social informatics in social work at the School of Social Work in Berlin. He developed SONETT, the on-line database and bulletin board and has researched in infant mortality, health care for foreign workers, urban affairs and planning. Bernd Kolleck has also recently completed a period as chair of ENITH.

Berndt Kirchlechner is professor of Social Work Studies at Fach-hochschule Frankfurt AM. His subjects include statistics, social research, computer literacy and IT. He develops software and chairs the national group on IT in training social workers and social services.

Contact: Professor Bernd Kolleck
FHSS Berlin
Karl Schrader-Strasse 6
D-10781 Berlin
Germany

Telephone: +49 (30) 21458 351
Fax: +49 (30) 2166411
E-mail: kolleck@comz.fhss-berlin.d400.de

9 Greece

Christina Vayas

HUMAN SERVICES AND INFORMATION TECHNOLOGY

Greece consists of the mainland and a few thousand large and small islands. The country has a population of ten million and an unemployment rate of approximately 9%. More than 40% of the population resides in the densely populated area in or around Athens. The country became a member state of the European Union in 1981. At present, there is stability in the economy with indicators of development. Social and unemployment pensions and benefits circulate through the tax system back to the public.

Social policy goals and major programmes are centrally planned, mainly by the Ministry of Health and Welfare as well as the Ministry of Labour and Social Security. Social legislation rests with the Central Government as well, through Parliament. The implementation of social policy appears at all three levels of Government: local authorities, the prefectures (regional state administration) and the national central administration. The human services follow a similar pattern. There are social agencies and organisations, both public and private, operating at the local, regional and national level. The regional and national welfare organisations usually develop a network of departments serving more than one community; however these public sector human service networks are insufficient to cover all unmet needs. In 1994 Greece legally recognised the second tier of Local Authority, and all centrally controlled and supervised public welfare departments moved under the auspices of the 54 prefectures.

Local authorities have no exclusive responsibility to plan welfare policies or organise local networks of services. This has contributed to delay in the development by municipalities of comprehensive and adequate human services. The gap in provision is covered by public agencies, church welfare organisations, the voluntary private sector, self-help groups and private profit agencies. Most human services budgets are financed by state funds, but also from private sources and European Union contributions. Welfare agencies are mainly under the supervision of the Ministry of

Health and Welfare. Social Security organisations are under the Ministry of Labour. Correctional and probation services under the Ministry of Justice and special schools under the Ministry of Education. It is evident that the different structures and the variety of decision making legal bodies have had their effect in slowing the pace of comprehensive planning, care management and integration of IT in the social and human service systems.

Human services and IT - the organisational structure

In late 1986, the government issued a law creating The State Council on Information Technology (SCIT) under the auspices of the Ministry of the Government's Presidency. This Committee is an advisory and supervisory body on matters of strategy development in information technology, as part of state policy for the social, economic and technological development of the country. The members are all ministers and the chair, always, the Prime Minister. The SCIT has the right to appoint different committees or groups to study IT subjects and make proposals. All public departments can receive assistance to develop plans for computerisation from the SCIT and its two service departments - the Technical Council on IT and the Office for IT Development. The State Council is a decision making body that regulates general information technology policy in the public domain and for public social services as well. However, it has remained relatively inactive.

In 1991 a new law (L.144A/25.9.91) laid the foundation of a private industry named *Organisation and Informatics Ltd* with a major mission to solve many organisational problems in public administration. A promising program, called **KLISTHENIS,** is in development to help the public domain join the information society.

In recent years, we have observed a fast-track development of the *General Secretariat for Research and Technology*, which operates under the auspices of the Ministry for Industry, Energy and Technology. This public service has its origins back in 1971, but took its present form in 1985. It operates ten departments and supervises eleven organisations for technology development and twelve research institutions, among them:

- the National Centre for Social Research,
- the Institute of Technology and Research and
- the Language Institute of Speech Processing.

Parallel and complementary to the public domain, a number of private agencies and software houses have assisted in the development of better health and social services through the support of the different European Community programmes (AIM, DELTA, ORA, TIDE, HELIOS, HORIZON etc.).

Data protection

In 1988 a specially appointed committee issued the first draft of laws to Parliament for the protection of citizens from unscrupulous use of sensitive personal information processed by computers. There was much interest expressed from several professional groups, including social workers, about the final content. So far, the proposal and three additional amendments in 1991, 1992 and 1995 have not become law. Greek law 2068/1992 ratified convention 108/28 of the Council of Europe for the protection of individuals in relation to automatically processed personal data. However the ratification document has not been deposited due to the absence of a national personal data protection law. Therefore there is no document, at present, to legally protect citizens, including clients of the human services, from unlawful processing of strictly personal data. Last year, the Greek state issued law 2225/1994 which marks the start of legal protection of confidential information in communications. A specially appointed national committee has supervisory responsibility in all state and private services and organisations (including databanks and mobile telephony enterprises).

Information technology in human services

The earliest endeavour to introduce and support information technology in the areas of social welfare, social security and health goes back to the late 1960s, with the foundation in 1969 of a Computer Centre for Social Services (CCSS). This is a partially autonomous scheme, funded by its clients, who are the local public social and health agencies. Today, it has five technical departments and employs about 400 IT professionals. It provides services, maintenance, software development and training of staff. Its work from 1970 to 1976 was 90% on the two major social security schemes (IKA, OGA) and up to 1985 it spread slowly to similar organisations. Only after 1986 did CCSS involve health services such as hospitals and medical centres in its IT development plan. In the social welfare sector IT assistance is still restricted to the transfer of financial benefits and to some limited statistical analysis. Today, the Computer Centre for Social Services serves:

- 20 social security organisations.
- 24 human services, with eighty information systems installed which consist of approximately 2,000 programmes.
- 120 hospitals and medical centres.
- 40 human services schemes and some seasonal users for the available statistical packets.
- Family benefit allocation and old age pensions for the Ministry of Social Welfare.

Quantitative information is very limited but it is clear that technological applications are being introduced, slowly but steadily, into the Greek welfare domain. The problem of availability of hardware and software walks hand in hand with that of how to use that which is available. A survey was conducted in the Spring of 1987 and repeated two years later by the TEI-Athens School of Social Work among 89 agencies - both private and public. Only a very small percentage were using computers, almost exclusively for office automation. The questionnaire was given to Human Services managers and to professional social workers. The first group showed interest in management information systems and decision making software. Social workers expressed a desire to use computers mainly for less paper work, client oriented information and registration systems but were dubious about using the computer in their professional work with the clientele.

However, in a limited scale research in seventy human service agencies in Attica (TEI-Athens, SSW, Computer Lab, 1992) three years later, the prospects were more promising. Despite their ethical reservations, social workers no longer refused to use information technology in directly supporting and assisting their practice. A similar questionnaire in 1994 was applied to the professional staff of 24 computerised rehabilitation agencies in the Athens area. The agency staff were highly sensitised but partially educated in using the computer as a professional tool. All reported positive responses to expanding its use in their work with parallel in-service training courses for staff development (TEI-Athens, SSW, Thesis by Alexander Tassopoulos, 1994).

Large state welfare organisations are being computerised, as are several private agencies that are mainly serving people with disabilities. Most human services are still only using computers for office work, accounting tasks and client registration and tracking. The need remains pressing for decentralisation, suitably trained personnel and developing the technical infrastructures of services. More and more human service professionals are becoming computer literate and are introducing their expertise into their agencies in the form of diagnostic tools for assessment, evaluation, education, disability limitation and simulation. This is not an easy task, as most human services have a poor IT infrastructure, despite lower hardware costs.

The government is also providing public agencies with computers, but social work and other human services are hardly involved in the computerisation plans which are mainly for administration and greater control. Additional to the above problems, software for human services is not easily transferred due to language barriers. Since the bulk of such software is in English and not in Greek it is not encouraged, in order to preserve cultural differences. Locally developed social software is limited and lacks commercial promotion and opportunities.

INFORMATION FOR CITIZENS

In the last two years public information systems have been developed offering automated information supply to the broad public and to different professional groups. Information supply in the welfare domain is still limited. However by use of a personal computer with a modem, it is easy to access a number of databanks such as:

- Handynet
- the Disabled Hellas Bulletin Board System, (the earliest information provider which was started by Nick Voulgaropoulos in the late 1980s)
- any of the three banks on legislation information (including social legislation)
- the HERMIS databank for social and medical sciences.

In 1993, the National Organisation of Welfare developed the first data databank through the European program STAR with information on all social and welfare agencies throughout the country. Use of information from such electronic services is either with or without charge. The Hellenic Telephone Company installed the means to connect citizens with national and international databanks using the HELLAS PACK and other systems. The same company is initiating a speaking database through the telephone system to the general public. Human Services educators are linked with international or European networks through their universities. Also links to the Internet services are promoted through private commercial providers with some human services practitioners using it from 1995. There are three main commercial providers with their own international connections and more than 15-20 companies which offer full access Internet connection through one of these providers. This system facilitates individual subscriptions to the Internet.

Employment and financial support

The Hellenic Manpower and Employment Organisation (OAED) is the national scheme for vocational training and social provision for unemployed people. This national organisation runs many vocational training programmes including courses in information technology specialisation. It also supports training centres for disabled unemployed people in information technology and offers vocational consultation and rehabilitation services. These services are not computerised, but a few private agencies are working in the development of IT supported job consultation and job matching. Teleworking is also timidly promoted. The first scheme was initiated for deaf and partially deaf young people. Nowadays, there are quite a few efforts to develop distance learning and distance training projects for students with disabilities, unemployed youths or post lyceum students. Teleworking is not a task for human services yet as it requires a well organised and computerised environment, but a few experiments are operating through European Union funding - mostly for women and disabled employees.

Social benefit calculation systems

Sections and departments under the auspices of Health, Welfare have been using the services of the aforementioned Computer Centre for Social Services in order to calculate and issue:

- Additional security to farmers.
- Postal payment of monthly welfare transfer to 40,000 elderly people.
- Payment of family allowances to more than 25,000 cases.

Support for people with disabilities

The field of rehabilitation was the first to introduce IT applications for client support, with people who are mentally impaired as the initial client group. The voluntary agency THEOTOKOS, for children who are mentally impaired, in 1985 was the first to start a micro-electronic laboratory which provided programs such as: computer based assessment, drill/practice and special applications of the logo program. The Hellenic Association for the Protection of Disabled Children has been pioneering 'high-tech' devices since 1988. The Social Work Foundation is an old private, non-profit social agency, which in 1989 was the first to operate a training program in computer use and programming for young people with motor disabilities. In 1991 it was also the first to create an Assistive Technology Advice Centre - CRITON.

CRITON uses computers to evaluate candidates and trainees in IT careers and has a 59% job placement record. It has developed its own multi-media evaluation software and the first computer program for Greek Social Workers. Training programmes in computers for young adults with motor-disabilities, or who are deaf or blind, have spread quickly thanks to European Social fund support. These are public, private and municipal schemes using training in computers as a means of professional rehabilitation and social integration.

It is worth also mentioning some other initiatives by experts in private companies and in educational institutions to develop Greek software and CD-ROMs for special education, for children with learning difficulties or to create technological devices adapted to several disabilities. These include the Department of Informatics and the Department of Educational Science at the University of Athens, the Institute of Information Technology in Crete, the Department of Physics at the University of Patras, the National Technical University of Athens, the Pedagogical Institute of the Ministry of Education, Inte-Learn, Microelectronic Education and Pliroforiki Technognosia which develops programs for special needs using the multi-media Logo platform.

VOCATIONAL EDUCATION AND TRAINING

Over the last two decades a number of schools, initially private, were developed in order to train a new labour force - the computer literate employee. Today, there is training at all levels of formal education - elementary, secondary and post lyceum. Many private and local authority initiatives offer training programmes to whoever is interested. The Ministry of Education in May 1995 started an electronic network to connect all elementary schools in the country, starting with the remote areas. At the same time a CD-ROM based program, called **Polimathia,** was developed by the Language Institute for Speech Processing (LISP) to teach the Greek language to students.

All universities and Technological Educational Institutes (TEI) use computers in generic applications. Some also use them for training and as educational tools. However, there are hardly any introductory courses on IT use in any of the social and human sciences departments, with the exception of the three Schools of Social Work. These have included such a course in their curricula since 1985, but can only offer limited courseware that hardly meet the needs in the field. Constant requests from the human services agencies have resulted in curriculum changes for the welfare professions. Computers are now slowly being introduced in class work and fieldwork.

All departments of social work have IBM compatible computers. The School of Social Work in Patras has a well organised computer laboratory. The other two use the laboratories of the departments of information technology. Present learning goals include sensitisation, introduction to computer use, agency visits, guests speakers and field studies. In 1992 the Athens School of Social Work opened the first fieldwork placement for its students in an Assistive Technology Advice Centre and also in three more social agencies where social work students use the computer as a vocational tool. Four surveys on IT applications have been conducted by the computer laboratory students and instructors of the TEI SSW in Athens and more than ten graduation theses have been written by social work students on the subject of IT in human services.

In a study conducted by a graduating social work student (1989) of TEI-Athens, it was found that younger social workers and social work students were much more demanding and optimistic about using IT applications in social work practice than the older group of professionals. This however is not the case today. The demands for IT training from experienced social workers and other human service professionals are increasing. However the schools hardly respond to these needs within their present roles. The few computer training events for human services professionals have been by private schemes or within the agency (in-service training). An interesting initiative was undertaken by the Teachers College at the University of Patras in 1992 to train twenty unemployed teachers in Computer Assisted Learning (CAL) for special education. This included instructional design for students with learning difficulties, for blind children and vocal or non-vocal augmentation.

Research

There is still limited activity in the field of social research but it is increasing daily. In the welfare sector there is the Computer Centre in Social Services and the School of Social Work in Athens. Apart from these, all other fact finding and assessment about the state of the art in human services applications is done privately by agencies and only in direct relationship to their special interest. Earlier mention was made of research into meeting disability needs through technology. There is however, no specialisation course offered in the field of Rehabilitation Engineering or Assistive Technology at University level. On the positive side, the National Technical University of Athens is participating in European Union programmes for 'high-tech' developments in the field of Rehabilitation. The University of Crete is also using the Institute of Information Technology to train PhD students in special education software and the University of Patras is developing assistive technical devices.

Research in many fields of IT application has been supported the last three years from the General Secretariat for Research and Technology (GSRT). In 1995, over 2,000 research proposals came from universities, technological institutes, research centres and others to claim part of a three billion drachma budget. Out of these 16% represent the area of society and economy and 19% the health sector (GSRT Newsletter, Sept. 1995). Also Greece has been involved very actively in almost all European Union initiatives in fields such as health, assistive technology, communication, vocational training, distance learning and telematics. The GSRT has an Internet address (143.233.65.1 anonymous FTP server).

PROVISION OF SERVICES

Technological devices and home care technology are developing at a faster rate now, but we are far behind other countries, especially in social software and assistive technology. The Hellenic Red Cross was the first to introduce an alarm system service for elderly and disabled people who are home bound (since 1990). The same organisation and Sismanoglio, a major hospital in Athens, initiated about the same time tele-medical services to cover emergency health problems in remote, areas of the country. In the Red Cross, besides the medical staff, social workers are also using the program to offer social advice and make referrals. Tele-medicine is expanding in the private sector and technology for the health sector is rapidly developing and widely used in public and private hospitals and medical centres.

Other initiatives

- The Hellenic Social Work and Welfare journal, *Eklogy* has, since 1987, regularly published articles and news on Informatics, Social Work and Social Services.
- The Council on In-Service Training in Social Work and the National Association of Schools of Social Work organised, in October 1987, the first Hellenic Congress on computers in the human services with international collaboration. Ever since, educational activities have been organised to spread the word and sensitise welfare and IT professionals. Among them, two joint seminars organised by the TEI-Athens School of Social Work and the Department on Informatics.
- Greece was one of the countries that participated in the Maastricht Convention for the foundation of ENITH, in December 1989. The TEI-School of Social Work

became a founding member. The Social Work Foundation has represented the local ENITH node, ever since.

- The Ministry of Education has decided to develop World Wide Web (WWW) pages and promote them through the Greek providers (eg Forthnet). Whilst private organisations are constantly developing WWW pages to promote a variety of goods and services, welfare services promotion is still almost non-existent.

CONCLUSION AND FUTURE DEVELOPMENTS

Twenty years ago, the Greek Computer Society (EPY) was founded. Ever since, it has developed an advocacy role in support of many much needed changes in IT availability and development. It publishes a monthly journal and has a number of standing committees. In 1991 the Greek Computer Society formed a special committee on IT and Disabilities. This group organised the first national seminar on Assistive Technology in September 1991 with European participation. So far, the Greek Computer Society has not included human services applications in its lobbying subjects. However there is good will to start on this goal with the help of the Committee on Social Issues, which published recently (1995) an interesting book on *Information Security: Technical, Legal and Social Issues*. There is also support through its annually organised National Congress, which this year (1995) included a panel on the *Information Society and Citizen Protection.*

Information technology, in general, has a recent past in Hellas. As the trend seems to be in all European countries, the field of social and human services appears to be the last to catch up with the opportunities offered through information technology. For Greece, there are a number of factors contributing to this delay. These include the lack of expert help that is sensitive to the needs of the welfare domain, lack of home based production, financial constraints and the rigidity of some centrally operating structures. There are also the well known ideological and ethical constraints which apply to both worker and client/consumer resistance. However in the next few years developments will be quite rapid. The European Union and member states now realise that the Information Society is a fact (the Bangemann Report) and that a comprehensive strategy must be implemented to meet the challenges, opportunities and new problems.

References

Bangemann M. *Europe and the Global Information Society, Recommendations to the European Council*, 26th May, 1994, Brussels: European Commission. 1994.

Greek Computer Society. *Information Security: Technical, Legal and Social Issues*. Athens. 1995.

Author details

Christina Vayas is Professor of Social Work at the School of Social Work in Athens. She is a founder member of the Greek Social Work Foundation which set up the first Assistive Technology Advice Centre (CRITON).

Contact: Professor Christina Vayas
Technological Educational Institute of Athens
School of Social Work
42 El. Venizelou Str.
123 51 Ag. Varvara
Attica
Greece

E-mail: kasp@handynet.forthnet.gr

10 Ireland

Ann Lavan and Aisling Byrne

HUMAN SERVICES AND INFORMATION TECHNOLOGY

Following the establishment of the State in 1922, Ireland inherited the statutory social services of Britain. The rapid social and economic developments which have taken place in twentieth century Ireland have been matched by a prolific growth in the statutory social services. Contemporary social services, however constitute a complex array of statutory and voluntary provision (Lavan and Iredale, 1993). The Health Act (1970) rationalised the Irish Health services and provided the impetus for the creation of a range of community care services and the employment of social workers in significant numbers. There are a large number of relatively autonomous voluntary organisations in the country. While this country has a long tradition of charitable giving, to date there is no information on how Ireland compares with other countries in this regard. The 1994 published estimates in the Budget, included under Social Welfare voted an amount of £4.73 million in respect of grants to voluntary and community organisations (Budget, 1994). The National Social Service Board is responsible for some coordination in the social services field, the pattern of coordination however is uneven.

'Human services' is not a familiar description in Ireland where the more usual designation is 'social services'. The social services are the main instruments of social policy and are those which are provided by the state and other agencies to improve individual and community welfare. The main social services are income maintenance, education, health and welfare (or personal social services). The term 'social welfare' has acquired a particular meaning in the Irish context and is usually taken to refer to schemes administered by the Department of Social Welfare. There are two basic systems of social welfare (social security) provision: one of social insurance and one of social assistance. Social insurance involves entitlements earned through contributions and is financed mainly from the social insurance fund. Social assistance involves either universalist or means-tested payments to persons in need and is financed from general tax revenues. The term 'social security' is used by the Commission of the European Communities to collectively describe these two systems.[1] The main social services are income maintenance, education, health and welfare or personal social services (Curry, 1993, p1). Although the scope of social insurance in Ireland has widened in recent years to encompass the entire workforce,[2] it still does not provide full cover to some categories.

The Department of Social Welfare administers the main income maintenance functions in Ireland and has a staff of 3,600. It relies on various agencies, business firms and contractors in the delivery of payments. Social Welfare Services (SWS) has modernised (over the past eleven years) and the language of the service referring to 'partners' and 'customers' reflects the modernising attitude (O'Shea, 1995). The Department of Social welfare administers a scheme of grants for voluntary organisations in the social services area, a community development programme and a scheme of grants for locally based women's groups. Recent changes in the Irish social welfare system include:

- A new benefit came into effect in October 19 1994 - Health and Safety Benefit, which is effectively the same as Disability Benefit but for specific employed women who have to leave work because of specified risks. Maternity Benefit continues in the normal way. (Relate Vol. 22 No.3, 1994).
- Changes may be in store for the country's 80 or so Citizens Information Centres when the National Social Service Board (NSSB), moves from the Department of Health to the Department of Social Welfare. In line with the transfer of the NSSB to his Department Pronsias de Rossa, Minister for Social Welfare provided for an allocation of £250,000 in line with the Welfare Rights and Information Programme (de Rossa's, 1995).
- Computerisation of information files held by the NSSB, is at the stage of design of a pilot project which will enable the Community Information Centres to have direct access to a central source of information.

Key ethical concerns around the use of information technology

There is no central policy for funding or monitoring information technology initiatives in the social services. Thus developments in this area are not easily described, assessed or analysed. There is now a specific proposal for a European Council decision concerning the establishment of Europe-wide Trust Services for public information

---

[1] See *Guide to Social Welfare Services*, Annual Publication, Department of Social Welfare.

[2] Through the elimination of earnings ceiling in 1974 and the introduction of insurance cover for the self-employed in 1988.

services and the social services. This is to provide for confidentiality and digital signature for social services and the general public to conform with principles of subsidiarity and the need to find a balanced solution with the needs seen by national administrations related to public order and national social security (Bangemann Report, 1994). In the context of the development of the global information society, the question of privacy is going to become a very important issue as new communication technologies become widespread. Indeed the Data Protection Act of 1988 is designed to give effect to the Council of Europe Convention and its purpose is to regulate the collection, processing, storage, use and disclosure of personal information. For the purpose of the Act, the 'Data' is defined as 'information in a form in which it can be processed automatically'. A 'data controller' is 'a person who controls the use and contents of personal data'; a 'data processor' is 'a person who processes personal data on behalf of a data controller' and a 'data subject' is 'an individual who is the subject of personal data'.

The Data Protection Act 1988 makes special provision for access to health and social work data. Social work data is defined as 'personal data kept for, or obtained in the course of carrying out social work, by a Minister of the Government, a local authority, a health board or a voluntary organisation or other body which carries out social work and is in receipt of monies provided by such a Minister, authority or board.' In summary personal data obtained in the course of social work cannot be supplied if it would cause serious harm to the health or emotional condition of the data subject concerned. However, as much of the data as can be supplied without causing harm must be disclosed. These regulations apply equally to health data (Clark, 1990).

The implications of the Data Protection Act have attracted a range of comment and critical assessment (Scally, 1988; Sterne, 1987a, 1987b, 1989). Given the pattern of rapid innovation and utilisation, policy makers must assume that the computer field will be a dynamic technological environment in the future. Even in the past two decades file automation in the public sectors of OECD nations has proceeded in subject matter areas of administration, intelligence and research; however there is in general the problem of what happens to traditional relationships, to such prerogatives of the individual as personal privacy and to the ethics of and public controls over a new elite of information keepers, when social policies become increasingly technical, long-range, machine processed, information based and expert dominated (Westin, 1971).

Rather than drafting away in precise legal language the problems which new technologies create for data protection, the Committee of Experts on Data Protection opted for the publication of its working party's findings and conclusions (Council of Europe, 1991). Among them personal identification numbers (PINs) were by no means a neutral issue. In Ireland there are context-specific PINs in several areas of public administration which are used for specific purposes. File matching or relating personal databases by means of PINs deserves particular attention. Specific controls should govern the use of PINs so as to avoid excessive power accruing to public authorities. It is important to be conscious of new techniques for identifying individuals, for example, genetic fingerprinting, voice prints, iris identification (Harris, 1990).

In his annual report for 1994 (the latest report available as this chapter goes to print in February, 1996), the Commissioner concludes that data protection is all about protecting an individual's privacy. Privacy protection, he says. is at heart a human rights issue and while the Irish legislation was universally welcomed it is quite remarkable that the word privacy is used *once* in the Act and the word *computer* does not appear at all! (Data Protection Commissioner, 1994 p.5). The single most important influence on the development of data protection in the European Union in the future is likely to be the EU Directive on the Protection of Individuals with Regard to the Processing of Personal Data and Free Movement of Such Data.

INFORMATION FOR CITIZENS

'A tide waits for no man, and this is a revolutionary tide sweeping through economic and social life'. The words are at the heart of the European Union blueprint for facing up to the challenges of information technology (Bangemann, 1994). In Ireland there are indications that the Irish Government is to establish a WWW site (During 1996) to provide information about government services and e-mail access to government departments. When the WWW service is operating, public access to information will be greatly enhanced. A major limitation, however will be the lack of public access to computers. Working class households and homes of the unemployed where computer technology is not a primary concern will be relatively deprived. It is somewhat ironic that it is *Ireland On line* (see below) which is to provide free Internet access to 300 schools and 200 public libraries (*Irish Times*, 19.2.1996) Sally Sheils, president of the Irish National Teachers Organisation, regrets that the Department of Education is not taking the initiative in use of technologies, the absence of in-service training for teachers and limited resources means, in effect, that schools will 'go on line' in a phased basis. A pilot Internet project has been running at one of the Dublin Corporation libraries (the ILAC), but access in other libraries will be on a phased basis.

Individual and community support technology

The Public Information Point **(PIP)** project in Limerick is one example of a number of developments in the establishment of national information systems accessible through public media. It is notable that this system includes data on social services. A data bank has been established which enables the public, via a simple to use viewpoint information terminal, to access information twenty-four hours a day. The database is updated by public service organisations in Limerick City and topics include: taxation, child health, community and voluntary organisations, doctors, dentists, drugs, education grants, elderly care, employment, family support schemes, health services, helplines, homelessness, Minitel, pensions, training schemes and welfare entitlements.

Until the advent of IOL (Ireland on Line) access to the Internet in this country was generally restricted to large corporations. There is, however, evidence of increased competition among service providers and there are new Internet Service Providers (ISPs) appearing. Telecom Eireann (the Irish Telephone Company), is now providing Internet access via a local telephone number. After a year of research and development at the company's headquarters in Furbo, Co. Galway, Ireland on-Line went public in 1992 with an affordable and user friendly service. Colm Greely, Managing Director of the Company has introduced a distinctly Irish flavour to cyberspace. Referring to their initiative in providing access for schools and libraries, Grealy says 'We hope that through the schools and libraries, everyone in Ireland will have a chance to be part of the Global Village' (*Irish Times*, 19.2.1996).

Employment and training

Plassey Technological Park, Limerick provided the context for entrepreneurs to focus their interest on the role which small business and industry can play in the development of technology-based innovative activities (Ward, 1987). The distance learning program installed on the FAS (Foras Áiseanna Saothair, the Training and Employment Authority) mainframe computers **CML** (computer managed learning) trains people in their own home in business applications and microcomputers from a central source, this was designed to conform with the FAS/City and Guilds course *Introduction to Computers*.

FAS headquarters offers a self-service career information computer, if you want to assess your work preferences and match them to a database of occupational information, in addition it allows you to consult a United Kingdom database of occupational information. FAS through its training centre network provides training courses throughout the country of a technological and commercial nature. In November 1994 computer aided engineering courses such as CNC, CAD and CAM were offered in Shannon, Data/Telecommunications in Limerick and software development, software engineering and data communications in Loughlinstown, Cork and Waterford respectively. 1994 saw the completion of the FAS Euroform, NOW and Horizon projects which range from developing training activities for the development of a multi-skilled technician for the Electronics Industry and for the Clothing Industry to projects concerned with desktop publishing, childcare, guidance, assessment systems and accreditation of prior learning (FAS, 1994 p.4). FAS has been the National Coordinator of the FORCE Programme in Ireland since its launch in 1991.

Informal sector

As an example of an innovative initiative aimed at providing Public On-line Information, the Dublin-based voluntary organisation PATCH (*People Active Through Community Help*), has constructed a cost effective on-line communications and information service to enable local information exchanges. PATCH also provided the first cost effective service to the Internet and linked this to the various networks being utilised by the user base. PATCH developed a number of on-line databases including listings of politicians at local, national and European level (**POLI-See**), the **AMIGO** database on immigration and emigration, and **TOPPSI** (To Operate by Providing People with Service and Information) which consists of a listing of over 8,000 community and voluntary groups, enabling users to access and exchange information on grants and funding, FAS training programmes and schemes, enterprise opportunities and a range of additional information. TOPPSI is a member of FidoNet, linked to over 6,500 systems world-wide. TOPPSI is the Irish host for GreenNET and ChatNET and is a member of CUSSNet (Computer Users in Social services) and information broker for ECHO, the European Community Host Organisation. The TOPPSI connection is an electronic mail and bulletin board system which offers people such as service providers and administrators a forum for pooling information and ideas. TOPPSI provides information for social, community groups and youth organisations enabling them to make better decisions based on up to date information. Under the auspices of the TOPPSI project, PATCH supplied Rosemound Community Centre in Derry with all its information services creating a complete Desktop Information Exchange which is known as the **Com Cubed** (Community Communications by Computer) which aims to link peripheral regions in the European Community and create trans-European information networks. PATCH aims to increase IT by Voluntary Organisations and has developed the only electronic information base on the community sector in Ireland.

The services offered by PATCH are now divided into two main headings:

- **Connect-Ireland** provides the above services through a BBS (Bulletin Board Service) which has Internet access. The service is costed to allow everyone cost effective access. The organisation provides training for on-line products and services.
- **Connect-Ireland Communications** provides the full Internet service and also provides an information development service and is to shortly announce initiatives in the areas of Health, Education and Youth.

Independent living

The most innovative developments in computerisation and training for disabled people are being developed by the National Rehabilitation Board (NRB) which is engaged in a number of experimental projects. The principle role of the NRB is to advise on aspects of disability and to coordinate the work of statutory and voluntary agencies engaged in rehabilitation. The NRB is the central agency in Ireland responsible for processing European Community funding for projects concerned with disability. Minitel and Prestel are used creatively and the NRB is active in European projects such as STAR and PETRA. STAR was the first project the NRB became involved in outside of the ESF funding system. This feasibility study project was called **TeAPoT**

(Telework Applications and Potentials). This was very much pioneering into the field of new work practises not only for disabled people but for the general population as a whole. It received a lot of publicity at the time from the IDA and the Department of Employment, as well as agencies involved with disabled people, at home in Ireland and overseas (Kenny, 1995).

In line with the thrust of the STAR programme, a further aim was to explore the potential of telework to create new areas of demand for advanced telecommunications services. A case study approach was adapted in the project. Following the identification of suitable forms of telework, this involved the implementation of a centre-based initiative and a number of home-based teleworking arrangements, which were monitored and evaluated in the course of the project. The telework units were located in Dublin, Portlaoise, Galway, Donegal and Cork. Distance from the employing organisation varied from 8 to 240 kilometres.

The Home Delivered Training Project (HDT) 1990-1993. The Home-Delivered Training Project was an innovatory pilot project which set out to test the viability of providing training in IT to people with physical disabilities in their homes, using computers and modem links. It was organised in two stages. In the first stage stand-alone distance learning methods were used. Each student used IBM-compatible computers and a modem to complete their tests at the end of the course. In the second stage, the modem was used for tutorial support through electronic mail, as well as for the completion of tests.

Teleshare 1990-1991, This project was designed as a follow-up to the telework project to provide shared tele-community facilities to Small Medium Enterprises (SMEs) that were involved in Telework but were too small to afford the telecoms themselves such as X25 pads, and people with special needs such as those with physical disabilities. Telecommunications for deaf persons include: telephone aids (Ampliphone, Loudspeaking unit, Evicovax amplifier) - portable communication aids (talking discs, EASI-COM SIOS, SMAD Alphacom) - speech aids (Siemens speech trainer) - television and radio aids (teletext, microphones, adaptors and inductive loop systems). On the basis of the work carried out in TELESHARE the shared-facility model combining local access to equipment with on-line or remote access to more sophisticated facilities seems to be the most suitable one. Remote access to facilities hosted at a regional centre would seem particularly important for supporting telework and other applications such as development of videotex services.

HEART (Horizontal European Activities in Rehabilitation Technology) 1993-1994. The HEART study concentrates on six areas:

- Standards, testing and certification/specification of rehabilitation products.
- Coherence between and among rehabilitation technology industrial sectors.
- Rehabilitation Technology Service Delivery.
- Legal and macroeconomic factors impacting rehabilitation technology availability.

- Emerging areas of potential rehabilitation technology research and development.
- Rehabilitation Technology Training.

EXLIB (Expansion of European Library Services for the Visually Disadvantages) 1993-1994. Production is moving towards digital text. Electronic transfer of documents offers so many advantages to the libraries and production centres. Electronic publishing and the need for transparent text - preferably based on an internationally recognised standard such as SGML - is crucial for the future provision of text, whether directly as digital files or converted to braille, large print or synthetic speech.

TIDE (Telematics for the Integration of Disabled and Elderly People) 1990 - present. TIDE's objective is to promote research and technology development (RTD) to meet a social and an industrial goal, namely to improve the quality of life for disabled and elderly people and to improve the European industry and market in products and services that meet the needs of disabled and elderly people. TIDE deals with a number of action lines: Access to Communication and Information Technology; Integrated systems supporting education, work, leisure, mobility and training; Application of Manipulation and Control technology; Technology Transfer; and Compensation for impaired functions e.g. robotic arms for wheelchairs.

VOCATIONAL EDUCATION AND TRAINING

Social service organisations and agencies have been slow to utilise computer technologies. This may be because social work students and practitioners in the past have not received adequate training in the use of computer applications directly relevant to practice. However today, Mr. Pat Downes, who is the Head of IT support and services at University College Dublin says 'that no faculty in the university has remained untouched by the advent of Information Technology'. This statement applies right across the academic spectrum.

The National Youth Federation are the process of setting up a multi-media training centre for youth workers. Youth Science Ireland are creating a national model of Youth Services Information. Youthreach are the in process of networking centres for young disadvantaged people with the intention of sharing information and resources.

The integration of IT in the curriculum

Introductory training is offered to students in social work programmes in Universities. The current incorporation of computers in social work curriculum may be characterised by two major trends. The first focuses on research applications, the second on basic computer programming. The research courses offered in the Universities mainly emphasise quantitative statistical software such as SPSS, SAS, MINITAB and /or spreadsheet packages, such as, LOTUS 1-2-3 and Excel. Students taking a Bachelor of Social Science (B.Soc.Sc.) at University College Dublin can choose Information

Studies as a degree course. Subjects offered include: micro-computers hard and software; information systems analysis and design; electronic information resources; communication in science and technology; and database management systems among others. In addition to learning the specifics of information technology and hands on experience of IT there is a strong emphasis on the social, cultural and organisational implications of IT. Students learn how to *deal* with information (search, storage and classification issues, and government regulatory policies). It is hoped that graduates in social policy and information technology will provide a pool of computer literate entrants to the field of social services. The Information Technology Research Centre (ITRC) is a new entity within University College Dublin established on the initiative of the Colleges' President. The Centre's primary mission is to promote and encourage studies and research into IT and to provide a framework for effective cross-disciplinary academic collaboration in teaching and research.

A World Wide Web education software project of the Computer Science Department of University College Dublin has won a major computing industry award - the Education and Government Client/Server category of the first annual Apple Enterprise Awards. **WEST** (Web Educational Support Tools) is a courseware delivery system that provides a multi-media environment for teaching across the Internet or within other computer networks. Members of the WEST development team demonstrated the system at PC EXPO in New York in June, 1995, where the awards were presented. The other nominees in the category were San Joaquim Delta College from Northern California and the University of Texas at Houston.

How IT supports the teaching of other subjects and core disciplines

Students of Social Science in University College Dublin now use a computerised shared directory accessed to by their user-ID, this enables course leaders to deposit lecture notes for direct access by students and in turn students can use the directory as a mechanism for raising questions about issues. University Libraries, UCD and Trinity College Dublin have now actively adapted to the computer revolution rather than being left behind by it. These libraries now utilise the latest technology to produce abstracts, journal articles and directories on CD-ROM. The service of CD-ROM databases for students is very attractive. A vast amount of information can be stored on a single CD-ROM - one disk equals 600 high-density floppy disks. With libraries now churning out diskfuls of data CD-ROM provides an interesting storage alternative with the potential to form libraries on-line, enabling small providers to become potential specialist providers of vast amounts of information in discrete areas.

Pegasus Mail is one of a number of applications available for sending electronic mail (e-mail). One of the most popular uses of electronic mail is to access mailing lists. Mailing lists are a method of group communication on a particular topic. Some social science lists that are available are:

DATANET@TAUNIVM	-	Social Science Data List
SOCWORK@UMAB	-	Social Work Discussion List
METHODS@UNMUMA	-	Research Methods Instructions
SOC-REH@PLEARN	-	List on Social Rehabilitation
SOCIAL-POLICY@MAILBASE.AC.UK	-	Social Policy Discussion List.

One of the most useful tools of the Internet is the Telnet and FTP (File Transfer Protocol) facility. This allows students to connect up to different computers around the world and to sign in as a guest user. This can be very useful if you want to access a foreign library. FTP offers users the opportunity to transfer data from electronic journals and discussion documents to their own computer. All around the world there are anonymous FTP sites. ARCHIE is a database of most FTP sites in the world. With this database students can obtain information regarding a certain subject and the site location.

The Audio Visual Centre at University College Dublin broke new ground in educational broadcasting in Ireland with a series of live television programmes which began on 18th October, 1995. **LearnNet**, the name given to the live interactive series on Radio Telefis Eireann (Irish Television) Network Two, featured student participation through telephone, fax and the Internet. LearnNet is targeted at adult learners who will be encouraged to be active rather than passive viewers. 'Using the information superhighway to bring access to learning for the unemployed is just one of the commendable aims of the project' says Leo Casey of the Audio Visual Centre.

PROVISION OF SERVICES

Central to the working of the Information Society, or IS, is the computer and the myriad of sophisticated software packages permitting the compilation, storage, retrieval and dissemination of vast volumes of information without the historic constraints of time, distance and volume. This section deals with these developments and processes of information technology in service provision agencies.

Practice level

The main computer package used for the analysis of NSSB (National Social Service Board) data is called **SNAP**. This is a package specifically intended for the analysis of Market Research Surveys and has many features which are not found in other packages available for general statistical analysis (Vincent, 1994). It is intended to have a student version available shortly, this version will be limited in the number of variables and cases it can analyse. SNAP can be divided into four: variables; data; analysis; and graphics.

The National Rehabilitation Technical Aids Information Service is fully computerised and provides national information on non-medical technical aids and equipment for those concerned with the practical needs of disabled people. The NRB have also adopted **Apticom** which is the system developed in the United States for use in assessing vocational aptitudes, occupational interests and work-related mathematical and language skills quickly and easily. In this program the initial phase of testing involves the assessment of a wide range of aptitudes including General Learning Ability, Verbal and Numerical Aptitudes, Form Perception, Motor Coordination and Manual Dexterity. After the initial phase an Occupational Interest Inventory is completed and clients are helped to decide on the type of employment in which they are interested. A project also run by the NRB 'Design and Dissemination of Information (Electronically)' provides public information points and Minitel. Public Information Points, as previously mentioned, are systems displaying information on Social Services, Revenue, Health and NRB services. These systems are located in public places like shopping centres and in Dublin and Limerick public libraries. **Minitel**, another electronic information system which is accessible nationally and internationally has NRB information but has the added facility of lists of Irish hotels and guest houses which are both partially and fully accessible to disabled people (Kenny, 1995).

Information systems

In Dublin Corporations' Housing Welfare Department, computers are used for purposes such as overview of workload; resource materials and making available information for social work staff such as (a) client index (b) work procedures (c) directory of housing services (d) directory of agencies. Furthermore a computerised database is planned, specifically for senior citizens providing information on residential entitlements. LAN Communications, a computer network set up in 1993 is currently being used by Revenue Commissioners where computers spread out all over the country are networked to each other. It also provides e-mail integration to government departments. This allows the different systems used by each department to communicate easily with each other (*The Sunday Business Post*, 5.3.1995).

The Department of Education has recently[3] made a £50,000 investment in a video conference link between its offices in Dublin and Athlone. 'Another weapon in our communications armoury' is how Seamus McLoughlin of the information technology section of the Department of Education described its new video conferencing system. The system is the first of its kind to be installed in the civil service, and according to McLoughlin, other government departments are watching its progress with interest. The two site link between was installed by a British company,

[3] The system was installed before Christmas 1994 and was officially launched on 30 January 1995.

Satelcom UK, based in Ascot.

The Department of Social Welfare aims to provide a fast, efficient service. To achieve this goal, an increased emphasis has been placed on computerisation and telecommunications in recent years. Most areas of the Department of Social Welfare now rely on computer systems for the administration of social security schemes and the computer network is being extended to local social welfare offices to allow each office to handle queries and claims at a local level as quickly as possible. The main features of the Departments' Information Technology infrastructure are three computer centres and a telecommunications network **INFONET**, which links the centres to local department offices around the country. The Department formally adopted a hardware and software strategy based on Digital VAX systems and standard Digital software. Calculation systems are unique packages written by the Department of Social Welfare connected to **INFOSYS** - a computerised information system which provides one point of access to all client information obtained from claimants RSI number.

Managing services

In the education field, LAN Communications implemented a wide areas network linking the RTC's and a consultancy service to the Higher Education Authority (HEA) to optimise its wide area net. As part of this LAN Communications designed, installed and supported the campus computer 'backbone' in DCU. As with other countries Ireland has a national body with the responsibility of compiling and collecting important demographic data and statistical information. The Central Statistics Office contains the principal economic and social statistics for Ireland. In a similar vein the Local Government Computer Services Board administers and provides an IT service to local authorities, government departments and other related bodies. As already outlined, the use of computers is advanced in the social security system. Other computerised initiatives include:

- Claims for all the Free Schemes are processed automatically for approximately 800,000 claimants.
- Accounts: A computer facility assists with the calculation and payment of refunds of PRSI both to employers and insured persons.
- Remote Certificate Entry (RCE). This allows medical certificates to be entered at the Departments local offices and the relevant details are entered to the general benefits computer system, thereby reducing the time taken to process payments.
- Medical referral for Disability Benefit: This system selects cases for medical referral (i.e. a second examination by the Department of Social Welfare's doctor) and generates the necessary documentation.
- A major project during 1991 was the development of a facility to pay Child Benefit by means of Electronic Fund Transfer (EFT).

Social care policy

The use of information technology in social care policy is not in widespread operation in Ireland. However, one example illustrates the small steps that are taking place. Centre Care, a voluntary organisation, uses a computerised system for recording information on clients using their service. Kay Keary, a social worker in the Child Sexual Abuse Unit of the Children's Hospital in Dublin is currently involved in the design and establishment of a computer data base. In informal discussion one discerns a certain reluctance to entertain the idea of computerised decision-making in client practice, in the belief that the kinds of problems presented to social workers can best be resolved in a situation of personal interaction. Developments in artificial intelligence, however, may overtake the social work profession (Fox and Winett, 1990). Ireland is not unique in this way as surveys carried out in the UK indicate that from one-third to one-half of all social services own microcomputers, however they are used predominantly for word processing, administrative and financial management functions. Less than 5% of agency computers are used directly by clinicians for case management or clinical decision-making (Glastonbury et al., 1988 p.77).

If client counselling support systems are categorised into simulation and calculation support programmes and database information programmes then it is possible to claim that there is an embryonic social care system in existence, though not primarily for use by social workers.

CONCLUSION AND FUTURE DEVELOPMENTS

Much has been written about the problems of European information technology in relation to the rest of the world and about Ireland's role within mainland Europe. European manufacturers like Bull, Olivetti and Philips are struggling for survival against faster moving American and Asian competitors. From an all-European perspective, Ireland is much more notable as a place where computers are assembled and software packaged than for the genius of our computer users. On a per capita basis, we tend to be particularly low spenders on technology (Sterne, 1991). Within Ireland, moreover, there are enormous differences in the accessibility of IT skills. Some 90% of software employment is concentrated in just five areas - Dublin, Cork, Limerick, Galway and Leixlip.

Among the threats we face is a phenomenon known as 'telecolonisation' - the process whereby urban employers use online circuits to tap the best talent in rural areas. The efforts of outworkers like these may swell the profits of metropolitan corporations, while contributing little to the well-being of the regions where they live (Grace, 1991). One attempt to counter this trend is the 'telecottage' movement, which aims to channel IT resources into isolated regions. The concept comes from the Nordic countries, which have been able to integrate it with sophisticated social services and regional development policies.

Research into social and cultural impact of new technologies and communications technologies has been undertaken (Komito, 1992). Further work, however, is necessary to assess the impact of technologies on social work/social service employment. Leadership is evident: the Eastern Health Board is actively considering the use of video conferencing to link people in remote parts of its catchment area with medical consultants. In late 1995, the Health Board took part in a remote diagnostics conference which beamed 'telemedicine' events into conference headquarters (Doherty, 1995).

It has already become a cliché to talk about the 'hype' surrounding the information super-highway but just about everybody wants to get on the bandwagon. Almost overnight it has become the issue for IT afficionados and interested observers alike. As the name suggests, this is no quiet country lane. Users don't stroll contentedly along admiring the view: **they surf.** Turbo-charged action is what the Internet is all about and, from the White House to Dáil Eireann (the Irish Parliament): social services, businesses and enterprises are being urged to get on board.

References

Bangemann M. *Europe and the Global Information Society, Recommendations to the European Council*, 26th May, 1994, Brussels: European Commission. 1994.

Budget 1994. Presented by Mr. Bertie Ahern T.D. Minister for Finance to Dail Eireann. 26 January 1994.

Commission of the European Communities, Science and Technology Policy. *FAST Series No.21 The New Technologies and Local Development.* CK Ward. Social Science Research Centre, University College Dublin. 1987.

Council of Europe. *The Introduction and use of Personal Identification Numbers: the Data Protection Issues.* Study prepared by the Committee of Experts on Data Protection (CJ-PD). Strasbourg: Publishing and Documentation Service. 1991.

deRossa P. Speech to Dail Eireann (Irish Parliament). 9th February 1995.

Doherty C. Video Conferencing Drives An Expanding Technology 'Infobahn'. *The Sunday Business Post*, 3rd December 1995.

FAS (Foras Aiseanna Saothair: The Training and Employment Authority). *Training Course List.* Dublin Headquarters: FAS Employment Services Offices.1994.

FAS (Foras Aiseanna Saothair: The Training and Employment Authority). *Annual Report.* Dublin: Foras Aiseanna Saothair (FAS). 1994.

Fox EA and Winett SG. Using Vector and Extended Boolean Matching in an Expert System for Selecting Foster Homes. *Journal of the American Society for Information Science*. 41(1): 10-26. 1990.

Grace G. *Developing Information Services - A Practical Guide.* Workshop Session at NSSB's National Conference. Dublin: National Social Service Board, unpublished. November 1991.

Harris J. *Wonderwoman and Superman: The Ethics of Human Biotechnology.* Oxford:

John Wiley and Sons Inc. 1992.

Kenny S. *The Role of the National Rehabilitation Board (NRB) and Information Technology.* Report for IT Working Group. Dublin: National Rehabilitation Board, unpublished. 1995.

Komito L. Information Technology and Regional Developments: promises and prospects. In Feehan J (Ed.). *Dublin: The Environmental Institute,* University College Dublin. 1994.

Lavan A and Iredale R. Ireland. In: Colombi D, Rafferty J and Steyaert J (Eds.). *Human Services and Information Technology.* Antwerp and Southampton: ENITH 1993.

Martin W. *The Information Society.* New York: University Press. 1988.

O'Shea R. *Multi-faceted Modernisation: Some Public Sector Hypotheses.* Dublin: Department of Social Welfare, unpublished. 1995.

Relate. Volume 22 Number 3. Dublin: National Social Service Board. December 1994.

Ruddle H and O'Conor, J. *Reaching Out: Charitable Giving and Volunteering in the Republic of Ireland.* Dublin: Policy Research Centre. 1992.

Sterne J. *People are Still Important - The Limitations of Technology.* Workshop Session at NSSB's National Conference. Dublin: National Social Service Board, unpublished. 1991.

Author details

Ann Lavan, who is a lecturer in Social Policy and Social Work at University College, Dublin, teaches a course on Human Services and New Technology to post graduate students on the M.Soc.Sc.(Social Policy). Her interest in IT arises from her research on the development of record systems/client databases, her experience on the Commission on Social Welfare with regard to the computerisation of benefit calculation systems and her work with the Combat Poverty Agency in Ireland.

Aisling Byrne completed the M.Soc.Sc.(Social Policy) degree at University College, Dublin in 1995. As part of her project work she undertook to update material for the preparation of the chapter in this volume and assisted Ann Lavan in the completion of that work in a voluntary capacity. Aisling is now a freelance researcher.

Contact: Ann Lavan
Department of Social Policy and Social Work
University College
Dublin
Ireland

E-mail: Alavan@acadamh.ucd.ie

11 Israel

Yitzhak Berman

HUMAN SERVICES AND INFORMATION TECHNOLOGY

Israel's comprehensive welfare system is based on social legislation that provides for a wide range of social and community services. Under the Social Welfare Law (1958) every municipality and local authority in the country, of which there are some two hundred, is legally required to maintain a social services department that effects the delivery of social services at a local level. The Ministry of Labour and Social Affairs is the central governmental agency that determines social policy, initiates legislation and enacts regulations for day-to-day social service delivery within local authorities. There is a process of decentralisation of social service policy decision-making and planning within local authorities. Supervision of social services in local authorities is carried out both by the Ministry's national supervisors, as well as by its district supervisors four district offices.

The Ministry of Labour and Social Affairs provides 75% of the social services budget of the local authorities, and 100% of the budget for certain services which are provided on a nationwide basis centrally from the Ministry, such as probation services, residential services for the mentally handicapped, and services for juvenile offenders and delinquent youth. Areas covered by the social services units of the Ministry include:

- Division of Personal and Family Social Services - Welfare of the Individual and the Family, Care of the Elderly, Community Work and Project Renewal, Services for Children and Youth, Adoption and Services for Unmarried Mothers, Prevention and Treatment of Alcoholism, and Organisation and Management and development in Local Social Services Departments.
- Rehabilitation Services Administration - Rehabilitation of the Physically Disabled, Services for the Blind, Rehabilitation Centres, Sheltered Workshops and

Residential Facilities. Division of Services for the Mentally Handicapped - Residential and Community Services

- Division of Correctional Services and Youth Development - Adult and Juvenile Probation Services, Youth Rehabilitation in Vocational Centres for School Drop-outs, Residential Care for Juvenile Offenders, Services for Youth in Distress, and Services for Women and Girls in Distress.

An additional framework which provides social welfare services are voluntary organisations. These organisations are mainly women's organisations, which provide services in the following areas: day care services; boarding schools for children and services for women.

Five schools of social work in Israel's universities offer graduate and postgraduate training in programmes combining theoretical study and work in the field. A school of the Ministry of Labour and Social Affairs provides training at centres throughout the country for child-care workers and social work aides, as well as in-service training for social workers. Social and community workers are employed in a variety of contexts, including social service bureaux, community centres, immigrant absorption centres, mother-and-child health centres, schools, factories and hospitals.

The National Insurance Institute is the administrative body responsible for the implementation of social security policy in Israel. The national insurance payments include the following categories: old-age and survivors, general disability, employment injury, border and hostile action casualties, maternity, children, unemployment, army reserve service and income support benefits.

In Israel, in the area of information technology and human services we have identified the following groups of experts who design human service software and the users of the software for the social services:

- The larger human service organisations such as the Ministry of Labour and Social Affairs.
- The National Insurance Institute or the Joint Distribution Committee of Israel (a voluntary organisation) have their own computer departments where they design software programs for their own use, and for affiliated organisations.
- The social work departments of the universities also design software programs for social services in which they are involved in research.
- Other organisations designing software for the human services are commercial firms and not-for-profit organisations who develop programs by order of the social service delivery organisations.

The users of human service software include national and local government, voluntary social service organisations and a growing number of private-for-profit service organisations. Information technology has become a part of the organisational process in the human services on three levels of administrative applications; service and treatment of clients; information transfer.

Administrative applications: Human service organisations have rationalised their administrative processes through the use of information technology. This includes client information and tracking, budget control and office administration. IT programs used in this area are management oriented. Their use is for social service administrators and are not oriented towards the work of the social service provider within the social worker-client relationship. The Israeli Ministry of Labour and Social Affairs has developed a new program within this context which impacts on all ministry social service departments. A description of the program is included in this report.

Service and treatment of clients: Information technology programs have been developed in a wide range of areas regarding special populations. This includes a clinical support system for foster care, an expert system to support assessment of the ability to work, a computerised system to support decisions made by military clinicians whether to discharge a soldier due to mental health problems, a nation-wide information system for the social work departments of Israeli hospitals, and a client information system in rehabilitation centres for the handicapped. (Berman, 1993).

Information transfer: A number of programs for the transfer of information to social work professionals and citizens have been developed. This includes an information system on all services for the handicapped and the aged, an information system administrated through the Citizen Advice Bureaux network, and the information for citizens program of the National Insurance Institute. A number of these programs are described in the following section.

INFORMATION FOR CITIZENS

Computerised information system of rehabilitation services and services for the aged

This computerised information system was developed by JDC - Israel. The information system is based on the ORACLE database and runs on a DEC Micro Vax 11/VMS 5.1 computer. Included in the database are 2,700 services. The list of services can be retrieved selectively by any of the over 1,000 keywords or any combination of keywords.

A service is included in the information system when it is a special service for people with a long-term problem - impairment, disability or handicap. They are classified into eleven major types. They are medical (8%), paramedical (5%), mental health (6%), educational (26%), social (22%), psychological (14%), vocational (10%), recreational (8%), residential (7%) consultation and information (7%) and voluntary organisations and support groups (12%). The computerised information system provides updated information and endless possibilities of indexing the information for use of government offices; of the specific services that provide guidance; of professionals in the field such as social workers, physicians, paramedical professions etc.; and of the population in need and their families. A request for information can be made by phone or in writing. The response to a query, generally a list of services with addresses and phone numbers, is usually mailed on the same day or given by phone. More complicated requests for analysis of services are answered as well and prepared in tabular form. The system is being utilised for the purpose of comprehensive planning and for decision making for people with disability, by policy makers such as the Ministry of Labour and Social Affairs or the National Insurance Institute.

A similar computerised information system exists on services for the aged in Israel. It includes a database of 2,200 services. The list of services can be retrieved selectively by any of the over 1,000 keywords or any combination of keywords. A service is included in the information system when it is a special service for elderly people. The services are classified into eleven major types. They are medical (2%), nursing homes (19%), nursing care (12%), mental health (1%), educational (5%), social (7%), vocational (1%), recreational (40%), consultation and information (4%) and voluntary organisations and support groups (7%) and day centres (7%). Some of the services of the elderly overlap with the general rehabilitation services in the database and are not included in the description. The system is being used for the purpose of comprehensive planning and for decision making for ESHEL (a planning organisation for the elderly) and policy makers regarding services for the elderly, such as the Ministry of Labour and Social Affairs or the National Insurance Institute.

Citizen's Advice Bureaux on the Internet

The Citizen's Advice Bureaux were first founded in 1957 as centres operated by volunteers. From 1974 it became a service under the auspices of the Ministry of Labour and Social Affairs operated by the local municipal authorities, using volunteers. The goal of the service is to provide citizens with information regarding their rights and obligations and their full participation in society. The Citizen's Advice Bureaux staff provides information, follows up referrals to services and serves as a link between the client and the services until the client's problem is under care.

In 1995 the Ministry of Labour and Social Affairs Citizens Advice Bureaux secretariat put the information found in its database on the Internet with a WWW address. This e-mail access to the Israeli Citizen's Advice Bureaux is experimental and is in its first stage of a three stage development programme.

- The Ministry of Labour and Social Affairs Citizen's Advice Bureaux secretariat will test access of the database to the public, and its technical operation.
- The database will be closed to the public. The Internet address will provide the public with general information on the Citizen's Advice Bureaux and will make

accessible more specific information through electronic information sheets. It is during this stage that the secretariat at the Ministry of Labour and Social Affairs will develop an updating system of the Citizen's Advice Bureaux database.

- The Citizen's Advice Bureaux database will be open to the public. The database will have continuous online updating of the information in the database which will guarantee the public that it is receiving correct information.

VOCATIONAL EDUCATION AND TRAINING [1]

The development and application of information technology in the vocational training of social workers is varied both over time and place. Two schools of thought exist in regard to the teaching of information technology. The first is the more technological oriented approach in which the computer as a tool for social workers is the point of reference. The second school takes a more humanistic approach to IT education in social work where the perception is that computerisation can be integrated into social work and social work programming is the basis of the course. Most courses are given at the M.A. level.

A course outline representing the more technological oriented approach was developed by Dr Monnickendam at the Bar Ilan University, School of Social Work and Dr Cnaan at that time at the Tel Aviv University, School of Social Work. The course is constructed of two interrelated and integrated modules: theory and practice. In teaching the theory module, three alternate theoretical paradigms are discussed: systems theory, decision theory and organisational theory. The practice module is aimed at providing the student with basic tools to apply the theoretical function to concrete problems and situations. Students are introduced to the university mainframe and/or to micro computers. By means of a series of exercises they learn to use the operating system, file manipulation and some word processing. A term paper is required where the student has to propose a design of a computerised process in a human service agency. The paper consists of the following mandatory parts:

- flowchart of existing process
- decision table
- data dictionary
- flowchart proposed computerised process
- output
- discussion

In a later course outline Dr Monnickendam introduced an IT course with a more social work orientation. In this course Dr Monnickendam teaches theoretical issues in information systems and decision making and the practical applications of the use of

---

[1] Material for this section was obtained from the Schools of Social work of Bar Ilan University, Tel Aviv University, the Hebrew University (Jerusalem) and the Central School for Training of Social Welfare Staff of the Israeli Ministry of Labour and Social Affairs.

the computer in social services. Case management as a case study is used, demonstrating information technology within a social work administration and treatment process.

Dr Scherer of the Tel Aviv University, School of Social Work also gives courses on information technology within the more technological conceptual framework. In his course the Introduction to Computers, social work students on the M.A. level are taught basic concepts of the computer, its possible uses, how to use a PC and to use a word processing program. Social work students are also taught BASIC (programming language), a data sheet program and about computer networking.

In a second more advanced course in information technology, Dr Scherer teaches about the use of the computer in the social services. This course is also for students on the M.A. level. The course familiarises the students with the various uses of information technology in the social services. The methodology used is based on the development of information technology programs. This is done by identifying the need for such a program, formulating the concept of the program and building the structure for the development of the program. The students familiarise themselves with existing information technology programs which are operating in different social services organisations.

Ms Dorit Barak at the School of Social Work at Hebrew University takes a more service application approach to information technology in social work. Her course reviews the major trends in information systems in the practising professions with an emphasis on social work. Different information technology programs are reviewed with a view to see how they serves the different organisational levels. The programs studied are:

- IT programs used to improve service delivery - including decision support systems, expert systems and clinical information systems.
- Administrative information systems

The goals of each of the systems are analysed, the concepts behind the program, how they are implemented and their contribution to the social service organisation. The problems of developing such programs and their implementation are also discussed.

The Central School for Training of Social Welfare Staff of the Israeli Ministry of Labour and Social Affairs is an in-service training facility for all workers in the area of social welfare. These workers may be employed by the national ministry, municipalities or by voluntary organisations. Those attending courses at the Central School include social workers and other workers in the area of social welfare (i.e. day care, institutional, and community facilities).

A course on Information Technology in the Social Services has been given by Yitzhak Berman to social workers from municipal social service departments. The course was given on the occasion of the introduction of computers into the social service departments. The goal of the course was to familiarise social workers with the issues and possible uses of the computer in a social service setting. The social workers received 'hands-on' experience in a separate course.

The course included a presentation of the conceptual issues in the relationship between social work and information technology. The 'thinking processes' behind the use of the computer and that of social work. How the two processes can be harmonised is analysed. Various issues in the use of information technology in a social service setting is raised. This includes: philosophical issues, ethical issues, social responsibility, ideological issues, professional and organisational issues. The impact of information on the organisation in general and a social service organisation is particular is analysed. The use of information in a social service organisation is studied as is the use of information systems in social work. Various computerised systems which are operable in social service agencies are presented and analysed. The course concludes with a discussion on how to introduce information technology into a social service organisation.

This analysis of the varied courses for social workers demonstrates that what the student learns depends on the lecturer. There is no accepted approach as to what a social work student should know on receiving a degree in social work. As most of the courses are on the M.A. level it should be noted that a social worker who begins working in the profession after receiving only a B.A. degree will have no formal familiarity with information technology in a social service setting.

PROVISION OF SERVICES

The initial motivation for introducing information technology into the Ministry of Labour and Social Affairs came as a response to the overwhelming number of monthly and other payments required to individuals and organisations. Mainframe time was rented from an outside semi-governmental agency where the computer was located with access being gained via a point-to-point connection. Terminals were furnished to necessary staff in the computer department and were used to implement and control not only financial payments but also the Ministry's budget.

The first contact experienced by non computer department consumers of the technology was via voluminous paper printouts of processed data. In the two year period 1986-87 a massive and rapid introduction of personal computers in the Ministry occurred. The first direct placement of PCS outside the computer department was in the Research Division of the Ministry. Almost immediately following (but unrelated to this) secretaries and typists were furnished with machines, and then at a more gradual pace department administrators were introduced to the use of computers. Usually these administrators sat themselves in front of their secretary's computer or on more rare occasions received their own personal computer. The saturation of Ministry offices by PCS instilled the sense of an organisation functioning within a technological ecology.

The Ministry is the central governmental agency which determines social policy, initiates legislation and enacts regulations for social service delivery carried out by the local authorities. Supervision of social services in local authorities is carried out both by the Ministry's national supervisors, as well as by its four district office supervisors. Department administrators are responsible for the planning and administration of services and resource control, manpower and budget. National supervisors are responsible for the implementation and supervision of social services according to professional social work guidelines.

Until very recently the computerisation policy of the Ministry of Labour and Social Affairs has clearly placed priority on the development of information technology programs which are related to the transfer of payments to outside agencies. These provide services such as day and institutional care for children and the aged, medical payments for the needy, and social service manpower. These services comprise the major financial outlay of various departmental budgets of the social affairs section of the Ministry. They therefore demand the administrator's utmost attention. Resource related policy has priority for computerisation resources. In fact no specialised information technology programming has been made available for the national supervisors' use. They remain dependent on paper reporting and tend to use the computer only for the administrative aspects of their tasks.

The main client reporting applications used in the Ministry of Labour and Social Affairs is the Basic Data Questionnaire (BDQ). The BDQ is a data form filled out by local social workers at intake of all families requesting services from the local social services department. The form contains basic family and head of household demographic information such as date of birth, family data, health status, education and the general reason for the family's approaching the local social services department. This expressed reason is not an operational definition of the presenting problem, but rather an indication of the area of family concern such as problems between spouses or a handicapped child. The unit of analysis of the questionnaire is the family.

All Israeli citizens are assigned an identification number. Each family member's number is recorded on the BDQ and is used as a control device to assure registration of all family members before they receive services which are related to payment transfers. Some locally initiated IT development has taken place during the past few years. These were designed for PC use, were administrative in nature, but represented only expansions and specialised modifications of the BDQ. Although other programs were designed, their basic purpose was to count people receiving services.

In the Ministry no 'social work' IT computer applications exist. For example no decision support systems or management information systems, which link families in treatment to services delivered, are available. A decision support system is however in use in the Juvenile Probation Service. Data available via the payment transfer programs enables the determination of who is served by whom, but there is at present no systematic way to evaluate service outcomes. All accumulated information concerns that which is needed to effect a payment. The only other source of service information is via the BDQ. It however does not furnish data regarding the diagnosis of problems in an operational context, types of services and treatment given to family, progress made, or evaluation of services.

The technology in place in the Ministry is administrative and not service oriented. It is within this frame of reference that the directors of the Ministry of Labour and Social Affairs decided to 'computerise' the ministry. It was in 1993 that the process began of a systematic, coordinated and standardised reorganisation of the use of information technology and the development of a management information system in the ministry. The information technology program which is being developed provides an example of the information needs and administrative processes of a centralised social service management system. The goals of the management information system (MIS) are:

- To provide information on populations receiving services and on the services which are delivered.
- To administer the supply and demand of services.
- To rationalise the system of payments.
- To rationalise the system of grants given to the municipalities and the budget adjustments made with them.

The MIS is made up of three modules, which are described in more detail below, and are:

- Population Module. Basic data on those people receiving services.
- Service Module. Information on those organisations providing services including identifying information of the population receiving services within those organisations.
- Budget and Bookkeeping Module. Information on the budget by services, status of transfer of payments to municipalities and all organisations providing services.

Population module

The population module is basically a client records and information system, which is based on the basic data questionnaire (BDQ). At present, in the 200 social service bureaux in Israel, there is an information system that is used in the policy, planning and administrative process (Berman, 1992). The Basic Data Questionnaire (BDQ), is the basic form for collecting data on a family that comes to a social service bureau for any type of service.

Over 215,000 families are in the information system, which is about 15% of the total number of families in Israel. The BDQ has been in use since the early 1970s, but has undergone changes in content, the way it is analysed, used and processed. Local social service bureaux send the BDQs directly to the Ministry of Labour and Social

Affairs. Those social service bureaux which use computers can send the BDQs by disk or tape to the ministry. There are three classes of information included in this system:

- Data on the head of the family.
- Data on other members of the family.
- Data on the household.

Functional use of basic data questionnaire by level

The Basic Data Questionnaire is used on four functional levels: administrative, statistical, planning and treatment.

Level	Micro	Macro	Macro	Macro	Macro
Stages	Basic Data Questionnaire	Statistical Output	Data Analysis	Problem Identification	Individual Problem Identification
Functional Use	Administrative (a)	Statistical (b)	Statistical, Planning (b)	Planning (c)	Administrative, Treatment (d)

(a) **Administrative** - The social worker records identifying data by head of family, data of other members of the family and general household information. This information includes the identification number of each member of the household. This identifying information is the basic data needed by a social worker to relate to a client and draw up a treatment plan. Within this framework the use of the BDQ remains on a micro level.

(b) **Statistical** - The total of all BDQs provides data of a statistical nature - the number of clients, the number of unemployed, the number of clients by type of problem, etc. It also provides the basis for data analysis, like measuring an increase in a specific problem, who has the problem, where does the problem exist. With this function, the BDQ data system is put on a macro-level.

(c) **Planning** - On the basis of statistics and the data analysis, the BDQ data system now takes on a planning function. On the basis of alternative information sources, such as analysis of trends, political pressure and public opinion, certain planning questions can be asked. The focus the data analysis into providing operational questions regarding problem identification and the setting of priorities. Through data analysis, problems can be identified and given priority, and the number of clients with the problem are ascertained, including the characteristics of those who have the problem. At this stage we are still operating on the macro level.

(e) **Administrative-Treatment** - In order for the BDQ data to take on an operational nature, those clients with the problem which has received priority are identified. It is at this stage that the BDQ data system is broken down to the micro or individual level. At this stage the social worker re-enters the process to deal with the individual. By using the identifying information of the BDQ, the social worker can relate to the client and draw up a treatment plan.

One of the key variables in the BDQ is the identifying problem as presented to the social worker. The BDQ records two identifying problems. The first, for the family which is general by definition. The second, for each family member who has a problem. This problem is defined in an operational manner in order to provide a course of action for the social worker.

Service module

The service module includes information on all organisations providing services to clients, which are funded by the Ministry of Labour and Social Affairs and/or the municipal social service departments. This includes institutional services, day care services and community services. The module includes information on the cost of services.

The major component of this module is data on who is receiving services. The Service Module is integrated with the Population Module therefore providing information on who receives which services. This enables correlating the identifying problem with services received. The service module also records those waiting for services by type of service. This information was found to be an indicator of services which are in need of development and expansion.

Budget and bookkeeping module

This module, which is for administrative purposes, keeps track of information on the budget by services, status of transfer of payments to municipalities and to all organisations providing services. One can see that the new management information system of the Ministry of Labour and Social Affairs is oriented towards management issues and provides very little information for the social work component of the organisation. After the implementation of this MIS program a more practice oriented information system is planned.

Other human service systems - information system for foster care agencies

The Information System for Foster Care Agencies was designed by Professor Rami Benbenishty of the School of Social Work of Hebrew University in Jerusalem (Benbenishty, 1996). The goal of system was to provide professional social workers with an information tool that could be integrated in daily practice, and enable monitoring of each case regarding client characteristics, interventions and outcomes. The system generates data for practitioners, supervisors, regional administrators and policy makers, although its main focus is on front line workers.

The data gathering instruments included information on historical background, the background to the current placement, the current situation, the foster parents, a report from the teacher, the biological parents and changes in placements. The unit of information gathering was the 'child in placement'. The system's output is both at the level of the individual child, providing information needed for service provision, and at the aggregated level, providing information for management and policy use. The system is partly computerised, but not within agencies because of lack of equipment. Practitioners use forms that are mailed to a central processing unit and receive output reports within days for inclusion in the client's file. Centralisation of individual client data allows aggregated analysis.

The system was developed in the Hebrew University School of Social Work and transferred to the Israeli Ministry of Labour and Social Affairs. This transfer was not successful and continuing improvement to the system was not achieved. Workers identified limitations in the current system and did not receive the feedback promised. It therefore has a limited impact. There are recent attempts to re-examine the system and create a process that ensures responsiveness to the needs of front line workers.

Information system for hospital social work

The case study reported here concerns the development and implementation of a nation-wide information system for social work departments in general hospitals in Israel (Auslander, 1996). It was organised by the three main providers in health care services, the Ministry of Health, the Kupat Holim of the Histadrut (a health fund) and the Hadassah Medical Organisation. These organisations own 97% of the country's general care beds. The project was carried out by the JDC-Brookdale Institute.

The scope of the project is the development and implementation of a country-wide information system for social work departments in general hospitals in Israel. This includes twenty eight hospitals and about 500 social workers. Information is being gathered in all social work departments by all social workers on their clients. So far data has been collected on over 10,000 cases.

The aims of the information system are to provide relevant information to persons on all levels of work concerned with hospital social work: the service providers, the supervisors and the local and national management. However, there is a strong focus in principal on quality assurance, rather than on decision support.

The procedures used in this client information system require social workers to record all their interactions dealing with patients on paper-based recording forms or directly onto the computer. As Steyaert (1992) noted 'While these forms were intended to replace all existing case records, their adoption for that purpose is limited. Total integration involves a more advanced and comprehensive use of information technology and a higher ratio of computers to social workers, which goes well beyond the aims of the project'.

However, the system goes beyond a mere recording of quantitative information on clients by including names and addresses of clients and allowing some information to be entered in free-text format. The forms are assembled and processed by a uniform computer program run on micro-computers at local hospital social work departments. This was developed in Magic, an Israeli database program. It allows data-entry, printing of case reports, a set of pre-defined frequency distributions and extensive queries. Users can also include information on up to four 'free' variables, thus allowing for information entry and analysis on items particular to certain hospitals. Finally, users will be able to decide on elaboration of some of the classifications used to make them more precise and valuable for clinical use.

The output of this information system is two-layered. At first, reports with frequency distributions on the major items are provided. These reports not only provide important information themselves, but also are an important incentive to request additional data analysis and reports, which can then be provided. This two-layered strategy specifically aims to avoid an overwhelming stream of data beyond the capacity of the users. A second aspect of the hospital social work information system is the introduction of protocols for data use. Assuming the capability of users at service level to use the provided information to be rather limited, guidelines were drafted containing selected issues being addressed, the data needed to answer them, the data analysis needed to get the necessary information and the plausible responses on the service or managerial level. This issue is related to the quality assurance aim of the system.

The issue of quality assurance is central to the development of the hospital social work information system and involves both the development and setting of professional standards for practice and monitoring and assessing them by using thresholds. These standards and their assessment are situated at three different levels - structural, processes and outcomes. At each level, the quality of social work needs to be guaranteed to accomplish an acceptable overall quality level.

DSS for vocational rehabilitation centres for people with disabilities

Israel has about eighteen centres providing vocational rehabilitation services for mentally or physically disabled people. Clients are referred by the National Insurance Institute, the Ministry of Absorption (new immigrants to the country) or local authorities. The rehabilitation centres assess the capacities of clients, provide appropriate vocational training, try to find placements after training and give up to six months continuing support. During training, which is from a few weeks up to one year, clients receive some payment for work done. The total number of clients at any time is about 2,000 across the country.

The decision support system currently being developed for the Israeli rehabilitation centres (Barak, 1996) is supported by the Joint Distribution Committee of Israel, the Israeli Vocational Rehabilitation Fund, the Ministry of Labour and Social Affairs and the Hebrew University. System and software development and implementation is being tested as a pilot project in the rehabilitation centre of Ashkelon (on the Mediterranean coast) in close contact with the other centres. The goals of the system are:

- reorganising the work more efficiently by planning the treatment process,
- improving the decision making process of the multi-disciplinary staff,
- assurance of equability of each member of the staff,
- developing knowledge in the area of vocational rehabilitation of disabled people,
- decision support in management decisions in vocational rehabilitation centres.

The planned system consists of six different modules - social worker's, evaluation, workshop, vocational training, vocational placement, management -all connected in a network. The existing modules centre around the social worker's module which gathers and structures all information about clients from the initial intake until discharge. Information includes factual data, checklists, short descriptions and lengthy text reports. One can indicate the extent as well as the presence of a problem, thus avoiding one of the shortcomings of social work classification. The systems support a task-centred approach, by inducing a description of the problems, the desired ultimate and intermediate outcomes, the interventions required and the time schedule for their achievement. The information systems follows the client throughout the treatment process and requires follow-up data to be collected. Among others the following reports can be produced at the request of the social worker: intake, treatment plan, monitoring of treatment, treatment summary at end of treatment.

The other modules assist the worker in their specific tasks at each stage of the rehabilitation process including planning and carrying out client treatment plans. The process requires workers to monitor and evaluate the progress of the client and they receive reports which are relevant to their role in rehabilitation. The social worker responsible for the case receives information from each module, studies the data and makes treatment decisions. In 1995 all the modules were completed and were implemented in one vocational rehabilitation centre. From 1996 two additional centres will use the decision support system.

DSS in the youth probation service

The purpose of this decision support system in the context of probation disposition decisions is to assist Youth Probation Officers at the Jerusalem District Office to make more consistent, equitable and reliable recommendations in the assignment of juvenile offenders to dispositions (Shapira, 1990). The system aims to develop in a gradual and evolutionary way, policy rules to eventually replace case-by-case discretionary judgement which is potentially arbitrary and inconsistent. The system has been in use since 1984 and covers over 500 youths assigned to the Jerusalem District Office of the Youth Probation Service. It is planned to implement the program at the Tel Aviv District Office. The software of the decision support system is programmed in D-Base III application program language. It handles:

- the interface, which allows communication between the user and the machine,
- computation of a rule-generated decision for each case by application of empirically driven rules embedded in the model,
- the compilation and continuous updating of a database.

The system also includes SPSS statistical software which enables retrieval and statistical analysis of data. An important aspect is the capability to continuously update, refine and modify the system of rules embedded in the programme.

The DSS process: The probation officer enters information on each youngster in a standardised, pre-coded form using a question-answer dialogue. On completion the program prompts the probation officer to enter a disposition recommendation. Using eight key variables, the program displays the disposition assignment calculated for the particular youngster by applying the rules embedded in the model to the information entered. The program then displays numerically the extent of disparity/agreement between the disposition selected by the probation officer and that generated by the model. The program continues by questioning the probation officer and his/her response to the system generated decision. Finally, the program permits later entering data on the court's decision in the case. The system provides facilities for monitoring and reporting probation officer decision making, as well as for continuing surveillance of implementation of probation service policy and identification of problems.

CONCLUSION AND FUTURE DEVELOPMENTS

Decentralisation is seen to be the dominant factor in the future development of information technology in the human services. Decentralisation will be a policy within organisations as the Ministry of Labour and Social Affairs and on a geographic level. In the Ministry of Labour and Social Affairs each social service will be expected to develop its own information system to answer its unique information needs. Each services information system will be compatible with the Ministry's MIS. It is expected that the services own information system will be geared to social workers needs, thereby enabling them to use information technology as part of the work process. This will help counter the dominant managerial aspects of information technology use as it exists in the Ministry of Labour and Social affairs at present. The development of such programs will begin with the completion of the Ministry's new MIS.

Local social service departments, especially those of the larger cities which have manpower and technical expertise are and will continue to develop their own information systems to answer local needs. These systems will be compatible with the Ministry's MIS, but these are local initiatives. Smaller municipalities which do not have the resources to build information systems will essentially remain with systems which meet central government requirements and not local needs. The gap between the information rich and information poor is expected to grow and has implications for future planning and project initiatives. There is no central government policy to provide 'know how' to social service departments who cannot promote such a project on their own.

Organisations and municipalities are developing computerised information systems for their clients and populations. The National Insurance Institute is a case in kind. It is expected that such systems will not only make the information more accessible to users but also empower the user in his or her relationship with different service organisations.

References

Auslander G and Cohen M. Reliability Issues in the Development of Computerised Information Systems. In: Rafferty J, Steyaert J and Colombi D (Eds.). *Human Services in the Information Age.* New York: Haworth Press. 1996.

Barak D. Decision Support Systems for Planning and Evaluation Interventions in Vocational Rehabilitation Services for the Disabled. In: Rafferty J, Steyaert J and Colombi D (Eds.). *Human Services in the Information Age.* New York: Haworth Press. 1996.

Benbenishty R and Oyserman D. Integrated Information Systems. In: Rafferty J, Steyaert J and Colombi D (Eds.). *Human Services in the Information Age.* New York: Haworth Press. 1996.

Berman Y. A Decision Support System in Resource Allocation: the Political Process in Rational Decision Making. In *New Technology in the Human Services*, 6(1), pp. 8-14). 1992.

Berman Y. Israel. In: Colombi D, Rafferty J and Steyaert J (Eds.). *Human Services and Information Technology: A European Perspective.* ENITH. 1993.

Shapira M. Computerised Decision Technology in Social Services: Decision Support System Improves Decision Practice in Youth Probation Service. In *International Journal of Sociology and Social Policy.* 1990.

Steyaert J. *The Use Of Client Information Systems In Israel.* Jerusalem: Ministry of Labour and Social Affairs, p. 8. 1994.

Author details

Yitzhak Berman is the Director of the Department of Planning and Social Analysis in the Ministry of Labour and Social Affairs, Jerusalem, Israel. He is a Research Project Director at the European Centre Information Centre of the European Centre for Social Welfare Policy and Research, Vienna. He is also a Lecturer in Social Welfare Policy at the School of Social Work, Bar Ilan University, Ramat Gan, Israel.

Contact: Yitzhak Berman
Ministry of Labour and Social Affairs
Department of Planning and Social Analysis
PO Box 1260
Jerusalem 93420
Israel

Telephone: +972 2 708346
Fax: +972 2 731640
E-mail: yberman@netvision.net.il

12 Japan

Tomofumi Oka and Tomiko Hayashi

HUMAN SERVICES AND INFORMATION TECHNOLOGY

An ageing society

The Japanese social welfare system is based on Article 25 of the Constitution of Japan. It says, 'All people shall have the right to maintain minimum standards of wholesome and cultured living. The state must make every effort to promote and expand social welfare, social security and public health services to cover every aspect of the life of the people'. Upon these principles, six basic social welfare laws have been instituted. They are the Public Assistance Law of 1946 and 1950, the Child Welfare Law of 1947, the Welfare Law for Poor People with Physical Disabilities of 1949, the Welfare Law for People with Intelligence Impairment of 1960, the Welfare Law for the Aged of 1963 and the Law for Maternal and Child Welfare of 1964.

This system is changing itself because of an ageing society. Japanese male and female average life expectancy were 76.57 and 82.98 in 1994. This is the highest in the world. The total fertility rate and birth rate have been declining since the 1970s. In 1993 the total fertility rate was 1.46, and the birth rate was 9.6. The result has been a rapid increase in the proportion of the elderly population.

Under these circumstances, the government amended social welfare laws in 1990 to restructure the system of supplying welfare services. The new laws authorise municipalities to provide home and residential care services for the aged and people with disabilities, whereas prefectural governments managed welfare services in the previous system. Under the new system, prefectures support municipal governments by offering information and coordinating municipalities' welfare services.

To operate welfare services efficiently in each municipality, information technology is helpful. Organising information is essential to meet various needs of individuals and families in complicated systems of community services, including welfare, medical, health, and housing services. In 1994 the government announced a plan to promote the use of information technology in providing public services. In accordance with the plan, the Ministry of Health and Welfare set up a committee which published, in 1995, a report for the introduction of information technology into health, medical and welfare services. Meanwhile, in 1994, the Ministry of International Trade and Industry announced *The Advanced Information-Oriented Program.* The Telecommunication Advisory Committee submitted to the Minister of Posts and Telecommunications a plan for an *Information Superhighway* that forms a network of fibre optic cables all over Japan by 2010. The Ministry of Posts and Telecommunications is trying a 'distant health counselling system' in which doctors examine and social workers support distant patients through video phones and video conferences. This system is working in a trial at twenty nine places with hospitals, visiting nurse stations, home care companies and health institutions for the aged, and so on. The system has been shown to quickly respond to changes of diseases.

The General Information System for Public Health and Welfare Services is working. It has an information on-line network of about 870 public organisations including the Ministry of Health and Welfare, prefectures, municipalities, public health centres and hospitals. This network keeps an infectious disease surveillance, a community health and medical planning system, and so on. The present focus is on training staff, including more information and expanding the network to more municipalities.

Comparing health and medical services, welfare services use less information technology so far. In 1994 the Ministry of Health and Welfare sponsored a study on local welfare service offices for the aged use of information technology. The study classes their use of information technology into four categories.

- The first is use of computers in welfare offices. Almost all the welfare offices use computer software to administer welfare services and to prepare statistics. Commercial companies usually develop the software and modify it according to each user's requests.
- The second is welfare information systems providing citizens with information. Ten per cent of municipal governments and thirty per cent of prefectures keep the systems.
- The third is the availability of care management systems. Few municipalities or prefectures have these.
- The fourth is emergency notice systems. Eighty per cent of municipal governments maintain this system.

An obstacle in the use of information technology in welfare services is, probably, computer illiteracy amongst social workers. Some feel that their 'human' work is away from computers. Some fear that information technology could reduce their employment.

This illiteracy is not particular to Japanese social workers. Japanese ownership rates of personal computers is low (13.9% in 1994) compared to other developed countries. Because of their language's characteristics of ideogram, Japanese people tend to use dedicated word processors (the ownership rate was 37.8% in 1994) rather than personal computers. While European languages use tens of letters, the main Japanese language uses thousands of letters. This complicated system of language hindered the Japanese from using computers for writing. However the development of computer technology has now completely overcome this language problem and personal computers now interest many Japanese people.

In particular children are educated to increase their computer literacy. Ninety nine per cent of high and junior high schools in Japan already have personal computers and teach pupils how to use them. The Ministry of Education plans to set a ratio of one personal computer to every two pupils from elementary schools up to high schools by the year 1999. This educational trend will contribute to improving computer literacy. Additionally the giant Japanese telephone company, NTT, is planning a computer dedicated low cost public network by the fiscal year 1996. This network will drastically change existing computer networks.

INFORMATION FOR CITIZENS

Individual and community support

Automatic telephone answering systems are familiar to people. Municipalities and prefectures use the system to provide free information on health and welfare services. The toll-free telephone service is not only for commercial use but also for public and non-profit use, with some services provided on a twenty four hour tape-basis. For example users can choose to know about services for AIDS or pensions. Some clinics, pharmacists, and lawyers provide counselling services by **dial Q2.** This system makes the callers pay the information charge to the carriers through telephone offices.

As the Japanese language uses so many letters, telex is only used for international business. In consequence fax services have been developed to a greater extent and are used for transportation, housing, sports, sightseeing, and so on. Some are virtually free (line charge only), and some are not free or only for paid subscribers.

CAPTAIN (Character And Pattern Telephone Access Information Network) is a Videotext service that started in 1984 and is available in all cities. Although some municipalities and prefectures use this system to provide information, most services available through the system are on a commercial basis. Because use of this system is costly, many users are commercial companies, not individuals. Few information services on social welfare are available yet through the CAPTAIN system.

More interesting are online services with computers. The number of the users was about 2,600,000 in 1994, which represented a thirty two per cent increase over the preceding year. An example is **NIFTY-Serve** that started in 1987 (the name is from the

English word and is not an acronym). It has about one million members and a variety of services. Concerning health, it has an on-line database service with information on health, diseases, AIDS, medicine, hospitals and doctors. The information is up to date, and this is important because modern medicine is developing rapidly. Also, this on-line service permits anonymous access to information on stigmatised diseases like AIDS.

Another type of service is a knowledge based system. After answering 349, if male or 373 if female, questions from the computer, a user gets a diagnosis about thirty one organs. The fee is 3,000 Yen per diagnosis (about $29) and an accuracy of diagnosis rate of 86.1% is claimed. Additionally, NIFTY-Serve has numerous BBS (electronic bulletin board systems) which help previously isolated people: patients, people with disabilities and people with special needs. Through these public BBS, people create CUGs (Closed User Groups) which are developing as new self-help groups.

Some prefectures have their own on-line services to provide the people with information. An example is **O-Net 24** of Osaka Prefecture which people access through personal computers. It provides information on health and welfare services, library, statistics, festivals, sightseeing, social education, labour market, and the projects and committees of Osaka Prefecture. This net is available all the time and users only pay for line charges. It can also be accessed through on-line services like NIFTY-Serve.

The Ministry of International Trade and Industry initiated **Mellow Society Project**, and started **Mellow Net** for the aged in 1992. This project materialised on the assumption that personal computer communication promotes the social participation of elderly people. The Net has a BBS in two commercial online services; NIFTY-Serve and PC-VAN. The Mellow Net has over 6,000 members. According to a survey 80% of the members are men but the proportion of female members increased from 10% in 1994 to 20% in 1995. Seventy per cent of the members are over 50 years old, and 55% are over 60 years old. Thirty per cent are retired. The Net links with the American and Korean counterparts.

The Ministry of Health and Welfare plans to establish an information centre for people with disabilities by the fiscal year 1996. Through the on-line service, it provides information on volunteers, prosthetics, health and medicine, and so on. It is ready for people's safety in emergencies like the earthquake that destroyed Kobe City in 1995.

For child welfare, the Ministry of Health and Welfare is testing the use of information pillars in convenience stores in the Chiba Prefecture. Since 1994, in 100 stores 110 information pillars have been set up to provide information about child welfare. With these pillars, people can learn about public and private agencies for child care, health and welfare.

Concerning the World Wide Web (WWW), though many companies maintain their home pages, there are few pages about social services. Although the national Government has some home pages, the Ministry of Health and Welfare had not established one as late as mid 1995. However we can anticipate that the WWW will soon be used in the social welfare field.

Employment and training

Personal computer communications enable people with disabilities to have job training at home. For example, Osaka City Rehabilitation Centre for People with Disabilities has a department of vocational training. This department offers training in information technology to disabled people. Some trainees learn in business firms and get information technology employment with such firms or public agencies. Using computer communications, people with physical disabilities began to work at home.

Computer networks for vocational rehabilitation have been established for disabled people in three prefectures. Through this network people can know:

- which businesses employ people with disabilities,
- what social resources are available to employ people with disabilities,
- how to improve the environment for people with disabilities,
- who wants to be employed, with what disabilities,
- which businesses accept people with disabilities as trainees,
- how to evaluate the training programmes,
- what is the environment like for commuters with disabilities,
- statistics on vocational rehabilitation.

Because it takes too long for computers to work in this system, some workers consider it inconvenient.

Information technology also promotes employment in social services. Every prefectural council of social welfare has a personnel centre that offers jobs in social services. To match the needs of job seekers and employers, the centres developed a computer network which has operated since 1994. This network collects and provides data about social welfare employment in Japan.

The informal sector

Information technology is well used to promote volunteers' activities. An example is a database of NHK, the Japanese public broadcasting corporation. It provides, at low cost, the **NHK Volunteer Net** on-line database service on volunteers. This helps those who want to volunteer and those who need volunteers to meet each other. With the support of social welfare councils and voluntary organisations, it keeps information on volunteers' groups and activities, conferences, training courses, reference books, and so on. Another example is Osaka Volunteer Association's database which holds information on 300 cases of volunteers' activities . The association distributes floppy disks of the database to other volunteer centres and social welfare organisations every month at low rates.

As a local example in Osaka City, the **Prop Station** volunteer group supports the aged and the disabled with computers. A mother of a child with disabilities started this group. It aims to use computers to promote the employment and social participation of the aged and people with disabilities. It offers lectures on computers to people with disabilities, and helps software developers to produce computer hardware and software available to people with disabilities. It distributes software that people with disabilities can easily use.

Independent living

The Ministry of Health and Welfare provides prosthetic appliances such as information technology, teletext receivers, handy talking aids, and communication equipment for people with severe disability. The Ministry offers these appliances only to those who have been issued with an 'ID pocketbook' which indicates their degree of disability. This in turn determines eligibility for services. For people with visual disabilities, the Ministry established a braille information network which electronically distributes brailled information to thirty six braille libraries over the whole country.

The Ministry of Labour promotes the development of equipment accessible to people with disabilities. The Ministry of International Trade and Industry announced the accessibility guideline on information technology in 1990. A municipal example is Okayama City's *Community Welfare Fund Utilisation Project*. This started in 1992 and offers information technology training to people with disabilities. Through this programme, they learn to use personal computers and word processors. The target is people with visual disabilities and hearing disabilities with the aim of promoting their independence and social participation.

VOCATIONAL EDUCATION AND TRAINING

The IT curriculum in social work education

Many Japanese universities have undergraduate curricula for certificated social workers, which are usually divided into 'liberal arts' and 'specialised subjects'. Social work students typically study liberal arts mainly in the first and second year and move on to specialised subjects in the third and fourth year. They have an opportunity to learn about information technology as part of their liberal arts study. This course on information technology is neither compulsory or specialised for social work students. Some undergraduate courses of social work research, however, train social work students to use statistical analysis software such as SPSS.

As the information to be organised increases in the social work field, the community of social welfare agencies needs more social workers who are computer literate. In 1995 the annual national conference on community development had a division on information technology and social services. Several speakers presented examples of community welfare services with information technology. This trend will change the curricula of social work in universities.

CAL in social work education

Although few computers are used so far in teaching social work, some universities tried using satellites to broadcast lectures. A telephone company and sixteen universities attempted an experimental **On-line University** in 1995. The universities installed computers and offered the lectures to each other through optical fibres. This system enables students to participate in lectures from distant universities with lectures saved on a database for students to use whenever they wished to do so.

PROVISION OF SERVICES

In Japan, people usually receive welfare services only after they apply for them. As a consequence, people in need cannot use welfare services unless they or their proxies know the services. Additionally, the separated systems of services require people to apply for different services in different offices. Even to apply for one service, they are often required to visit different offices to have essential certificates issued. People in need usually have little information about what services they can use and how and where they apply for them. This shortage of information provision, combined with bureaucratic inefficiency, blocks the use of welfare services. On the other hand, service providers fail to discover enough information about the needs of people in communities. To overcome these problems, effective information systems are necessary in Japanese social welfare.

The practice level

Concerning welfare services for the elderly, **WHIS NET** (Welfare and Health Information System NETwork) links and supports the counselling and information centres for the elderly in every prefecture. A non-profit corporation manages this system. WHIS NET keeps data on social education, private services, case studies, prosthetic appliances, laws and policies, welfare and medical agencies, and so on. The users are welfare agencies only and use is free of charge. Some municipal governments have similar information systems. Some systems have not only database facilities but also expert systems that provide tailor-made guidance to clients. These information systems help counselling and information centres by offering them information on appropriate services according to the identified needs of the clients.

However, the counselling and information centres have no discretionary powers to allocate services. Therefore, the clients have to visit service providers to apply for the services. The counselling and information centres help the clients to identify appropriate service providers and to apply for the services. Linked to WHIS NET, a total of 10,000 home care support centres are planned to open by the year 2000. These centres will be responsible for care management in the community, and they are expected to operate as comprehensive welfare information providers.

Another example is that the Osaka branch of the National Federation of Health Insurance Societies developed the **Hospic** computer system to provide its members with information about hospitals. Access is through the member society to which individuals belong, not by direct client access to the system. The service, which started in 1994, displays a list of hospitals near clients' homes that can provide the service needed. It also offers detailed information on medical services at about 1,400 hospitals in Osaka and five nearby prefectures. Although the Ministry of Health and Welfare stored information on all hospitals, Government regulations prevented disclosure of the information. Recently revised regulations enables the Osaka branch of the National Federation to collect and publicise the information. Through this information system, patients check their medical services and fees. Although the system is accessible from computers, most people telephone requests and receive information through faxes. Current information suggests its use so far is limited.

Information systems

Community care requires workers of different professions to share information about clients and to coordinate their services. In a municipality, public health nurses and home helpers enter client data into a networked computer immediately after visiting the clients. This system enables different professionals at different locations to share the up-to-date information about their clients on-line.

To share information on clients among human service providers of various professions they need a common vocabulary. In 1990 the National Council of Social Welfare developed the Standard Code and Keywords of Social Welfare. This code and the list of keywords make it possible to manage, classify and search the data in welfare and related fields with a computerised information system. All of the counselling and information centres for the aged and all the social welfare councils in Japan already use the code and keywords. It is not easy to codify data about individual needs for social welfare. The Standard Code and Keywords of Social Welfare was revised in 1994.

Since 1988 the Ministry of Health and Welfare has attempted an 'IC' card or optical memory card system in two municipalities as pilot models. The aim is to promote computerised national medical care. In this system, a card records personal medical records such as individual case histories and examinations. The user takes charge of their card. This system makes medical treatment quicker and more accurate. One of the two municipalities changed the system to put into the cards, not only users' medical records, but also records about their use of social welfare services. To protect privacy, this system sets passwords that prevent service providers from reading records that are irrelevant to their services. Protecting privacy is one of the principles established by the Ministry of Health and Welfare to promote these card systems.

Managing services

Office workers in social services use information technology in over 60% of municipalities. They use computers to manage the information about service applications, service eligibility, public assistance, prosthetic appliances, residential and domiciliary services, and so on. Many residential institutions use various computer programs to manage workers' timetables, and clients' and workers' files. They also use them to calculate budgets, workers' salary and nutrition levels of meals. Some are developing systems to document their daily treatments. These systems work in place of hand-written records. Furthermore, some workers are developing a system that analyses and organises social work processes from intake to evaluation. Through this system they seek to identify trends and correlations within social work processes.

Social care policy

Japanese nationals are required to register their name, sex, birthday, address, household, householder, household number, the date when they became residents etc. The resident registration system issues resident cards. The computerised system is useful when the municipalities undertake social surveys on their residents to develop their social policies.

On the other hand the government is discussing the Citizen-Number-System, where every citizen has a number and the government manages the information on citizens comprehensively. However, it may be difficult to protect personal privacy in such a system and this issue is blocking plans for its introduction.

CONCLUSION AND FUTURE DEVELOPMENTS

The 1990s is the first decade for Japan to develop computerised information systems on social welfare. Many municipalities and voluntary agencies have developed and managed their information systems. Unfortunately, as their systems have different formats, they are not compatible with each other and are unable to share information. The government has failed to establish common standards for information systems.

In particular, social insurance for care of the elderly starts in 1997. To achieve social insurance an effective information system will be needed. This system must provide information on health and welfare services, and organise information on the needs and conditions of clients. Additionally it must operate to maintain care management for many clients and realise care planning in the community. Such as system is not feasible without information technology.

Under these conditions, computer literacy is becoming a necessity in social work education. Social welfare agencies realise that they need social workers who are familiar with computers and computerised information systems. We can anticipate a rapid spread in the use of information technology in all areas of social work.

Despite this optimism, we should note some social questions. Firstly, these social trends will widen the gap in the information available to information-skilled people compared to the information-unskilled. The poor, aged, disabled, or less educated could be alienated from the world of information technology despite their severe social needs. Therefore, they need public assistance to use information technology. Secondly, we need to agree on how we put individual information into on-line networks. In other words, we must guarantee that individual privacy is protected.

Author details

Tomofumi Oka is a full time lecturer on community welfare services and community development in the Department of Social Welfare at Sophia University. He studies self help movements in Japan.

Tomiko Hayashi is a social worker with Osaka City Counselling and Information Center for the Aged. She is in charge of a database on social welfare services for the aged in Osaka City.

Contact: Tomofumi Oka
Department of Social Welfare
Sophia University
7-1 Kioi-cho
Chiyoda-ku
Tokyo 102
Japan

Telephone: +81 3 3238 3645
Fax: +81 297 72 3118
E-mail: t-oka@sophia.ac.jp

13 Micronesia

Arlene Cohen and Janice Shriver

HUMAN SERVICES AND INFORMATION TECHNOLOGY

Micronesia, meaning tiny islands, consists of 2,200 small volcanic and coral islands spread throughout 4,500,000 square miles of the western Pacific Ocean. 'Lying west of Hawaii, east of the Philippines, south of Japan and north of Australia, the total land mass of all these tropical islands is less than 1,200 square miles with a total population base estimated at no more than 300,000' (Cohen, 1992, p. 285). The region can be divided geographically into three archipelagoes: the Marshalls, Carolines, and Marianas. Not only are the islands of Micronesia spread over a large geographic area but each island group has its own unique culture and language. 'The inhabited areas vary from idyllic villages with no cars or electricity to the high rise resort developments of Guam and Saipan' (Bendure, 1992, p. 9). Micronesia can also be divided into five separate and distinct political entities:

- The Territory of Guam, an unincorporated territory of the United States, and the most developed island in the region.
- The Commonwealth of the Northern Mariana Islands (CNMI), a territorial possession of the United States, with Saipan being the best known and most developed island.
- The Federated States of Micronesia (FSM) consisting of the island states of Pohnpei, Chuuk (previously known as Truk), Kosrae, and Yap.
- The Republic of Palau.
- The Republic of the Marshall Islands.

This chapter addresses the development of services and the use of information technology (IT) in the field of human services within these five separate and different political units.

Guam

Guam is considered the metropolis of Micronesia. It is the largest island geographically (212 square miles) and the most populous; the 1990 census cited the population at 133,152. At that time, United States military personnel and dependents accounted for 15,198 people stationed at the military bases on Guam. However, with the downsizing of the military in the past few years, many military personnel have left the island.

The social service network on Guam is located primarily under the Department of Public Health. Modelled on the United States Social Service system, it offers the United States categorical assistance services of Aid to Families with Dependent Children, Food Stamps, General Assistance, Child Protective Services, Adult Protective Services and Medical Assistance. Social services are also offered by the Guam Memorial Hospital and the Public Health Outpatient Clinics. The Department of Mental Health and Substance Abuse offers the full range of mental health and counselling services to all age groups. The Department of Education, which includes a Head Start Program, also offers some social services. It employs school social workers, guidance counsellors, and pupil personnel workers. They offer counselling services to pupils and have a number of special outreach projects for new immigrants from Micronesia.

Other agencies within the public social service network include Sanctuary (a private, non-profit shelter for adolescents with an office located on the University of Guam campus), Guma Mami (services for the developmentally disabled), Department of Vocational Rehabilitation, the Rape Crisis Center and a counselling service attached to the Superior Court. The United States military offers services to uniformed service personnel and their dependents. Some social services are also provided under the auspice of the Catholic Church. The Catholic Social Services maintains shelters for abuse victims of all ages, a shelter for the homeless, and offers a variety of services to the elderly. Guam also has an AIDS referral program and a chapter of the American Red Cross.

Commonwealth of the Northern Mariana Islands (CNMI)

Social services in the CNMI are located under the Department of Public Health and Environmental Services. The Division of Mental Health is housed in the Commonwealth Health Center in Saipan. It provides a variety of mental health counselling and substance abuse services to clients on the islands of Saipan, Rota and Tinian.

Karidat is a private, non-profit Catholic social service agency in the CNMI. It provides services to families and youth, including victim advocacy and a twenty four hour crisis hotline. The United States Department of Public Health has a presence in Saipan, the major island in the CNMI. Medical and allied health personnel are stationed in Saipan to provide assistance in the development of human service programs.

Other Micronesian islands

Compared to Guam and the CNMI, there are considerably fewer social services offered in the other areas of Micronesia and only a handful of social service workers. Extended families play a greater role in these areas and social service needs are often filled by families. Consequently, fewer Western models of social service provision are utilised.

The Federated States of Micronesia (FSM), The Republic of Palau, and The Republic of the Marshall Islands have located their social services under their Ministries of Health. The services which seem to predominate are mental health services, health education services, and services to youth. In the past several years, the United States Department of Public Health has sent mental health and substance abuse professionals to islands throughout Micronesia to help develop their social services. These projects seem to have focused predominantly on the development of mental health and substance abuse services.

INFORMATION FOR CITIZENS

With the exception of Guam, there is no remote online access to local information systems in Micronesia. On Guam, the only local online public information system is the RFK Library catalogue at the University of Guam. Users can dial-in or access the database through the Internet. There is also a World Wide Web site in the early stages of development at the University of Guam[1].

The Guam Community College Library and the JoeTen-Kiyu Public Library in Saipan have in-house on-line catalogues. Plans are underway to implement dial-in and Internet access to these libraries in the near future.

Internet access is available in Guam and Saipan with the rest of Micronesia slowly beginning to develop the capability. In 1986, a low-cost commercial packet-switched data communications link with Hawaii became available in Guam and Saipan. This link provides connectivity to commercial service providers in the mainland United States.

The University of Guam installed the first permanently connected Internet host in the region in 1994. However, to date, very few people outside the University of Guam can access the Internet through this host. There is a commitment from the Government of Guam to provide island-wide Internet access for government agencies; although at present this is only in the early stages of development.

To meet an increasing demand for Internet access, a local commercial Internet provider has developed a thriving business providing low-cost public access to the Internet[2]. This provider also serves several government agencies and has some public information available.

The introduction of the Internet on Guam (approximately 18 months ago) is offering an exciting array of opportunities to overcome the problems created by distance and smallness. It is now possible to access an enormous amount of information almost instantly. One can seek resources, ask and receive answers to questions, and chat with other professionals on a variety of special interest bulletin boards.

Throughout the rest of Micronesia, Internet access is theoretically available through the **PEACESAT** (Pan-Pacific Education and Communications Experiments by Satellite) satellite network, a project funded in part by the United States government. Although PEACESAT provides access to low-cost voice and data communications at forty one sites in twenty two countries in the Pacific Islands, its use for Micronesian Internet access is limited.

PEACESAT is headquartered at the University of Hawaii in Honolulu. All Internet connections from Micronesia must go through the Honolulu hub; consequently, PEACESAT is not a viable Internet access option for most of Micronesia. The limited number of channels, enormous time differences, heavy traffic creating competition for use, and lack of sufficient training work against the regular, easy use of PEACESAT and dissuade the novice. An upgrade to the PEACESAT system is being proposed which would eliminate many of the limitations, but with shrinking United States federal budgets, the outlook is not very hopeful.

VOCATIONAL EDUCATION AND TRAINING

The term 'social worker' is used in a very broad sense in Micronesia. It may refer to someone holding a Masters Degree in Social Work or it may be used by someone with as little education as high school. Only recently have social workers on islands other than Guam received college training. Of those with college training, most hold a Bachelors of Arts degree from a United States university. A few now hold Bachelor of Social Work degrees from the University of Guam. With the exceptions of Guam and Saipan, the majority of people working in human services in Micronesia are not college graduates.

Although the Bachelor of Social Work program at the University of Guam offers a fairly traditional social work curriculum, this curriculum does not yet incorporate any IT. A few students have been introduced to SPSS (Statistical Package for the Social Scientists) for their Senior Project data analysis during this past year. However, it is not yet a regular part of the curriculum.

The *RFK Library* at the University of Guam provides CD-ROM based indexes. These indexes include the **Child Abuse and Neglect Index**, **PsyLit** (covering the area of psychology), **ERIC** (covering educational materials), and **CINAHL** (covering nursing and allied health). Very soon, due to a recent legislative appropriation, a social sciences full-text CD-ROM system will be available in the *RFK Library*. These CD-ROM products are available to the public and are used by human service providers on Guam.

Although the University of Guam does not have sufficient resources to offer students Internet accounts, access for the social work students has been arranged. A number of social work students have acquired sufficient Internet skill to seek information and communication with other social workers throughout the world. The Internet is of particular importance to these students because of the paucity of social work publications in the university library.

PROVISION OF SERVICES

The geographical expanse of Micronesia posed a challenge to the authors in gathering data about information technology use in the region. Consequently, the authors decided to use a sample of convenience to gather much of the information for this section.

The Guam Association of Social Workers (GASW) holds an annual conference each March and invites participants from throughout the region. The 1995 conference was well attended by people working in human services throughout the islands. The theme was *The Rhythm of our Ancestors* and included many presenters from the various island states and nations of Micronesia.

The authors used the conference as an opportunity to survey the attendees and to discuss the use of IT in their work. A questionnaire was distributed at the opening session of the conference and sixty nine completed questionnaires were returned. The questionnaire gathered identifying information from the respondents and asked about their agencies' possession and use of computers, their knowledge of the existence of software programs, the software programs used, and the use of e-mail and the Internet.

Since there has been little marketing of software that has been specially developed for human service providers, the authors theorised that there might be limited knowledge about the various types of programs available. To address this problem, the authors offered the respondents two lists and asked them to indicate those functions of which they were aware.

- One list contained software functions that might be used by clerical and administrative personnel and included word processing, agency appointment management, desktop publishing, accounting and bookkeeping, billing, budgeting, client statistics, client satisfaction, and research and research calculations.
- The second was a listing of functions that might be used by social workers. It included eligibility determinations, welfare calculations, client databases, client charting, client tracking, social maps, diagnosis and assessment, and treatment planning.

Most respondents were familiar with software packages for clerical and administrative functions; in fact, nearly all agencies used computers for word processing and many used graphics programs, spreadsheets, calendar programs, and databases. There was considerably less familiarity with programs that social workers and other human service workers might use in their work. Respondents indicated some awareness of social work application software; but it was clear that most had never actually seen any in use. The small minority of human service workers who do use computing software packages seemed to use them mostly for word processing and/or checking information stored in databases.

Guam

All of the major social service agencies in Guam were represented at the conference and responded to the questionnaire. Most of the agencies are presently using software packages to collect client and statistical information for reporting purposes. The Department of Mental Health and Substance Abuse recently obtained United States federal funding to develop a customised software package for intake assessment. The Government of Guam Admissions, Demographic Data and Mental Status Assessment System was tailored to meet the unique needs of the island population. There are plans for developing other customised software for treatment planning and evaluation that will link with this system.

Sisyphus, a software program for treatment planning and clinical report writing, is installed on some computers at the Department of Mental Health and Substance Abuse. Few professionals are trained in its use and not many clinicians are currently using the program.

The Department of Public Health and Social Services has three separate custom developed online systems for determining eligibility and calculating benefits. These systems address the three individual assistance programmes: Food Stamps, Medicare and Public Assistance. They were developed independently between 1985-1987. An integrated system covering all three programmes is seriously needed and planning is underway, although lack of funding may inhibit the project. There are also plans to link the proposed integrated system to other information systems, including the child support system in the Attorney General's Office. Access to the Motor Vehicles information system at the Department of Revenue and Taxation is currently available.

Although not directly related to the provision of social services, another effort worth mentioning is the Guam demonstration project for the State Immunization Information System. Resulting from the United States Centers for Disease Control Childhood Immunization Initiative, the online system is designed to track all immunization activity. Future plans include links to the Guam Memorial Hospital the United States Naval Hospital, the Guam Department of Education and private health providers throughout the island.

The Navy Family Service Center uses a variety of IT packages. Currently in use are statistical information databases, client charting and tracking software, a system for treatment planning and the **Quality of Life Information Management System**. Sanctuary is using the **Runaway and Homeless Youth Management Information System**. This comprehensive system, contracted through the United States Department of Health and Human Services, profiles clients, tracks them through the social service system, and provides data for research.

Telecommunications on Guam

Since the University of Guam is an Internet node, the authors assumed human service agencies would have arranged for Internet access through the university. This is not the case. Only a few human service workers have access to the Internet through the University. A few other human service workers are using a commercial provider. Most respondents were uncertain as to whether or not their agency had e-mail or Internet access. Moreover, many did not appear to know anything about e-mail or the Internet. This lack of knowledge was surprising as the Pacific Daily News, the local Guam newspaper, has carried many articles on the Internet in the past months. Sanctuary and the United States Navy Family Service Center are two notable exceptions.

Sanctuary, as part of the United States National Network of Runaway and Youth Services, has access to the Center for Substance Abuse Prevention's **PREVline** (PREVention on-line) computer based message and information service in Washington, DC. They access the Regional Alcohol and Drug Awareness Resource (RADAR) Network; and **YouthNet**, the National Youth Network Electronic Bulletin Board systems. However, since they do not yet have a local direct Internet connection, a costly long-distance phone call must be made for the access. The United States Navy Family Service uses the local military data communications network to connect to the Internet. Although not all of the social service workers at Navy Family Service Centers use the Internet; those that do, use it for general social work and counselling information, locating software, and for inter and intra agency e-mail.

Commonwealth of the Northern Mariana Islands (CNMI)

Saipan, the main CNMI island, is closest to Guam in terms of Western development. With the exception of Guam, it is more advanced in the use of IT for delivery of human services than other areas in the region. The CNMI Social Services utilises software packages for eligibility determinations, welfare benefit calculations, establishing client databases, client charting, client tracking, social mapping, and treatment plan writing. The Department also has access to e-mail which is used for locating information resources, conferences and programmes, and networking with other agencies. The **Ayuda Network**, a local bulletin board system (BBS) was established in Saipan a few years ago. The word 'ayuda', meaning 'help' in Chamorro (the local language) was chosen to express the nature of the BBS. It was established to enable social service providers to share information and client referrals. Although active for a few years, when the individual running the system was no longer available, the BBS died.

Yap and Kosrae

The authors have no direct information about the use of human services IT on Yap or Kosrae as no one from either Yap or Kosrae attended the GASW conference. It is unlikely that any human services software is used in Yap. Yap maintains a more traditional lifestyle than any other Micronesian state or nation. The traditional lifestyle, which includes a hierarchical caste system, discourages western values and 'westernisation'. One notable exception is a medical doctor in Yap who has connected to a commercial Internet service provider through the local telephone company on a 300 baud connection. Although this commercial access is available, it appears not to be promoted.

It is also unlikely that Kosrae is utilising computer technology in the provision of human services since it is 'one of the least developed areas in Micronesia ... most of its 7000 inhabitants still rely on subsistence farming and fishing. It is estimated that less than 15% of the population works in the money economy.' (Micronesia, 1992, p. 88.)

Other Micronesian islands

Several human service workers from Chuuk, Pohnpei, Palau, and the Marshall Islands attended the GASW conference. Responses from the conference attendees in these other Micronesian islands indicated that although a few computers were owned by their agencies, these computers were used predominantly for word processing. With a couple of exceptions, there was little familiarity with IT in general.

About half of the respondents said they used computers but no one used any software packages for human service providers. Usage seemed to be confined to word processing and the occasional use of a database. Chuuk, Pohnpei, Palau, and the Marshalls do not have access to the Internet or e-mail in any reliable and inexpensive way. In fact, a number of our respondents from these islands had never heard of either the Internet or e-mail.

CONCLUSION AND FUTURE DEVELOPMENTS

Micronesia lags behind much of the western world in terms of application of IT in the provision of human social services. In some of the islands, administrative and accounting systems and some degree of office automation has been introduced, although few specific applications in the social services appear to be in place. Given the geographic barriers, lack of financial support, and maintenance of a traditional lifestyle, the application of IT has not occurred in most parts of the region. Micronesia is still in the stage of building infrastructure such as roads, electricity, and water. Unreliable (and in some cases nonexistent) electrical and phone systems and the lack of IT awareness and training are major barriers to the use of IT.

As an increasing number of Micronesians go 'off island' for education (mostly to the United States) it can be expected that their utilisation of IT will increase rapidly if local support is provided. Of those Micronesia residents responding to the survey, many wrote comments indicating their interest in learning more about computer technology and software programs for human service workers.

The authors found that social service workers in Micronesia are typical of other service providers in the region. In a recent paper discussing the problems of librarians in the region, the writer noted that:

> *Island librarians face numerous challenges. Remote locations mean increased costs ... On most islands, the basic infrastructure is still developing. Consistent power supply is not guaranteed; telephone service can be erratic. Networking within one's own village, much less the island or the region is difficult, to say the least. Those working in island libraries are often untrained, often overworked and have limited opportunities for training or attendance at professional conferences.* (Tarpley, 1995)

These same challenges are faced by all human social service workers in Micronesia and must be addressed before the use of IT can fully develop.

References

Bendure A and Friary N. *Micronesia.* Australia: Lonely Planet Publications, 260 pp. 1992.

Cohen A. *The Pacific Libraries Association of Libraries and Archives.* FID News Bulletin, 42(12): 285-286. 1992.

Tarpley J. *Pacific Islands Association of Libraries and Archives: Training in the Island.* ASSOCIATES: The Electronic Library Support Staff Journal, 1(3): Feature -Tarpley. 1995.

World Wide Web sites referred to in this chapter

1.The University of Guam.
http://uog2.uog.edu/

2. Commercial Internet provider - low-cost public access to the Internet, plus public information including from government agencies.
http://www.kuentos.guam.net/

Author details

Arlene Cohen is the Systems Librarian at the University of Guam RFK Library. She is the System Administrator for OCEAN, the RFK Library online public access library. She holds a Masters of Librarianship degree and has a background in computing, technical authoring and in academic library work in the USA. Her work in Micronesia is on library automation, resource sharing networks and telecommunications. She is currently Executive Secretary of the Pacific Islands Association of Libraries and Archives.

Dr Janice Shriver is an Associate Professor of Social Work at the University of Guam in Mangilao, Guam. She previously held faculty positions in the USA where she also obtained her Master's Degree and her Doctorate. Dr Schriver has extensive experience in social work as a practitioner, trainer, administrator, educator, consultant and psychiatric surveyor for the HCFA (Health Care Financial Administration). The latter agency is concerned with health care standards.

Contact: Arlene Cohen
Systems Librarian
RFK Library
University of Guam
UOG Station
Mangilao, Guam 96923
Micronesia

Telephone: +1 671 735 2345
Fax: +1 671 734 6882
E-mail: acohen@uog9.oug.edu

14 The Netherlands

Jan van der Sluis and Albert Visser

HUMAN SERVICES AND INFORMATION TECHNOLOGY

Like most Western European countries the Netherlands have been through a rather turbulent period of diminishing government resources and low economic growth. As a result succeeding administrations were forced to find solutions, some involving drastic reduction of support for non-governmental organisations (NGOs). At the same time policy makers 'discovered' the idea of a market driven welfare industry. Following that thread, they sought to stimulate more efficient use of resources. In fact, some savings were achieved by so-called 'efficiency kortingen' (efficiency reductions)! In the end, resources were allocated and institutes were forced to become more and more market oriented. Output and budget financing, work registration and management information systems all became popular. As a consequence policy makers expected improvements with slimmer and more efficient organisations. In real life, many organisations were forced to raise caseloads, employ more flexible workers and find new markets, or else they just did not survive.

This new way of thinking also had implications for the information needed by national organisations. Seven of them - amongst them the Social and Cultural Planning Bureau, The Central Bureau of Statistics, The Union of Dutch Municipalities and the Netherlands Institute for Care and Welfare - started, as a result of an intervention of the Dutch Ministry of Care and Welfare, a joint platform called PWI. In short, PWI now tries to set standards and improve data collection processes. It is in this setting that use of technology for information for citizens was supposed to bloom ...

INFORMATION FOR CITIZENS

Information for citizens has been available for a long time and until recently was distributed mainly on paper. Leaflets and memoranda were 'printed matter' offered to the public via, to a more or lesser extent, attractive displays or by mail. However to obtain the particular information needed, the citizen had to know about the existence of that information. In practice only generic information like new tax laws was brought to general public attention through nationwide campaigns and brochures. Information on specific rights like social security and welfare was usually only available on request or through the organisation that implemented the rules. One reason for this phenomenon is that it was considered to be impossible to produce general brochures on information with very specific consequences for individuals. The Dutch welfare acts are a well known example. The structure of these acts make it (almost) impossible to give general information as the acts are aimed to provide 'custom made' assistance. This is an essential observation as it underlines a non-technical aspect of information dissemination: people have to be able to ask a precise question.

Information for citizens is somewhat confusing concept. At the heart of the information matter is data and only in adding value does data become information. This implies that only citizens themselves can define 'information for citizens' which in turn implies that all data should be available to the public. This is not the case as intermediate organisations determine what to make public and what not. This dilemma has led to interesting discussions about government information which intensified as a result of the fact that computers - particularly telematics - enabled many people to manipulate raw datasets. In other words, the argument of complexity seems to have lost importance.

Central government policy

The distribution of information for citizens through telematics has been a major issue in the Netherlands. The reason can be pinpointed. From December 1994 to June 1995 several memoranda were published that moved the focus away from isolated experiments towards larger and more ambitious projects. In particular the Department of Trade and Industry and the Department of the Interior discovered new opportunities. Each produced memoranda describing ways to put the Netherlands on top of the wave that gushed across the world.

The Department of the Interior[1] published its memorandum in Spring 1995. *Terug naar de Toekomst* (Back to the Future), is clearly oriented towards societal effects. Although it also lacks sufficient financial background, there are topics addressed that are relevant for this chapter. *Terug naar de Toekomst* addresses the issue of government information. It covers a rather broad range of topics varying from the network **GemNet** to ideas about using telematics in relation to new ideas on democracy. In doing this the Dutch government is making its first moves on and towards the electronic highway.

The Department of the Interior seeks to coordinate all governmental actions. However, at the same time the Union of Dutch Municipalities made its first moves on this terrain. As a result there is now in operation a project coordinated by the

Department of the Interior called **Overheidsloket 2000**, aimed at establishing a 'one-counter situation'. This is seen as a way to stimulate efficiency; citizens do not have to apply to different counters for assistance.

The Department of Trade and Industry[2] stressed economic opportunities offered by new technologies, especially the new Electronic Highway. They identified the need for fewer regulations for industries using or developing the Electronic Highway and suggested pilot projects, adopted by different Dutch departments, should be started. The goal of these projects was to demonstrate how telematics could be used in different spheres of society. In summer 1995 the distinguished departments searched for projects. One is the **BVE-net**[3], a network for secondary vocational education, apprenticeship systems and adult basic education which is intended to support teachers and students.

As a direct result of Department of Trade and Industry intervention, De Balie, a centre for culture and debate in Amsterdam, realised an interesting concept. The **Digital City**[4] (De Digitale Stad or DDS) starts from a clear concept that it should be possible to use telematics, in effect the Internet, to strengthen relationships between government and citizens and between citizens. DDS should be a community network, freely accessible and providing new ways of communication and information retrieval. At first DDS was mainly accessible using dial up modem connections. Using the Amsterdam area code the information provided through DDS was available at low cost, but all of that changed rather quickly. From a freenet-like structure DDS developed towards a high end entity on the Internet. A significant change was made with the transition from a text oriented system towards a graphics oriented one. In this respect DDS follows the general trend of the Internet to become more and more graphics oriented. It is fascinating that by so doing, DDS manoeuvred itself away from its original goal of being as open and freely accessible as possible. The techniques now used have become a serious threat to this goal.

DDS nevertheless is very significant as the concept has been copied by other Dutch cities and regions with around ten digital cities operational. The information provided is quite incomparable. Amsterdam for instance is now able to provide its inhabitants with a quite acceptable governmental information system (**PIGA**). DDS users can search the Amsterdam database for minutes of meetings and significant policy papers. Other digital cities are still in the process of convincing local authorities of the spin off of 'being digital'. One of the most wanted sources of information, the House of Commons (*Tweede Kamer*), is still not available to the annoyance of many people. The same goes for how the Dutch Central Bureau for Statistics (CBS) operates. It now offers a WWW site[5] but users can not access datasets - the information available is tables and figures as they are, or would be, published on paper. As a sideline, the basic facts about the categories of information offered and sought indicates the type of users of these sources - it is clear that they can not be classified as the average citizen. This distortion biases discussion of the use and effects of telematics for information sought by citizens. In general, the result is an overestimation of the user needs and consequently a too optimistic view of chances.

The Department of Public Health, Welfare and Sports is also involved. Together with the National Centre for Information on Health, public libraries have been awarded a grant by this department to establish a network of information for clients and patients. This government program **Transparent** funded 55 projects of which some 18 aim for better information provision for the citizen, client or patient. The projects range from multi-media applications providing information on cancer and heart diseases to electronic patient records for use by GPs for patients with psychiatric problems, and the Diet Diskette.

Municipalities

Citizens of several Dutch municipalities can obtain information from their local government. In Amsterdam the aforementioned DDS-linked information system PIGA is an example. In Eindhoven **EGIS** offers quite a lot of information to the public, varying from addresses to environmental information. **SPIRIT** in the city of Rotterdam offers similar services and more. It is perhaps not that surprising that municipalities have sprung forward. Databases, information systems and e-mail are increasingly used by them for work management. The step not yet taken is opening up these systems to the general public. GemNet for instance is a network to enable communication between municipalities and some related services. It is still limited to local government, but the name discloses a more ambitious goal: designing a network capable of transporting more information than the obligatory core business. If GemNet matures it could be a valuable asset.

Closely linked to information for citizens are experiments to increase involvement of citizens with politicians and politics. Apart from the web-sites or BBSs, political parties like the Labour Party or Green Left have funded two experiments that are of interest. First there were the so called city debates (*stadsgesprekken*) in Amsterdam. A local television channel organised a series of city debates on topics relevant to policy makers, politicians and citizens. In the studio all parties were invited to debate a specific subject. The interesting aspect was that viewers were able to give their opinion by telephone, intervening and influencing the discussion by giving support to either side. Although the city debates were successful, they died as a direct result of that success. It transpired that the professionalism of the broadcasts and the choice of really 'hot' topics made them apparently too threatening to politicians.

In Rotterdam a similar setback was experienced. The Citizens Consultations (project *Burgerraadpleging Hoogvliet*) in Hoogvliet was an experiment in 1993 about government renewal. The main goal was linked to that of social renewal: improving the quality of life - here the quality of government administration and politics. The borough of Hoogvliet started the initiative, deciding on five Citizens Consultations using teletext. The situation in Hoogvliet allows two way communications over television cables. Technically all conditions to make the experiment a success were met. But it failed ...

Evaluation of the project produced valuable information. Firstly it transpired that fewer people were interested in participating in the electronic version of Consultations than in the paper versions. Especially older people hesitated. Secondly, although politicians seemed enthusiastic, they were unwilling to put really hot issues on the agenda. It was also unclear to what extent the results of the Consultations influenced policies - leading to disbelief amongst participants that they were taken seriously. As a direct result the level of participation dropped for each new Consultation.

Non-governmental organisations (NGOs)

Information for citizens is clearly not limited to that provided by authorities. There is a wealth of information available through other channels. Bulletin Board Systems (BBS) for instance have been around for a long time. They are 'proven technology', widespread and many are interconnected through Fido-net. BBSs can be organised by topic or group, or used as a means of communication.

There are BBSs for people with disabilities, offering specific information and software. The Dutch organisation *WoonZorgFederatie* has a BBS offering a broad range of relevant information for nursing homes, such as standard allowances, collective labour agreements, model nursing plans, etc. Pandora, an organisation for influencing public opinion about former psychiatric patients, has a BBS. NPCF, the Dutch federation of patient and consumer associations, uses a BBS to provide addresses of patient organisations. NIAD, the Netherlands Institute for Alcohol and Drugs, exploits a BBS with detailed information on drugs and alcohol abuse. This is part public, part only accessible to subscribers. NIZW, the Netherlands Institute for Care and Welfare, uses a BBS as an experiment on new means of communication and to exchange information. NIZW will make the transition to a Web-server during 1996 and the trend is for more organisations to take this step.

Dutch libraries are also major players. Their role is less as information providers, although they have extensive databases, as that of intermediaries. Amongst public libraries the idea is gaining momentum that they can become key figures in the near future: (electronic) information retrieval is already possible in the larger libraries and librarians are trained to search for information. So, not only are more and more libraries putting their catalogues on line, they are also creating a distinct profile as information brokers.

Information for citizens does not necessarily require telematics. There are numerous examples of stand alone Points of Information. In Amsterdam for instance a system to support house hunters is up and running. Installed in displays, detailed information is provided on available houses which users can select and print. Similar displays are used to disseminate information for elderly people (Roosendaal) and patients (several hospitals). The CD-i medium used has yet to be explored by many

Dutch municipalities but the city of Nijmegen has made a CD-i, which is being evaluated.

Information available

What kind of information is being provided for citizens? For those with fairly fast Internet access, by no means typical, there is already an interesting range of information sources available. Some government departments are active: none very innovative and in most cases scanty. The Dutch tax authorities have opened a site which supplies citizens with (interactive) information on taxes. Job Centres have started to use displays and telematics to inform people about available jobs. All university libraries are on-line accessible and some public libraries going on-line.

VOCATIONAL EDUCATION AND TRAINING

Special focus on computer use in social work education started in the Netherlands in 1984 with a governmental plan (*INSP: informatics stimulation programme*) with substantial governmental funding. Up to 1989 the results were that seven schools were supplied with pilot networks and there were newly developed curricula or courses:

- a basic course in informatics applied to the field of social services;
- a curriculum on the social effects of automation of information processes;
- a curriculum on social and organisational aspects of systems development;
- a curriculum on managerial and supervisory support of social welfare institutions and those involved in social and development work;
- a curriculum on telematics and the use of external databases for social purposes.

The schools selected for these projects received material and financial support from the Ministry of Education to set up further training schemes and curriculum development. This action was crucial for social work education to apply computer use in their curricula. In 1989 the first plan was followed by another: the *VIT-program* ('a renovation policy concerning information technology'). The VIT-program Social Informatics lasted from 1989 until 1991 and produced an overall curriculum for computer use in social work education, based on substantial research. Finally a third nationwide innovation programme: ISI (*Innovation for Social Informatics*) delivered learning materials for all Social Informatics modules and trained teachers. This programme was managed by CAUSA at the Hogeschool Eindhoven.

Did all these actions lead to a vast application of IT in social work education? Although there was no massive shift, central stimulation by national government led to important changes in the use of computers in social work education in the Netherlands. Use of computers in schools for social work increased and for a better understanding we will highlight two main application areas:

The first concerns curriculum development which includes learning about the application of IT in social work practice and studying social informatics. As students are educated to be professional social workers they need to learn how to handle computers in the daily practice of social work. Not only do they need to know how to use computers and software, but they also need to know about the social, psychological and ethical impact of computer use in their profession. Therefore this has become a part of the curriculum in most polytechnics. They start with a course in basic informatics, followed by courses that are more or less tailor made for the available specialisms. This implies specialist computer courses for social and legal services, for arts therapy, in community education etc. These courses are a full part of the curriculum with contents tested.

The second application area is the use of information technology to support educational and managerial processes. These area can be considered under four main topics:

(a) *Computers used as a general tool* - a fast growing area. It is a tool because its main function is in replacing other equipment (overhead projector, typewriter, etc.); the processes stay the same. Students use school computer facilities to write their papers. The computer is also used as a computing machine in small research projects.

(b) *Testing.* Several schools are experimenting with automated testing and exams, moving to full interactive testing - a rather drastic change in the learning process. It allows more student centred learning in the students' and not the school's time schedule and decides when they are ready for a test or exam.

(c) *Information retrieval.* Through a modem or network, the computer is used to contact databases and libraries and retrieve information (still on a small scale but increasing). The main innovation in data-communication is use of networks, mainly the Internet which is rapidly replacing use of bulletin boards and other online databases. Actual applications are:

- local area networks with a computer lab;
- campus wide systems that access databases and libraries;
- e-mail for students, staff and teachers. Staff increasingly use the Internet and e-mail whereas there is still little student use of electronic mail or data exchange. The main application is communication with students studying abroad (as in Europe the 'Erasmus students');
- WWW pages with extensive information on topics, not forgetting the extensive list of discussion groups, list servers and Web pages distributed by CUSSNET, ENITH, HUSITA etc.

(d) *Distance learning* is hardly developed in social work education. Most experiments in this subject concern economics and technical faculties.

(e) *Computer Assisted Learning*. This area of computer use is growing but depends on development of courseware (defined as self-contained educational software). Schools experiment with applications as soon as they are available. Of relevance here is the courseware development project of the Hogeschool van Utrecht and STOAS-CMN (a courseware developer) which developed sixteen courseware packages for the social work curriculum. These include:

- In Hogeschool van Utrecht, School for Social Work there is a special course for non resident students with deficiencies in the Dutch language. They receive extra training through a fully computerised language course. It uses drill-and-practice which is the most effective method of training deficiencies in vocabulary and grammar, rather than in pronunciation.
- There are several computer courses in the area of social and legal services. This topic area contains much formal knowledge, which is not easy to learn, and often dull. Here interactive computer courses, with case material that students have to analyse and find solutions for, helps motivation. Teachers feel relieved at having to teach less law and can focus on a more supervisory role of work with small groups of students.

(f) *Use as a management tool* is widespread, at least for student registration and keeping track of results. This was mainly induced by requirements of the ministry regarding students numbers and registration for student allowances. Also schools are financed on the basis of the results of their students.

Support

Schools of social work that wish to implement certain aspects of IT, either in their curriculum or in administration, can get assistance from a special consultancy service which emerged from another project financed by the ministry. At a national level there was a project called *Implementation of Information Technology in Higher Education,* (ITO) managed by the Open University (distance learning). This project developed a model for the implementation of Information and Communication Technologies (ICT) in higher education. One result of the project was a consultancy organisation which provides support for IT implementation in schools at a very reduced price.

Contact between teachers

At present the main form of contact takes place around course development in the VIT-program. Almost all schools for social work participate. CAUSA, the main contractor, distributes *Interactief*, a quarterly newsletter which informs on curriculum development for computer use in Social Service Education. Informal contacts play an important role and initiatives are undertaken to formalise these contacts. Contact through the Internet is also increasingly important.

Evaluation

Most Schools of Social Work have a considerable number of computers for educational use. Disappointingly the most widespread use is for word processing. This means that computers are often used as a current model typewriter and we do not fully use the opportunities available. Often it depends of the attitude and skills of teachers whether they make more advanced use of the computer. If a teacher stimulates or demands it then students are more likely to use computers and SPSS for research projects.

The expected massive switch to computer assisted learning did not take place. Teachers, especially in our profession are not very progressive. The mainstream is not about to make a rapid change but will remain with known procedures. This attitude is probably due to Dutch education being an 'ivory tower'. The whole system was fully subsidised, the money mainly covers personnel and with little money for innovation. There were no market activities and no competition, but this is changing. Polytechnics now have more responsibility for their own finances and can go to the educational market to sell courses to generate extra money for innovation. Also a more competitive climate between schools is now stimulating teachers to innovate and use new technologies to make courses better and more attractive - they need to attract young people who are raised with computers, the Nintendo-generation! These innovations will inevitably also lead to more distance learning, more multi-media applications and greater use of the Internet.

PROVISION OF SERVICES

The diffusion of technologies, other than telematics, in the human services in the Netherlands is slow. Looking back it seems that there was just a little progress. In the social-cultural work sector, such as community centres, the decision on which registration system to implement was made by the Union of Supporting Agencies (VSW). They chose on the basis of a neutral assessment one system, **WIDA**, out of four options, proclaiming it as the standard to be developed further. However there are very different systems still in use and sold (eg **SOCURIS** and **Crosstabs**). The chosen system is being redesigned, but there is some doubt as to whether different organisations will use this standard as they are still defining their own requirements.

Earlier there were great expectations of the use of telematics. BBSs for instance could be used as a platform for workers to exchange information and get answers to practical or urgent questions. This never happened and systems developed on this premise failed. The ones that survived are based on either some duty to provide information or on a manifest need for information. In the field of care for young people there is an example of the former kind of BBS. The Netherlands Institute of Alcohol and Drugs Prevention (NIAD) is an example of a developing a BBS based on a manifest need for information. They offer for instance access to their databases with information on alcohol and drugs, access to their publications and an e-mail forum to discuss addiction related topics.

There are also a few successful initiatives on the Internet. The aforementioned Web sites of ENITH and CUSSnet are good examples of how things can be done. Another example is the mail list SOCSEC-L which provides communication for over one hundred workers in the social sector. An intriguing observation is that SOCSEC-L also serves the needs of some fifteen non-Dutch subscribers who are nevertheless interested in developments in the Netherlands.

Also of interest are experiences with 'larger scale' networks. They all tripped over the same problem: how to get the right, reliable information in the network. The Dutch MIP-projects are a good example of how things can go wrong. Not only technical problems, but certainly also problems with the content, made evaluators conclude that MIP-projects somewhat failed. They recognised certain positive effects and concluded that MIP was premature and too ambitious to succeed. Projects now aimed at developing local networks use this information and try to get the provision of information in order before the network goes on line. In the southern provinces of the Netherlands successors of MIP are being set up but whether they will succeed is unknown.

As of 1996, 'Information for the Handicapped' has become part of NIZW which means that information on disability from both organisations can be offered on one CD-ROM. **NIGSYS** will be updated, reviewed and extended during 1996. NIZW information sources are now quite widely used. The developers of **ADDI** (guidance and calculation software for the social sector) use NIZW information in their **SOKI** social map program). NIZW's own products indicate similar interest for this kind of social information. *Grote Almanak voor Informatie en Advies* has over three thousand subscribers and requests are made for subsets of this volume. The Internet shows that people are indeed looking for customised information. Regrettably NIZW had to suspend their on-line Videotext *Raad en Hulp* (Advice and Help), but this information - and probably more - will become available on an RDBMS and the Internet in due course.

One sector seemed to make significant progress. In youth care a system of data collection and dissemination was set up to meet department and managerial information needs. The project almost failed and is still heavily criticised as ineffective. However experience was gained of new ways of electronic exchange of information. The technical side of the project seemed alright. The problem was, again, in expectations of what could be done with the system. As youth care is a field where quite a lot of software is already used there seems to be some reluctance at looking at opportunities. Youth care is for instance acquainted with things like registration, expert systems and decision support systems. There are several products available: DSM, the COM-procedure, KWIS, ABL, CLIK, Gas, PIPER, KISIT, GRIP and Daisy. It is interesting to learn that all these means of support, whether or not paper based, are especially useful to structure and make explicit the processes through which help is given. None of the instruments do, or were meant to, take over the counsellor's own responsibilities.

A need for registration and management was one incentive to migrate the **GIRST**-method towards software. GIRST was not developed from a computer perspective but from a clear cut view on how things should be orchestrated in home care. Nowadays the Integrated Information and Registration System for Homecare (GIRST) has become an internationally marketed product. Although there are competitor packages available, the strength of GIRST seems to be in its content driven concept and design. Now operating under Windows GIRST provides a rich instrument for all people working in home care. It provides managers with relevant management information and homecare workers with day care planning materials.

In addition to developments for registration, some organisations are making their first timid moves towards the use of techniques like simulation and geographical information systems (GIS). The latter seem to be popular with several being developed. Coincidently or not, two important examples of Dutch GISs are both for use in the sector for elderly people to support policy makers, for example, in deciding on suitable locations for elderly people. The Amsterdam based *Foundation for Applied Gerontechnology* made a GIS that uses actual distances travelled, while the Heerlen based *Expertcentre Policies concerning the Elderly* developed a mapping system that uses distances measured as the crow flies. Both systems have to be fed with data extracted from different sources on population, property use and finance. This demonstrates a major vulnerability of these systems in their dependence on the accuracy of other databases.

Another development in this area is towards more intelligent systems. NIZW for instance is building a demonstrator of a simulation model to support policy makers and workers in predicting the consequences of certain policy decisions. Technically speaking, building such a simulation model is not that difficult. The difficulties are at a very different level. How to decide which rules apply to the model. How to decide which algorithms to use in those rules. And, most defiant of all, how to include some intelligence into the system to make it less rigid? Economists have experience of building models, but the care and welfare sector lacks these models. NIZW is trying to close this gap but it will take several years to build and validate such a system. A similar project is being carried out by Cap Volmac in the Dutch city of Alphen aan den Rijn.

As a direct result of the aforementioned *Overheidsloket 2000* program, an expert system is being developed to support front office workers in decision making on legislation concerning provision for people with disabilities. This will be a tricky task as municipalities have a discretionary competence.

A gratifying feature is the entrance of 'new' parties. During 1995 one Dutch college of higher education had its Department of the Arts, after consulting NIZW's **Spits**, develop a computer program to support trainers working with people with dementia. It still yet to be decided whether to migrate the program to CD-i, CD-ROM or fixed disk. The program enables trainers to visualise the personal lives of people with increasing dementia problems: photographs and sounds connected to their own lives, training sessions to keep the level of word and sentence recognition at an acceptable level, and more. The first experiences with this concept are very promising and the program is scheduled to be marketed in 1996.

New technologies are being introduced: CD-i, for instance. Although it is not clear whether CD-i will become the success Philips thinks it is, there are clear cut advantages. The little silvery disk can be used without any knowledge of computers - just plugging the player into the television set will do. This, in fact, is the major advantage of CD-i over CD-ROM. Another difference is the quality of moving pictures. At present CD-i is capable of better resolution than CD-ROM which in classes, courses and neighbourhood centres is a valuable asset.

CD-i technology is being used in several ways, mostly in training or information settings. Subjects addressed using CD-i are: coping with asthma, (health care and some of the prejudices); introduction courses for refugees (help with understanding language and customs); training nurses to lift patients; information for families and others on coping with dementia and so on. Nevertheless, some titles intended for CD-i are now being produced on CD-ROM, such as **Streetwise** on youth health. The same will probably apply to NIZW's product on dementia. The reason is mainly economic; producing CD-i is expensive and the expected installed base of CD-i players is too low.

Finally there is progress to be noted in a completely different field. As observed earlier, the Union of Dutch Municipalities (VNG) is leading the way for local government. IBA, their information policy department, has set landmarks by developing dataset standards in cooperation with other organisations. These *GFO*s, as they are called, lay down rules for several sets of data with the aim of reducing incomparability. GFOs exist for policies such as real estate, social services and welfare. Many software developers now use GFO-standards in their software and the organisation of employers in the Dutch welfare sector (VOG) used GFO implementation as a criterion when they assessed registration software.

CONCLUSION AND FUTURE DEVELOPMENTS

A main objective for the coming years will be to answer the question of how to implement technology in a sensible way into the daily work of people concerned with our care and welfare. First, there is the question to be answered as to what extent technology is capable of supporting that work. Work that is dominated by more or less fuzzy processes and interactions between human beings. In the next decade software developers and engineers will undoubtedly try to tackle this problem from a technical perspective. The first (demonstration) projects are now being carried out on topics which can be characterised as complex: decision making based on social security legislation; establishing the effects of (social) policy decisions; making diagnostic judgements on for instance delinquent juveniles or on people with multi-layered problems.

The second question is about the driving force behind technological innovation. Most people will support the assumption that innovation should be driven by real needs. Who is to define those needs? Two probable institutions can be identified: the workers themselves, and the educational and supporting systems. In the present situation, one can have serious doubts as to the extent to which workers can generate enough energy to make their wishes explicit. Staff at schools for social work may be better equipped. They can be addressed on this issue as they have a distinctive task of training future professionals. So, rethinking the changing content of professional acts should be a part of their core business. The same goes for supporting organisations which viewed from a similar perspective: are helping professionals in keeping track of societal changes.

One final remark needs to be made on the speed of change and the conditions for implementation. Dissemination of technology is a slow process. This cannot be emphasised enough. People tend to think of technology as just a product that needs to be marketed. But the products discussed in this chapter and book are of a very different kind then a dishwasher or washing machine, even if modern ones are now equipped with fuzzy logic based instruction sets. The products discussed here have implications far beyond those of domestic appliances. They redefine the role of professionals and clients. In that sense they are threatening, as they will fundamentally change relationships. The same goes for aspects like acting by professional standards; are they to be dismissed as decision support systems and expert systems are being introduced?

Not acknowledging this aspect will cause frustration, from the perspective of policy makers wanting things to speed up, as well as from the perspective of developers wanting change to be embedded in daily work. This in turn means that the conditions for change are rather critical. People will not support any change if they do not see any benefit for themselves. In essence, it is as simple as that. Getting social workers to use a complex management information system that has no gain for them will only lead to less and less accurate completion of forms, and less and less usable forms of management. So, even before developing new tools one should invest in getting people a bit more technology minded. There should be a way of thinking about technology that is fed from the idea that technology might be of interest to your daily job; not hard core technology driven nor hard core technology hatred. Another condition to be considered is the ultimate question: who is going to pay for all this? The Dutch government has set examples: in trade and industries, in public policy, in municipalities, and in studying and rethinking democracy. There is however an absence of structural (financial) support for projects and experiments in the care and welfare sector.

World Wide Web sites referred to in this chapter

1. The Department of the Interior.
http://www.minbiza.nl/

2. The Department of Trade and Industry.
http://www.minez.nl/

3. BVE-net. Network for secondary vocational education, apprenticeship systems and adult basic education (to support teachers and students).
http://www.pi.net/%7Ebvenet/

4. The Digital City (De Digitale Stad or DDS).
http://www.dds.nl/

5. Dutch Central Bureau for Statistics (CBS).
http://www.cbs.nl/

Author details

Jan van der Sluis is currently working as project manager for information technology with the Netherlands Institute for Care and Welfare (NIZW). He previously worked as a senior researcher at the Department of Sociology of Leyden University and at the Social and Cultural Planning Bureau. His publications include work on long term unemployment, social and welfare policy, and information technology and society.

Albert Visser is a social scientist who specialises in the application of new technologies in social work education. He is a member of the policy staff in the Faculty for Social Professions of the Professional University of Utrecht (Hogeschool van Utrecht). He has also been a member of the executive committee of ENITH since December 1989.

Contact: Jan van der Sluis
NIZW
PO Box 19152
3501 DD Utrecht
The Netherlands

Telephone: +31-30-230.63.11
E-mail: janvds@knoware.nl *or*
J.vanderSluis@nizw.nl

15 Romania

Poliana Stefanescu

HUMAN SERVICES AND INFORMATION TECHNOLOGY

Like most countries in Central and Eastern Europe, Romania is a former socialist country which was led by the communist party for about forty five years up to the revolution in December 1989. Nowadays Romania is a country in transition from the dictatorial political regime and a centralised economy, to a democratic society and a market economy.

Social work in the former socialist countries is in a state of chronic under-development. During the communist regimes, social work in Romania was a passive and bureaucratic activity focused on providing the population with minimum but secure living conditions: wages, sick benefits, child allowances, old age pensions and free medical care.

The communist state presented a paternalistic image to the people, giving the impression that it was able to overcome all problems. In these circumstances, genuine social work that is orientated to solving urgent human problems in a personalised manner, was reduced to a minimum. Instead of professional social workers, the authorities hired ordinary clerks who handled papers and approvals. At that time, the schools of social work were abolished and the profession of 'social worker' vanished.

After 1989, social work made a new start. It is now considered as an important part of social welfare provision and is supported both at a national and a local level. The system for educating social workers is also developing and there are now four year university courses in the main cities in Romania for qualifying for social work.

Social work services are provided by government agencies and by NGOs (non governmental organisations). At a national level, there are several different ministries and institutions that are responsible for providing social services, including the Ministry of Labour and Social Protection, the Ministry of Health, the Ministry of

Education, the Ministry of Justice and The State Secretary for Handicapped Persons. At a local level, services are provided by the following authorities:

- Local Public Administration
- The Health County Office
- Minors Protection Commission
- The Handicapped Territorial Office
- The Education District Office

The multiplicity of these department affects the coherence of the social service system as a whole, which lacks a long term development strategy. Legislation is inadequate and many activities in social work are managed by old laws or by new, incomplete laws. This occurs because the dynamic and momentum of social problems during the transition phase is considerably faster than the legislative changes needed can be introduced.

The organisation and provision of good social work services in Romania requires the investment of funding on a huge scale that the state is not able to provide. Over the last few years a large number of NGOs have begun to support social service provision and social work activities in Romania. Many of these are funded from western countries including the European Union and the United States of America, but there is also funding from Romanian companies and private persons. It is vital that the state supports and stimulates the development of these NGOs. In the new context of reform of all forms of social protection for citizens, the NGOs have the potential to become trusted partners working alongside state provision. Some of the NGOs are using computers for recording client data and other information. We can note four examples of work by NGOs that includes an information technology perspective:

- A professional association of social workers, called ARPA (The Romanian Association of Social Work) which promotes new initiatives and methods in social work. It is editing a Bulletin of the association that includes articles on the use of information technology.
- The 'Institute for the Study of the Quality of Life' in Bucharest is undertaking research on the social costs of the transition, which focuses on unemployment, poverty, the level of education and standards of living. The results of this research, using computer analysis, are being published in the journal 'Quality of Life'. In 1993 in the same journal, the institute published an important paper 'White Book: A Commentary on the Social Work System in Romania'.
- The Research Institute for Labour and Social Protection is responsible for handling information concerning people with social problems or people who are socially or economically vulnerable.
- The National Commission for Statistics is also monitoring the economic standards of the population with results published periodically in a bulletin.

INFORMATION FOR CITIZENS

The transition in Romania led to critical social phenomena of unemployment, poverty, homelessness and children on the streets. As a consequence the social services are facing a large number of clients and demands for services.

Information for citizens in Romania is mainly provided by traditional means of books, leaflets and pamphlets for target groups such as pensioners, women, children, teenagers, young mothers and disabled people. There are developments which are outlined below using computers, the Internet, telephone and television services, some reaching specific target groups but with the potential to expand to others areas. Two examples of computer information software are databases that can be used either by professionals or by ordinary citizens:

- **Jurist PC** which contains text and comments on Romanian laws, starting from 1950.
- **FARMA-SOFT** which includes a medical dictionary, hospitals, pharmacies, emergency stations and a medicines index.
- **Unemployment services**. Unemployment affects young people and adults alike. Unemployed people are registered at the unemployed offices and their data is recorded on local databases. In many towns in Romania computers are used locally for recording the data but there seems to be little work on using computers for offering jobs. One initiative in this area is an annual 'Job-Fair' for new graduates who are offered jobs using a job database. This is a private initiative of youth organisations.

The Internet

In early 1993 the first connecting node to the Internet was established which aimed at developing research and higher education networking in Romania. Now every university is linked to the Internet , either having their own domain server or having terminals connected to an external server. The Central University Library (the main site) is linked to the Internet and is developing a bibliographical and retrieval database. These activities will be extended in the future to the local libraries of the faculties.

Some social work agencies are also linked to the Internet , for example Save the Children has an Internet connection and through this the opportunity to access social databases. The LOGIC telephone company offers individual connection to the Logicnet which is a network of public data that is available via dial up.

Television services

Teletext services are available through the national and private television stations. These contain hundreds of pages of information about television broadcasting, utility telephone services, cultural activities, etc. However only the latest television sets available in Romania are able to capture teletext so use of teletext is not extensive at present. Some private television stations have night-time special on-line broadcasts called 'hot-lines' that offer help and advice to those that phone in. The audience reached consists mainly of young people.

Cable television is extending in hospitals and a valuable example of this is the Marie Curie Children's Hospital in Bucharest. Through a private donation, the children who are patients there can watch special educational broadcasting.

Telephone services

Telephone information services are available twenty four hours a day from the Romrelcom company. There are non-governmental agencies that finance special telephone services such as:

- The 'WHITE telephone' which is dedicated to the needs of people with disabilities.
- The Save the Children organisation has a special telephone for children's questions (questions that they will not usually ask their parents).
- The ANIMA foundation receives telephone calls about people who are concerned about care of their animals.
- INTERTIN is a night-time telephone hotline for young people who need friendly advice and help.
- JOBTIN is the telephone number of a youth centre where people can call to offer or get jobs for young people.

VOCATIONAL EDUCATION AND TRAINING

In Romania, social work education is taught at the Universities of Bucharest, Cluj, Iasi and Timisoara. There are also post-graduate courses for people already working in social work, but having a different original background, to obtain a professional qualification. Besides these, the three different theological institutes - Orthodox, Catholic and Baptist - are developing their own courses in social work.

Because all of these schools were established after 1989, they had to be accredited to the Ministry of Education in order for their diplomas to be officially recognised. During the accreditation process, one of the requirements made about the curriculum was the integration of a special course in Informatics of at least one semester. This fact shows the importance of information technology in the higher education of social work professionals. Including information technology into the curriculum led on to specific aspects of:

- The faculties must have, or have access to, adequate technical equipment - computers, printers and modems.

- Teachers must demonstrate specific skills not only with computers but also in the socio-human field.
- Students must learn to use specific software applications in order to enhance their knowledge in social work.

Not all the departments of social work have their own computers and information technology teachers. Most use facilities that belong to the technical departments of the universities. The best equipped is the Department of Social Work at the University of Bucharest which owns a Novell computer network and other additional equipment. Their information technology teacher is also a member of their faculty staff. The software used in the departments of social work is varied and depends on the type of computer used:

- DOS - Microsoft Works, WordPerfect, SPPS/PC+, studentware
- Windows applications - WinWord, Excel, Access

Unfortunately there is no dedicated software for social work though we need it. As mentioned before, many agencies develop databases for client registration but these are local initiatives that cannot be generalised. During the seminars the students have opportunities to stimulate the structure and loading of sample client databases. There are no information systems of wide utility in social services.

In the educational process, knowledge of information technology is a goal as we discussed earlier, but it is also a tool in teaching and studying other subjects and disciplines. The curriculum includes a course called ‘Statistical methods in socio-human sciences’. At the University of Bucharest this course is computer orientated and the students learn how to use SPSS (Statistical Package for the Social Sciences) and how to write a statistical report based mainly on descriptive statistics. The other schools of social work do not use computers for this course. Computers are used by the students to simulate a budget and expenditure, and to create charts representing indicators for a course on ‘Sociology of the Family’.

Another use of computers is in organising a database of practice placements for students. This database includes only the institutions and offices from Bucharest and neighbourhoods. Each faculty of social work needs its own database for student placements. A valuable initiative with the University of Cluj in collaboration with other organisations is editing a *Guide to Social Work Agencies for the District of Cluj*. The information includes both governmental and non-governmental organisations.

Another use of computers will be the building of a wide database with bibliographic references for social work which can be accessed by students. This is an initiative by teachers and students in social work at the University of Bucharest and will be financed from a research project. The most important data from social research will be stored in an on-line social work archive that will be developed from 1996 onwards at the University of Bucharest.

Computers will also be used in an important research project concerning the integration into professional practice of young social workers who graduate from all universities in Romania. This project is supervised by the head of the Social Work Department from the University of Bucharest, Professor Elena Zamfir.

E-mail and file transfer protocols (FTP) are beginning to be used in the universities, especially by teachers and researchers. Starting in 1995, the Ministry of Education is financing a special project for information technology use by secretaries and administration within universities. This involves acquisition of computers, staff training and development of software packages. Five years ago the same ministry financed the acquisition of the first computer networks for universities for use in the teaching process. Although this equipment was insufficient, it was a valuable start and a wise way to invest the education budget.

During these years the faculties enhanced their equipment using either Tempus funds or other educational programmes and collaborations with foreign universities and organisations. Tempus is a project funded by the European Union which promotes staff and student exchange between the European Union and eastern European countries. Its primary purpose is to assist the Eastern European countries in developing their educational programmes.

Romanian social work higher education has been significantly stimulated by special programmes of teacher and student mobility, as much as by acquisition of books, teaching materials and electronic equipment. Besides these, curriculum development has also been an important area of progress for departments of social work. In the last few years, students' mobility has been enhanced with special periods of social work practice placements.

Teaching use of computers is part of some vocational courses for unemployed people or for young people who have recently left secondary or high school and need to find jobs. One example is a private initiative, the 'Computer Academy' in Bucharest which organises training courses on computer applications for young people at a 20% discount on normal rates. Larger trade unions also organise short term retraining courses for their members, including on the use of computers. As many job offers require computer knowledge, many people take this course.

PROVISION OF SERVICES

Use of computers in personal human services is only at the beginning. Only a few agencies have computer applications which record client data in local databases, and these are mainly in unemployment offices. In towns where the municipality had funds to buy and finance special software development, the Office of Labour and Social Protection records data about clients and makes periodic updates. From the summer of 1995, new laws for social support allowances increased the use of computers for data archives.

In some larger hospitals, computers are used not only for administrative purposes but also with sophisticated medical equipment to process and display health care parameters such as computer tomography and encephalography. Bed reservation is also computerised in a few hospitals. Use of computers for diagnostic and medical data processing is being experimented with in a special unit within the faculty of Medicine in Bucharest. It is planned that the USA government will support the opening of a telemedicine centre in Romania.

At present there is little corresponding development for using computers in the management of social work or directly in social work practice. However we can anticipate that software will be developed for use in these areas in due course.

CONCLUSION AND FUTURE DEVELOPMENTS

The use of information technology in social services is not very extensive at present. There are a few agencies that use the technology not only for word processing, but also for recording data in local databases. It is obvious that social services need factual information concerning their clients, the financial funds allocated and access to information on the whole network of governmental and non-governmental social help.

Use of computers must improve access to this kind of information that will be stored in specific databases. It is important to create client orientated applications in order to help social workers to guide and assist clients. Management orientated applications are also important because of the difficulties of getting money from budgets and the multiplicity of cases to be handled.

Computer applications orientated to daily life applications for people with physical or mental disabilities have not yet been developed. There are some initiatives such as psychological tests, ability tests or computer educational games but only in clinics and research laboratories of universities. It is important that students learn about these applications in order to apply them in their practice. For the future, Romania needs a generic national computer system for social security with human services as a part of it.

The educational system in social work must be the 'avant garde' of this profession. Students will be provided with updated knowledge and after graduating will bring a new wave into social work. This requires modern courses, IT equipment, video labs, exchange of teachers and students with developed countries, exchange of information and teaching methods, many practising hours and the allocation of a reasonable budget.

Use of e-mail and other file transfer protocols must be developed for the benefit of students and teachers. It is necessary to have free access to professional databases from important sites and to get information from electronic journals in social work. This is an important area where ENITH can help. Using IT in all aspects of social work will lead to modernisation of this profession but at present there is no long term programme for informatisation of the whole activity.

Because social work is at the beginning, the social worker will not only be a counsellor or therapist, the social worker must also be a 'sensor' of the society which involves the painful but necessary process of transition and determining human orientated democratic changes.

References

Colombi D, Rafferty J and Steyaert J (Eds.). *Human Services and Information Technology: A European Perspective.* ENITH. 1993.

Glastonbury B. *Human Welfare and Information Technology.* Van Gorcum, 1993

Grebel H and Steyaert J. *Social Informatics.* Hogeschool Eindhoven, the Netherlands. 1993.

Stefanescu P. *Using Computers in Social Work Training.* HUSITA 3 conference paper, Maastricht. 1993.

Stefanescu P. *Modelling the Dynamic of Subjective Poverty during the transition in Romania.* Research Report, Bucharest University. 1995

Zamfir C. *White Book: The Social Work System in Romania. Comments.* Bucharest University. 1994.

Zamfir E and Zamfir C (Coordinators) *Social Policy: Romania in the European Context.* Bucharest University. 1995.

Zamfir E. Social Work and Social Policy in Romania during the Transition. In: *Social Education in Selected Countries*, Japan. 1994.

Author details

Poliana Stefanescu is a lecturer in social work in the Department of Social Work at the University of Bucharest. She has previously published on the use of computer networks in social work training in Romania.

Contact: Poliana Stefanescu
University of Bucharest
Faculty of Sociology
Department of Social Work
BD. Mihail Koganiceanu, 64
Bucharest
Romania

E-mail: poliana@drept.unibuc.ro

16 Russia

Tatjana Serebjakowa

HUMAN SERVICES AND INFORMATION TECHNOLOGY

A complete overview of human services in Russia seems to be almost impossible because of the size of the country (more than 150 million inhabitants) and the difficulties of gathering local information. The following outlines are therefore necessarily incomplete and may serve as a first step on the way to a more detailed picture of a complex and difficult situation.

Following the breakdown of the communist regime Russia faces severe economic difficulties. The level of production has fallen dramatically and, although it now seems to have stabilised at a low level, the prognoses are still contradictory and insecure. Inflation and economic stagnation have rapidly impoverished large parts of the population and brought wealth to only a few.

Government organisations are insufficiently developed for the demands of a market society. This means that the taxation system is still not working very well and that the government loses a lot of income. In addition, the systems of internal security and justice are still lagging behind in their development, which opens up possibilities for arbitrariness, corruption and crime.

At the same time, however, the historically fundamental benevolence and charity of Russian society prevails. Help is generously given in families as well as to the needy in the communities. This is a major resource in a situation where a substantial number of the population earn the minimum wage of about twelve dollars a month and where prices are rapidly approaching world market standards.

Statistical indicators of wellbeing in the Russian population draw a gloomy picture. Mortality rates are increasing and were 15.6 per thousand in 1994. The birth rate, which has dropped in recent years, now stays constantly low and was 9.4 per thousand in 1994 (*Argumenty I Fakty*, Nr. 9/95). Life expectancy has gone down to 57.9 years for men and 69.8 years for women (*Iswestija*, 25.10.95). Infant mortality and mortality of children up to the age of four years is four to five times higher than in western developed countries and the mortality of mothers is fifteen to twenty times higher (*Argumenty I Fakty*, Nr. 9/95; *Iswestija*, 29.6.94).

The signs of poverty, social and personal problems coupled with lack of public resources are obvious in the Russian cities. Amongst the most needy are elderly people and children who have lost their families and homes. Elderly people with low income (pensions) and whose families have limited financial resources are dependent on public support. In many of the bigger cities there are private or public care organisations which offer shopping aids, nursery care and places to meet, get warm and eat. Charges are made for most of these services. There are also homes and shelters for elderly people run by the government but these are often overcrowded.

Young children who have lost their families or homes as a result of, for example, money problems or alcoholism or whose parents are in jail, roam through the cities, sleep in cellars or staircases and often suffer from drug abuse (sniffing gasoline or glue) and severe health problems. In St. Petersburg alone their number is estimated to be 4,000-8,000. Some shelters for children have been opened in St. Petersburg but the problems remain. Clearly, shelters on their own are not enough to help these children - care and commitment from professional pedagogues are also needed.

Along with the reconstruction of the economy a new social care system has to be built up. In the communist society, factories and administrations cared for old age pensions and many other social needs of employees and their families and medical treatment was free. Now, however, social insurances and government activities have to take over these tasks. Government social policy focuses on old age pensions, family care and homes or shelters for the elderly, homeless and pensioners from the armed forces.

Introduction to information technology

Where possible and where it can be financed, information technology is used in public and private social services. Many people know how to use computers and it is not difficult to find good computer experts. Children are trained in computer sciences at school and students take an obligatory IT course in the first two years at university. Pupils often have to learn, for example, programming in BASIC using paper and pencil as no or insufficient computers are available for them at school or at home. The number of computers is also limited in social services, and there is no market for specially adapted software.

INFORMATION FOR CITIZENS

While no example was found by the author of technologies for individual and community support and independent living, an interesting example of IT for employment and training was found in the city of Yaroslawl. The program was used in a public bureau for job consultancy and psychological advice. The bureau has a well equipped laboratory for the testing of sensual, motor and psychological capacities of people looking for jobs or planning their professional education. It also offers courses on job acquisition skills, personal performance and presentation. The individual capacities of those looking for jobs are analysed and the competencies and skills they developed during previous training and job practice are coded. The program then names and ranks a number of jobs for which the person has adequate skills. The basis for this ranking is a database of jobs with a detailed analysis of their demands on individual skills and competencies. A discriminant analysis is performed by the program each time individual data are entered to produce the ranked job list.

Unfortunately, a description of the program or its methodology is not available, so a deeper discussion of validity or privacy issues is not possible at this time. There is also no significant publication of the program in Russia, but it is used elsewhere. This example shows, however, that interesting programs may be found which are neither sufficiently published nor publicly discussed and that more examples of applications of the (once) leading Russian psychology may be expected.

VOCATIONAL EDUCATION AND TRAINING

Vocational education and training of social workers has only recently begun. Most new social work departments are integrated into or have developed out of the faculties of psychology and pedagogy. Application of computers in education is still unusual unless linked to the faculties of sociology and dealing with empirical social research.

PROVISION OF SERVICES

The Russian government is developing a system for payment of old age pensions in cooperation with the eighty two regions and states of the Russian Federation. The personal data of all pensioners is stored in the regional computing centres of the social administrations. The pensions are paid in the local dependencies of the regional administrations, data is coded locally and sent to the regional centres via networks. The regions send their accumulated data to the central administration in Moscow. The equipment of this system is quite modern and generous and much better than, for example, in universities. A high level of costs is met by foreign funders like the European Union.

Some of the larger non-governmental social help organisations use computer programs to keep their information updated, such as information on volunteer helpers or on storage of food, furniture or other resources for the needy. Programs are mostly local according to the demands of the organisations.

Networks and computers are set up locally in both governmental and non-governmental organisations by international technical assistance organisations such as World Learning Inc. on the basis of funds from national governments. At present, four regional Russian centres are equipped with computer networks and linked to the Internet. Along with the equipment goes a computer training program for local staff. Russian colleagues thus linked to the international networking community will welcome exchanges of information.

CONCLUSION AND FUTURE DEVELOPMENTS

Although Russia faces a severe struggle with economic and social difficulties, there is a high level of technical skills and a strong willingness to apply technologies that can help to cope with the enormous difficulties. In the future, computer networks will offer unique help with communication, especially as other forms of inner Russian and international communication media are slow and insecure. Social work itself is at its beginning, and international communication on methods and successful examples of practical help will be fruitful and important. For specialists and friends from other countries, a lot of interesting ideas, programs and solutions may still wait to be found in Russia.

Author Details

Tatjana Serebjakowa is the Dean of the newly founded Department of Social Work at Vologda University and is also Dean of the Department of Further Education at the same university. She is a member of the Russian Association of Social Work and Social Pedagogics and has published several books and articles.

Contact: Dr. Tatjana Serebjakowa
Dean at Vologda University
Pankratowa Uliza 88 B
kv 11160026 Vologda
Russia

Telephone: +7 8 1722 23625
Fax: +7 8 1722 21632

17 Spain

Mercedes García-Camino Burgos, Ana María Salamanca and Clara Suárez de la Llana Madrid

HUMAN SERVICES AND INFORMATION TECHNOLOGY

Social services in Spain reflect the political and administrative division and organisation of the Spanish State pursuant to the Constitution of 1978. The Constitution envisages three levels of government: local (municipal), regional (referred to here as 'autonomous communities' or 'communities') and national. There are a few exceptions to this general rule, whereby a great deal of responsibility for social services has been vested in regional authorities (in the Basque country, for instance). At the national level, the departments or ministries involved in social and human services are Social Affairs, Labour and Social Security, Health and Consumer Affairs, and Interior. There are essentially two sources of funding: the General State Budget and the Social Security Budget. In principle, the central authorities regulate and harmonise the activities of the other levels of government, and meet certain needs by providing services that can only be provided at a national level. Regional parliaments and governments have enacted their own laws and regulations. The central government is in the process of completing transfer of a number of social services and institutes to the regions.

Spain's political and geographic configuration is instrumental for social, economic or any other kind of activity. It is therefore essential to understand that each autonomous community has its own peculiarities and must respond to specific developments effecting social service provision. An important role is also played by the private, non-profit services managed by charitable institutions such as Cáritas, the Red Cross and many foundations and voluntary organisations.

The number of non-governmental organisations, foundations and private enterprises engaged in social services has grown substantially in recent years. The use of information technology in such institutions varies widely. Service companies, which have increased considerably in number, particularly in providing services for the elderly, tend to use them to a significant extent, for tele-alarm systems, for instance.

Likewise, the number of foundations engaging in social services that use IT in their day-to-day work has risen substantially.

Volunteer services are much less developed in Spain than in other European countries. Although this is improving, the resources available to such organisations are generally very scant, so IT is of little relevance in this sector for the time being. One of the areas of social services in which IT is more widely used is in the provision of financial benefits. A significant factor in IT developments in this area are that such benefits are paid by the national administration and therefore effect the entire country. The benefits include:

- Non-payer Social Security Pensions. Pensions that ensure a minimum income for people who have not paid sufficient social security contributions to receive normal benefits.
- Pensions under the Act for Social Mainstreaming of the Handicapped (LISMI), the only benefit currently in effect being the mobility allowance or subsidy for transportation costs.
- Family benefits for dependent children.

At the regional level, many Communities have enacted legislation to provide complementary economic benefits to compensate for certain social inequities. IT is often used for management of such payments (social and labour, educational, housing or health needs and so on).

Legislation effecting the use of IT essentially refers to the use of recorded data, statistics, files, etc. The national Organic Act on the Regulation of the Automatic Processing of Personal Data (LORTAD) has been in effect since January, 1993. The main characteristic that differentiates this Act from others in effect in the rest of Europe is in being less restrictive about data exchange between ministries and departments for government controlled files. This does not apply to privately owned files. A European directive is under discussion in Brussels on protection of automated data in the European Union, to provide a more homogeneous framework for data protection legislation in the various member states.

The Ministry of Social Affairs, the highest-ranking national body, has national, regional and local databases throughout the country containing information on entities, foundations, centres, services and benefits. These data are shared and can be consulted by the Ministry of Social Affairs and the Autonomous Regions through the Social Services Users Information System (**SIUSS**). This is in the final implementation stage in nine of the ten regions that have signed an agreement to this effect with the Ministry. Another four regions already have their own information system and bridge software connecting the various systems is being implemented. Of the remaining three regions, one is in the process of signing an agreement, while the other two will neither enter into such arrangements nor implement systems of their own. Information and statistical results will be produced once the process is completed, in order to ensure proper planning of the services to be provided.

INFORMATION FOR CITIZENS

Individual and community support

CEAPAT is the State Centre for Personal Independence and Technical Devices and is a division of the Social Services Institute (under the aegis of the Ministry of Social Affairs). It carries out nationwide information and advisory functions for users, professionals, businesses and institutions on technical devices and adaptations to improve the quality of life for people with disabilities and/or the elderly. CEAPAT participates in several Spanish Standardisation Organisation national committees on technical adaptations and accessibility, represents Spain in the European TIDE research and development and the HELIOS **Handynet** project and collaborates in COST 322.

CEAPAT is also the Spanish data collection centre for the Handynet Network. Handynet is a European multilingual automated information system, a communications and cooperation network that provides services to people with handicaps and to professionals working in this field. Because of its specialised activities, the CEAPAT collects the technical and functional data for two sub-modules:

- technical adaptations for people with motor handicaps and
- technical communications devices.

Two other centres cooperate in the data collection process: the Centre for Curricular Development (under the aegis of the Ministry of Education and Science) for the educational software sub-module, and the Aids and Devices for the Blind Unit of the National Organisation of the Blind for technical devices for the visually impaired sub-module.

CEAPAT's documentary database provides both general and detailed information on the major parameters of each and every product, prescription, etc. The guide contains information on assistance for therapy and training, prosthetics, assistance for personal protection and care, personal mobility, communication, information, technical devices for computers as well as information on access to services and devices.

With the support of the Horizon initiative, CEAPAT has set up a network of Information Counselling Centres (**CAI**) which use Handynet as an information and exchange tool in their day-to-day work. This nationwide network embodies centres of very different kinds: Regional Government centres, local and municipal centres, centres belonging to associations, foundations, universities and research institutes. Each CAI receives information on the network on a regular basis and a CD-ROM with an updated database every four months. Information is currently furnished on the following, through the various centres:

- Technical devices for people with a handicap: products, features and manufacturers.
- Organisations providing services for people with handicaps.
- Procedures used to acquire technical devices.

Information for citizens

Special attention should be drawn to social services' libraries and documentation centres, where nearly all information is computerised. Foremost among these centres is the SIIS, the only one specialising in handicaps, which covers all related subjects. This is a private, non-profit institution under the aegis of the *Fundación Eguía Careaga*. In 1980 it inaugurated a centre in Madrid whose activities are coordinated through the Royal Foundation for Prevention and Care of Persons with Disabilities.

Moreover, the publication of a *Gueda de Recursos Sociales* (Guide to Social Resources) in Aragon on electronic media represents an important step forward in the use of IT in social services, which will gradually be implemented in all other regions. It is divided into eleven sectors: population at large, childhood and youth, the elderly, the handicapped, drug abuse, the homeless and other social groups, integration into the work market, education and health and social services. The *Guía de Recursos* program can be used to process queries under the following selection criteria: geographic area, community social service, town, industry. It is also possible to access legal regulations, classified by industry.

The Social Services Authority of the Regional Government of Galicia's Department of Health and Social Services has been particularly active in the implementation of IT for user information systems, tele-assistance, etc.

Independent living

Tele-assistance and tele-alarm systems for the elderly and people with handicaps are currently being developed under the sponsorship of public and/or private institutions. Such systems are wholly or partially subsidised in all regions. One of the first regions to implement a system to help the handicapped and the elderly to live independently was the provincial government of Alava with its **Telephone Assistance Service**, inaugurated in 1986.

Employment and training

In Spain, most workers with disabilities using some sort of electronic device for work site adaptation are blind people. There are, of course, people with motor or hearing impairments who work with computers, but they usually do not need special tools to access information systems. However, there are centres and projects that address the issue of specific, work-site computer modifications for cases of severe motor disability (Barcelona's Municipal Patronage for People with Physical Handicaps).

Activities sponsored by the Technological, Employment and Disability Advice (ATED) Group relating to handicapped, the elderly and professional integration deserve special mention. This Group was created in 1990 by the Foundation for the Development of the Social Function of Communications (Fundesco) and Telefónica's Association for the Handicapped (ATAM). The latter provides care of all kinds for people with disabilities through its own centres or using outside resources. Fundesco, in turn, has promoted and cooperated in studies and research on the application of IT to enhance the quality of life of handicapped, elderly and other people with special needs. Since 1994 Fundesco has provided World Wide Web services[1], which include information on their activities, access to its bibliographic databases and purchasing its publications using electronic media.

Two of the most important IT projects for employment and training are: **Estrella** and **Delfos**. Estrella was developed under the Empleo-Horizon initiative. It is a computer application which, in addition to the management, development and follow-up of programmed action, provides the opportunity to expedite and harmonise processes such as introducing a common language in all the provinces falling under the scope of the project. The objective is to facilitate the integration of people with disabilities in mainstream social life and employment. Its functions are as follows:

- Register people with occupational disabilities.
- Organise and manage professional and vocational training courses.
- Draw up a resource map (training/employment).
- Study training/vocational supply on a district or local level.

This application provides employment technicians with support and updated information through expediting procedures (issue of printouts, reports, etc.) and speedy access to databases relating to these people (training, employment, technical devices). The project, developed between 1992 and 1994, is broken down into four large Plans for Action:

- Job classification, counselling and placement: information on the group of people involved; identification of needs; implementation of information and guidance systems; drawing up of resource maps; coordination of the bodies and agents involved.
- Training: professional and vocational training for people with disabilities; training of technicians.
- Employment promotion: enquiries about the labour market by sectors; information, guidance and support; counselling for employers; itinerary to the job site; encouragement of self-employment.

- Transnational information, dissemination and action: dissemination of innovative programmes and measures; exchange of experience; dissemination of methodology for promotion of employment; drawing up and dissemination of guides, leaflets and informative material.

Essentially, Estrella consists of five inter-related databases. The hardware has been upgraded by installing a CD-ROM, which enable professionals to access other databases, such as Technical Devices, as well as legislation relating to the community of people with disabilities.

Under the Horizon initiative, the *Confederación Gallega de Minusválidos* (Galician Confederation of the Handicapped) has implemented the Delfos project. It is a system of computerised distance learning and evaluation that runs on two levels (basic education and vocational training). This computer aided learning system is designed so that communication times are as short as possible, messages being written off-line. The system allows for both teacher-pupil and pupil-pupil communication. There are four communications areas:

- Two basic classrooms: one for basic education and the other for vocational training (where the pupil uses teacher-remitted educational materials).
- Magazine: deals with non-educational issues.
- Playground: for the exclusive use of pupils.
- Work environment: used to provide pupils access to the various areas.

Communication is via e-mail, for which purpose a user-friendly 'message editor', which runs on Windows, has been developed. The Occupational Training module develops hypertext-type material. Pupils engage in an independent learning process which is complemented with personalised attention from their tutor. E-mail is also used in the classroom, as a speedy way of performing tasks such as correction of exercises, proposing activities, answering questions or reporting test results. It also provides speedy interaction between teachers and pupils. A computer program has been implemented to review each pupil's link-in to the local area network. This also has an evaluation function that provides for working flexibility and accommodates different timetables.

VOCATIONAL EDUCATION AND TRAINING

Despite numerous attempts to collect detailed information on the use of IT in training social workers, the data collected depicts the situation in only a few regions. In Spain, the use of IT for social work training depends on the degree of development reached in each region where school of social services are located. Thus the information provided shows both the overall situation and the specific situation in each region.

With regard to how IT is included in curricula, until recently there was often a unit that dealt specifically with new technology, covering issues such as centre management, social projects and computerisation of services; there was also a course specifically devoted to information technology applications in social work. With restructuring of the curriculum, both training perspectives were eliminated. It was thought that these are basic skills that should be acquired independently of a university degree. Nonetheless, the curriculum does envisage elective courses in which some of these technologies are used, albeit from a statistical standpoint or as a convenient document storage system.

The Huelva School of Social Services has general subjects that covers issues such as 'Definition of science, technology and practice', and other elective subjects such as 'Effect of scientific and technological progress on the characterisation of current society'. Moreover students can volunteer to learn how electronic media are used to find sources for social service studies and how to use such media: Internet, access to specialised libraries, census data, etc.

Similarly, in the Valencia School of Social Services' programme, IT training consists of two subjects: 'Introduction to information technology in social sciences', which provides pupils with the basic skills needed to use a computer; and 'Information technology applied to social services', where pupils are expected to become acquainted with standard computer tools commonly used in their profession: Database management and statistical package tools.

Generally speaking, IT is not used as a teaching aid (Computer Assisted Instruction), due to the low ratio of computers to students and the lack of an IT laboratory equipped to accommodate so many students. Nonetheless, in the schools of social services in Barcelona there are specific programmes for the organisation of in situ training in Social Service centres. In the Huelva University, there is an informatics room for students, but with few computers for independent study of complementary subject areas. An Internet connection is planned for most schools of social services. IT use for teachers is more widespread than for students, with many having e-mail addresses and Internet access. Huelva University is representative of most Spanish university libraries. Its central library is connected to the Internet, but students have no address. The school's library is computerised, but without student work stations. Moreover, the central library is in the process of computerising its resources and the new system is to provide work stations for student and faculty use. This university has a server[2] which teachers can use to put their addresses on the Internet.

The Salamanca School of Social Services is implementing a Gopher through which both general and scientific information will be available and accessible by faculty and students via a computer terminal and various query areas on the different campuses. An information technology laboratory is planned for the use of faculty and students.

The use of IT in the overall professional development of social workers is still uncommon. Nonetheless, there are certain specific cases, such as the Provincial Government of Huelva, with social workers using portable computers to computerise user records or to develop a nationwide social services user card, an experiment which is currently under way. Moreover, social workers are beginning to consult bibliographic sources through databases and so forth, more and more frequently.

PROVISION OF SERVICES

At the practice level the information technology used for social services in the autonomous regions usually consists of systems that are accessed directly by social workers and management staff in these departments. One areas of social service in which IT is more widely used is the management of economic benefits for users. Most of the regional government use automatics systems for welfare benefit calculation. An example of a higher level application is the Integrated Management System (**SINGES**) in the region of Castile-La Mancha. The objective is for this system to administer all the benefits processed by the regional social services, automatically computing all amounts to be paid, etc.

Similarly the Madrid regional government has case management systems for calculating benefits paid periodically. The major systems address: benefits for people with handicaps, large families, family support, social assistance fund, Madrid Integration supplement and a computerised non-payer pension system.

In a different task area, the region of Murcia, in conjunction with the Royal Foundation for Prevention and Care of Persons with Disabilities, developed a Windows application for the International Classification of Impairments, Disabilities and Handicaps (**CIDDM**) as part of the social, health and/or educational care it provides for this community of users. Other DOS applications are also used, with a database for analysing accessibility to public buildings in the city of Murcia.

Information systems and managing services

In Spain each autonomous region has reached different levels of development of computerisation of Social Services, depending on resource availability. In the Andalusian Institute of Social Services, IT is used essentially for management of social benefits, allowing for retrieval of quantitative data on beneficiaries and services rendered. It also handles queries on the Social Assistance Fund, Handicapped Social Integration Act, complementary assistance, standard application for assistance, child care centres, homes for the elderly, benefits for large families, subsidised public transportation, etc.

As far as computerised office systems are concerned, the Andalusian Social Services Institute has the normal package of word processors, databases and spreadsheets on its local area network. An electronic mail facility is being installed. Other computer applications implemented include, in the Castile-La Mancha region, the Social Worker Information Subsystem (**SIAS**), intended to expedite access to computerised files to obtain data, profiles and case status reports for a particular area.

Once all the data are collected they are conveyed to the provincial delegations' Integrated Management System (**SINGES**). In regions where social workers are equipped with portable computers, information can be retrieved at any time and place.

SINGES has been operating since 1994; an open system, it includes benefits other than those currently managed by social service authorities in the Castile-La Mancha region. This system entails a higher level of IT application. The point of departure is the INFRES (Social Information, Recording and Appraisal System) basic document. Besides collecting data, a social diagnosis of problems is run and a course of action is proposed to solve them. Social workers have been upgrading their equipment with modems to send Social Worker Information Subsystem information to the Integrated Management System. In addition, they are able to access information on user status such as amount and justification of benefits at any time without moving from wherever they are. This is most convenient when evaluating the social situation of a particular area or providing users with a progress report on their cases.

Regional government of Greater Madrid

The Social Integration Department's section on Information Systems, part of its Research and Appraisals Bureau, reports directly to department authorities and performs the following tasks:

- Design and operation of a Social Services Information System, providing updated data on programmes, customers, resources and demands on a permanent basis.
- Participation in any activity involving the implementation of sub-systems within the Social Services Information System, to ensure that decisions concerning hardware and software are in line with the needs of social service planning and organisation in the region.
- Coordination of activities with local or national level institutions to compare and check criteria and data collection methodologies.
- Providing other units and services with support for the design of their own applications and the selection and formulation of the variables to be processed, as part of the current general information system.

Social care policy

With regard to the use of databases for statistical purposes in resource planning, the system used is the Social Service Users Information System (SIUSS). It is employed as a planning aid to match resources to user demands: since the social records show the demand level citizens make of primary care social services, the actual resources available can be compared to the ideal model. The Provincial Government of Alava has a Social Service User Demand Database for the purpose of producing routine user statistics, as well as specific statistical analyses as required.

CONCLUSION AND FUTURE DEVELOPMENTS

The apparent shift in the application of IT to social services from purely economic benefits to technological aid, entails a gradual increase in the use of IT by social service providers: computers, modems, CD-ROMs. While the use of IT in tele-alarms, elementary education, general information services and service management is developing rapidly, employment and household IT are much less common tools. Incipient development is observed in the implementation of information networks linking centres and services engaging in these activities. Nonetheless, there is some risk that the various regions may develop different information systems to manage the same services and demands. The implementation of Counselling and Information Centres (CAI) - over 50 are operational at this time - is an important development. As noted earlier, these centres, which use Handynet as an information and exchange tool, receive an updated version of the database on CD-ROM every four months.

World Wide Web sites referred to in this chapter

1. Fundesco - activities, access to bibliographic databases and purchase publications.
http://www.fundesco.es/

2. Huelva University (central library links for teachers).
colon.uhu.es/

Author details

Mercedes García-Camino Burgos is Group Coordinator of the ATED. Technological, Job and Handicap Counselling) ATAM-FUNDESCO Group.

Ana María Sánchez Sánchez Salamanca has a degree in Psychology from the Universidad Pontificia and is a member of ATED (ATAM-FUNDESCO) Group.

Clara Suárez de la Llana Madrid has done post-graduate studies on Library Management and Documentation. She has worked with disabled people since 1982 and is a founder member of the ATED ATAM-FUNDESCO Group.

Contact:	Mercedes García-Camino Burgos
	Grupo ATED Plaza de la Independencia
	628001 Madrid
	Spain
Telephone:	+34 1 330 06 00
Fax:	+34 1 330 06 59
E-mail:	mercedes.garcia-camino@fundesco.es

18 United Kingdom

Bryan Glastonbury and Nick Gould

HUMAN SERVICES AND INFORMATION TECHNOLOGY

The Human Service system in the United Kingdom[1] is dominated by public services, having their origins in the formation of the Welfare State in the 1940s. The core objective of the Welfare State was to provide a framework within which the population could live satisfying and productive lives, with a reasonable material standard of living, from birth to death. Hence the major components of the system were measures to promote full employment, education for all, a comprehensive health service, a national sufficiency of affordable housing, and a fund to make payments when a family was not in receipt of income from normal employment. It was recognised in the post second world war years that some people would not be able to cope, even with this level of support, so a further range of services were provided. These were sometimes referred to as 'a safety net' or 'casualty services'. They included payments for adults who had neither employment nor enough contributions to qualify for unemployment benefit, help for homeless people, and welfare services for neglected children, juvenile delinquents, those with physical or learning disabilities, and those who could not care for themselves unaided as a result of chronic illness or old age.

As time has passed the UK's commitment to the Welfare State has loosened to the extent that the label is no longer commonly used. The population has shown a stronger commitment to some elements, such as the National Health Service, but has been prepared to see others, such as public housing, fall by the wayside. A number of reasons have lead to these changes. Economic recessions have dramatically increased the cost of services (such as unemployment benefits), and undermined a welfare

---

[1] Although this chapter is entitled United Kingdom (UK) it primarily concerns England. There are similarities with Wales, Scotland and Northern Ireland, but also differences.

system which was dependent on a stable and flourishing economic environment. The development of some services placed comparable pressure on resources (such as the cost of health care technologies). Political attitudes have also changed. For several decades there was support across the political spectrum for strong public services, but since 1979 the majority Conservative party has favoured a lessening of dependence on public services, an increase in the private sector, and a focus on targeting services to areas of need, rather than making comprehensive provision.

Regardless of changing political attitudes, the human services (more commonly referred to in the UK as *personal social services*) have grown substantially. This relates to a massive growth in identified need, with a range of causes. Sporadic economic recessions have not only impinged directly on levels of unemployment, but have spread more widely to increase, amongst others, social breakdown and deviant behaviour. Demographic changes, especially the increasing proportion of very elderly people, have increased the number of people who cannot live independent lives without the help of health and welfare services. Changes in social attitudes and linked legislation, such as making divorce easier and cheaper, have pushed up the numbers of broken families and children at risk. New areas of need have also been exposed, such as child abuse, without clear knowledge as to whether they represent new forms of pathological behaviour, or enhanced sensitivity towards activities which have always been part of social life.

National policy for the personal social services has gradually developed a clear focus on community care. Starting around the middle of the 19th century the UK built up a substantial level of institutional resources. These included long stay hospitals for people with learning and physical disabilities or mental illness, children's homes, homes (workhouses) for destitute families, prisons for adult offenders, and other institutions for younger offenders. Over the period which started with the 1958 Mental Health Act, this policy of dependence on institutional resources has come under increasingly detailed scrutiny, leading to the view that many thousands of residents could and should return to life in the community. The commitment to community care is a direct outcome of the view that, if at all possible, people should be helped to live normal lives in the community, with institutional care as a measure of last resort. The new Community Care Act came into force in April 1993. Parallel measures relating to children (Children Act 1989) and offenders (Criminal Justice Act 1991) have been implemented, although more recently there has been a sharp reversal to increased use of imprisonment for offenders. Community care is a much more complex system to administer than the relative tidiness of institutional care, and this has placed particular emphasis on the role of IT.

Organisation of services

Organisationally the UK has three central government ministries primarily involved in the personal social services. The Department of Social Security, through a network of local offices, directly administers the social security system, in relation to contributory and non-contributory benefits. The Department of Health oversees the National Health Service and the major personal social services (Social Services Departments), though the former are administered by regional and district health authorities, and the latter by local councils. The Home Office has responsibility for the penal system, including the Probation Service, which also is administered from within the local government framework.

Welfare services developed in a somewhat haphazard fashion in the UK, until it was felt that action needed to be taken to deal with the resulting fragmentation. In 1968 all welfare services in Scotland were brought together into social work departments. In 1971 all welfare services in England and Wales, except for Probation, Hospital Social Work and Educational Welfare, were brought together into social services departments. The Probation Service in England and Wales has remained organisationally separate. In 1974 some remaining social work services which had developed as part of the hospital system were also brought within social services departments. This overall structure remains today. Social work and social services departments are run by local authorities, and vary substantially in size. Strathclyde in Scotland is commonly cited as one of the largest local authorities in Europe, and its social work department as one of the biggest welfare agencies in the world. At the other extreme several London local authorities have populations of around 250,000, and their social services departments are correspondingly small. Generally, however, the UK's social services agencies are large, with widely ranging functions, and this has perhaps enabled them to afford and make better use of information technology opportunities than smaller organisations. To an extent this position may change as a current round of local government reorganisation is implemented. It is expected to lead to the break-up of most of the existing large social services departments and the emergence of 45 new ones.

While the state system remains dominant, there is a growing independent sector, based on voluntary organisations, non-profit organisations, and a small but growing number of private companies. Voluntary organisations have had a traditional role in the UK as pioneers of new methods for meeting needs, many of which have subsequently been taken over by the public sector. Voluntary groups have also taken many of the initiatives towards consumer involvement and empowerment within the welfare system. The private and non-profit sectors have been more concentrated, with a particular focus on sheltered housing and nursing homes for older people, and pre-school child minding. However, under a succession of Conservative governments, the independent sector has taken on a different role, as the contracted providers of services which were previously offered directly by local authorities.

The independent sector is making greater use of information technology, but it is becoming apparent that non-statutory agencies may have different priorities from the statutory services. For instance, for some voluntary organisations their foremost information technology need is for geographical information systems and linked databases which can analyse information on actual and potential financial donors, rather than systems built conventionally around client index systems (for a full discussion see Sparks, 1996).

Information technology infrastructure

The UK has little centralised information technology provision related to the social welfare system. Although the Department of Health (the government agency with overall responsibility for the personal social services) has an information strategy for social services, the emphasis of this is upon the specification of requirements for various statistical collections in relation to areas of policy concern. The Department has not seen it as its role to direct local authorities as to how those requirements should be met. Similarly, the information implications of government policy are regarded as being for social services departments to work out in the context of their own practices. Some local authorities do liaise informally over information technology activities through such groupings as the Association of Directors of Social Services Information Management Group and the Foundation for Information Technology in Local Government (FITLOG).

Various pressures are building on the Department of Health which may lead towards some reconsideration of its previously laisser-faire approach to information technology and information systems. These developments include: the monitoring of community care implementation which shows weaknesses in information systems as a significant factor in preventing good progress; the demonstrated failure of some local authorities to be able to extract the data required for central statistical collections, particularly in relation to children in public care; the methodological problems which social services are experiencing in establishing population-based planning; and not least, the current process of local government reorganisation which is highlighting the problems of disaggregating and amending unwieldy ad hoc systems.

A small but significant indication of change has been the Department's commission of the University of Bath's Social Services Research and Development Unit (SSRADU) to develop a database (LACCS) for local authorities to record information relating to children in their care. LACCS is also able to generate the annual statistical return relating to looked after children, in the electronic format required by central government. It is optional for authorities to adopt this system, but it represents for the first time the availability of a software system developed to a prescribed national standard.

The Probation Service, which is overseen at central level by the Home Office, is moving more proactively towards a national system. This is part of a central government initiative (Coordination of Computerisation in the Criminal Justice System) which aims to make the criminal justice system operate more effectively by improving the flow of information between its constituent organisations. The probation **CRAMS** system, currently being implemented, will provide local probation services with the means to record referral details, monitor progress of individuals through the criminal justice system, and record and analyse outcomes (e.g. patterns of re-offending). CRAMS has been developed as an Oracle database which will be located on a UNIX server at local departmental administrative centres networked to PC terminals in local offices. Implementation is following 'business process re-engineering', i.e. consultancy over a department's information needs and flows before installation of hardware and, finally, staff training. The intensive nature of the planned implementation process means that this is being achieved via a rolling programme for individual probation departments over a period of several years.

There is no national network in the UK for statutory personal social services. There would be both organisational and ethical obstacles to be overcome, should such national networks be proposed. Many agencies have local networks, connecting central to local offices, and some are part of a wider local authority network. Inter-agency networking is rare, except in the voluntary sector. Similarly there is no national database for welfare services, though databases exist within agencies. **Volnet** is an on-line database about voluntary services, accessible on payment of a subscription fee. The Internet hovers over this scene as an enormous opportunity. Some developments have taken place, such as a number of relevant discussion and information networks, but any major shift of social services agencies towards Internet usage has still to take place.

Professional staff in the personal social services in the UK have traditionally looked upon themselves as poorly supported in terms of office infrastructures. There is a widespread view of the insufficiency of such areas as clerical service, telephone lines and aids to increased efficiency. Electric typewriters were introduced many years after they were commonplace in other sectors of the economy. Many offices still do not have dictaphones or other aids to record keeping. Telephone lines are often shared. Given this tradition it is no surprise that UK social services agencies are not in the forefront of office automation. Word processing is common, though often with old or obsolete equipment (such as dot matrix printers). Office networks are growing slowly. Just a few agencies (eg. Hampshire Social Services Department) have substantial multi-purpose networking and computer systems. Many agencies are now working quickly to develop integrated financial information systems in order to be in a position to respond to the much greater emphasis the central government is now placing on service costing and purchasing.

Ethical and legal framework

The UK has made two legislative moves in recent years which relate to personal data, such as client information systems. One is in the area of data protection, where attempts are being made to improve the security of personal data, and limit the extent of authorised access. Traditionally in this country information given to a social worker was likely to be considered totally confidential, known only to the social worker who received the information plus one or two immediate colleagues.

Since computerisation, and since agencies have grown much larger, such privacy is no longer available, given the big increase in the number of those with authorised access to client records. Hence formal data protection activities are likely to have a limited impact for the clients of the personal social services. The second legislative area concerns client access to files. Most clients of social services departments now have a statutory right of access to view their files. In practice very few clients have taken up this opportunity, and most agencies have declined to make or advertise easy routes for such access. A few have instituted deterrents, such as long waits or a fee. Given the long tradition of treating client records as the private material of the agency, it follows that the use of these records has been limited to their serving as a backup for the professional counsellor or service provider.

There has been considerable public debate in the UK about ethical issues surrounding the use of IT. The traditional area for such debates has been around the notion of confidentiality, but in recent years it has extended to include debate about equal opportunities and discrimination, and the role of computers in aiding or inhibiting consumer empowerment. For a full discussion of these issues see Glastonbury and LaMendola, 1992.

INFORMATION FOR CITIZENS

There are a number of national information systems accessible through public media (eg. teletext), but except for disability networks these rarely have material of specific relevance to the human services. Generally networking has made little progress within the human services area. Some local libraries, community centres and citizens advice bureaux are networked to information sources, but despite the wide use of home computers, few of these are linked to networks. Later sections mention a number of computer programs which are directly accessible by consumers, and are used by them.

The ones most widely in use relate to welfare benefits calculations. Ferret Information Systems[1], in addition to Maximiser, has several more specific calculation programs, and these are available on a low-cost hand-held computer as well as a PC. The authors know of no decision support systems made directly available to the public. Any individual can, of course, buy those that are openly marketed. A voluntary organisation, Citizens' Advice Bureaux, is increasingly using computerised data sources for its advice and information service to members of the public.

Probably the nearest to a publicly accessible national databank in the general area of human services in Britain is Volnet, which offers information about voluntary services. National databanks do exist in the statutory service sector (eg. in social security), but not for public access. Nevertheless, some movement can be anticipated in the area of public access information as part of the process of implementing commitments to information provision given by the Government in a range of citizens charters.

In the future the most significant medium for public access information may be the Internet, as more groups and individuals come to have access to modem links and graphical browsers. There is a problem with the transience of sites on the Web, but the availability of browser software is complemented by the appearance of directories dedicated to human services interests. An example is the **People's Internet Directory** (e-mail *pid@ cosmos-uk.org*), which is produced from London and currently lists approximately 250 mail-lists, news groups and World Wide Web addresses which are relevant to human service workers and service users.

Information for service providers

Many social services agencies have computerised databases of their own service resources and those of other agencies in their locality, often integrated with the broader information system. The Department of Health, largely in the context of seeking to offer nationally valid sets of performance indicators, is gradually expanding a computerised framework for annual agency reporting, and the Office of Population and Census Studies (OPCS) offers comprehensive and detailed demographic data which is used widely in the human services.

Many agencies use this demographic material to build up computerised profiles for their areas of specific situations which might imply a social need (such as the numbers of single parent households, or those living in properties lacking basic facilities). Some also use OPCS population projections to identify and plan for future services. This approach has been encouraged by the Department of Health's Economics and Operations Research Division which has taken forward workshops with social services and voluntary sector representatives to disseminate good practice in relation to population needs assessment. Examples include SSRADU's **Resource Allocation Decision Support System**, and **Balance of Care** from the private consultancy, Secta.

Training support

In the specific context of social worker clients, the main developments of training supports have been individual ventures, mostly in probation. David Colombi, for example, has written programs, **Drugs**, **Alcohol** and **Driver**, with training potential, the first two offering information about drugs and alcohol respectively and the impact of their use and the third a guide to the link between self-assessed aggressiveness/fearfulness and careful car driving. Such developments have been limited, a major impediment being the lack of equipment for direct client access. There is no tradition and little sign of future plans to allow social work clients to use agency computers. In a broader context there are central government ventures to retrain unemployed people, and/or offer useful training to school leavers who have been unable to find a first job. Motivation for these comes in part from changes in employment skills resulting from the technology revolution, and hence a common subject of training is new technology and its uses in specific industrial or other employment sectors. However, the main motivation since the mid 1980s has been economic recession and the high numbers of people out of work. European Social Fund grants have been used in this area.

For many years there has been sporadic criticism of the education system (schools and higher education) for not adapting curricula and courses quickly or sufficiently thoroughly to meet the changing needs of the technology revolution, and the new skills in demand in many forms of employment. In addition to general exhortation and pressure to improve matters, a more specific development starting from the late 1980s is the opening of a number of dedicated technology colleges with a mix of public and private funding.

Supported work for people with disabilities

In the UK there is a system of registration for disabled people, and special provisions are made both during the normal age span for education and, subsequently, in relation to employment. There is a national framework of Disablement Resettlement Officers (DROs). Within this context grants are available to enable disabled people to purchase and use adaptive technologies. Several more specialised grant aiding bodies (eg. CCETSW) will fund technology aids to help overcome any disadvantages which a person with a disability might have in education.

The design and production of adaptive technology and linked software is extensive and diverse, and a full description is beyond the scope of this overview. However, there are a number of contact points for detailed information. The British Computer Society (13 Mansfield Street, London, W1) has a Specialist Group for the Disabled. In the area of employment there is the Computability Centre at Warwick; SKILL provides campus access information; ENTER aids students wishing to find out about the provision of technology aids to study at higher education institutions; ACCESS Centres in a number of colleges offer individual assessment; and there is a National Council for Educational Technology. These are not the only organisations, but can serve as starting points. The Disabled Living Foundation can serve a similar role with regard to adult disability.

VOCATIONAL EDUCATION AND TRAINING

In 1989 the Computer Board for Universities and Research Councils established a number of centres under its Computers in Teaching Initiative (CTI). The aim of each Centre is to promote the use of computer applications and computer aided learning within its subject area in higher education. The CTI Centre for Human Services[2] is based at the Department of Social Work Studies in the University of Southampton, and produces the journal *New Technology in the Human Services*. CTI Human Services has, since 1995, an additional responsibility to promote awareness of equal opportunities issues across all CTI subject areas. Conventional short training courses, with 'hands-on' experience, are widely available in welfare agencies to train staff in the use of computer applications. For the most part these courses are specifically related to the agency's own computer uses, and are only available for the agency's own staff, as part of in-service training activities. Computer or new technology based teaching/learning in relation to the personal social services has made limited progress in the UK. The Central Council for Education and Training in Social Work (CCETSW) jointly with John Hall (Video Consultancy Service) have developed interactive video disk applications in the area of social care. A few agencies are using computer-based courses to teach office automation (such as word processing).

Computer aided learning

Some educational institutions are currently developing computer-based curriculum material for social services students. In a few instances (eg. Maximiser at the University of Southampton) a well established computer program has been used within the framework of a training course (a monitored comparison of the effect of teaching welfare benefits by conventional means or with the use of Maximiser is reported in *New Technology in the Human Services*, Vol.5 No.3). The Social Work Training Council (CCETSW) has published *Unlocking Care Management,* developed by SSRADU, and joined with the Universities of Southampton and Cardiff in publishing *Social Work and IT*. This is the Council's first venture into software publishing. *Unlocking Care Management* consists of a working version of a relational database with various care management functions such as needs assessment, care planning, financial management, and a resource database. A series of case studies which can be loaded from floppy disk enable students to learn core care management skills whilst also developing an appreciation of information technology applications in social work. *Social Work and IT* is a computer-based set of materials designed to be taught/learned in a practical context, and give students an understanding of the growing role of information technology in the personal social services.

In 1993 the Higher Education Funding Council (HEFC) started a Teaching and Learning Technology Programme (TLTP) to develop courseware in a range of subject areas. The ProCare project is one of the TLTP projects, and has launched a computer-assisted set of courseware on interpersonal skills, and during 1996 will launch courseware on research methods. Possibly more significant in the long run is the increasing recognition of the link between open learning and technology assisted learning. The Open University and Open Learning Foundation both have a strong focus on learning materials in health and welfare, and are planning the greater utilisation of technology.

Human service research

The main national funders of human service research are the Economic and Social Research Council (ESRC) and Medical Research Council (MRC), both of which focus on basic research linked to universities, the Department of Health (health and social services) and Regional Health Authorities, the Home Office (offenders), and a number of foundations. All have funded research involving IT though none have given it a high profile or identified it as a specific theme. However, in the broader context of developmental work, a significant initiative has come from the National Health Service Executive Information Management Group (NHS IMG). While the main focus is on health research and development, two projects closely impinge on the social services: the projected extension of terms development (the Reed thesaurus and codes) into the social services arena, and the emphasis on shared information between health and social services, as for instance in the 1996 Community Focused Healthcare project. Many local agencies have research officers or small research teams, mostly working on short term projects closely related to agency developments.

PROVISION OF SERVICES

Benefits calculations systems

From the point of view of IT the most interesting developments in the social security area arise from the calculation of eligibility for benefits which are not universally available, but are based on the establishment of eligibility criteria, and may be subject to discretionary interpretation. As the government of the UK has moved more towards a preference for targeting benefits where there is need, so the range and complexity of such benefits has increased. The perceived tasks for the computer programs are:

- To check whether the potential applicant for benefits has the needs which establish eligibility.
- To ascertain (means test) whether the applicant has a sufficiently low level of income and resources to warrant state provision.
- To assess which of the total range of benefits are appropriate to the type of needs and the level of income and resources shown by the applicant.
- To advise on the type, amount and frequency of payment for all benefits for which the applicant is eligible.

A number of microcomputer (PC) programs operate in this field, and have achieved considerable success. Two are in widespread use, Maximiser (from Ferret Information Systems) and the Lisson Grove Benefits Program. Maximiser is part of a suite of linked programs in the field of benefits calculation and associated activity (eg. the relationship between levels of earning from employment and benefits eligibility). Each program works by asking questions about the applicant's circumstances, and then, on the basis of the information received, goes on to ask further questions or provide a calculation of benefits eligibility.

In principle, each of these programs can be used directly by a potential applicant or with the help of a service professional. All have a *Help* facility, to explain the eligibility criteria, the legal framework, and the process of calculation for each benefit under consideration. These programs are sophisticated, accurate, updated very fast to relate to changes in the benefit system, and subject to continuous development. They are exemplars of excellent PC applications in the personal social services. The Department of Social Security has itself shown considerable interest in computerised calculation programs. It has a process of computerising the calculation system in all local offices, though based on staff rather than applicants using the system. The commercial products mentioned in previous paragraphs are used in social security offices, and increasingly in social services departments.

Client information systems

Computerised client information systems are widely used in social services and probation agencies. They are commonly generic in nature, and usable for a range of functions in addition to the provision of information (such as assessment, treatment and evaluation). Information systems are highly developed in the UK social services, and form the core of most agency IT systems. Broadly speaking the first of these had a framework comparable to the essential features of a statistical or survey analysis package. That is, data could be entered for a number of subjects (clients), and the database could then be analysed to produce composite descriptive statistics. The data was normally in coded form, and the calculations were usually used to provide annual figures about the overall activity of the agency, such as the number of clients in each category, the numbers receiving a particular service, and so forth. Generally they could only function on a batch system (ie. they were not on-line), and some computing skills were needed to make use of them. They were not user friendly and were not used for interrogations relating to individual clients. In effect they were management information systems about clients.

Subsequent developments saw the expansion of these management information systems into genuine client information systems. Substantial improvements were made to presentation, accessibility and user friendliness. Coding was largely dropped. Fast on-line interrogations became possible. Terminal extensions to local offices opened up access to a much wider range and number of agency staff. Coverage increased from, perhaps, one or two screens of material on each client in the early systems, to up to sixty screens of material on each client. Flexibility for data entry and editing was much improved. Scope to use free text became much more widespread. In short, over the last decade, client information systems have moved from being computerised card indexes through to the point where, currently, they are close to being the equivalent of full client records. This trend will undoubtedly continue in the 1990s, though many, certainly the smaller ones and probably a majority, will opt to retain their traditional approach to case files alongside computerised developments.

In the absence of an up-to-date survey of social services departments, the extent and form of computerised information systems have to be inferred from anecdotal and secondary sources. These do suggest that such systems are now universal, although they vary between quite rudimentary in-house systems, and comprehensive integrated systems. Rapid developments in the capabilities of processors and general PC technology are changing the hardware configuration in agencies. The trend is from applications running on a mainframe computer and accessed from locally situated dumb terminals, towards wide and local area networks of PCs connected to a corporate server. Some networks are potentially large, as for example in Hampshire, but current local government reorganisation is reducing the size of these very large local agencies (for example, Hampshire Social Services Department has around 7,000 staff, but is being divided into three agencies) and may weaken the development initiative they have shown in the field of information technology.

Perhaps the most important single feature of the last decade has been the transition from a system which was primarily used for composite analysis (such as annual statistical returns), to a system which is now primarily used for the interrogation of individual client files. Scope for composite analysis has not been lost: indeed, it has been enlarged, to allow for more sophistication in the analysis, particularly related to service costs. Nevertheless, the switch in usage has tended to move the spotlight away from the quality of composite output towards the quality of individual records. Some problems have been experienced during these developments. The initial formation of the database and its subsequent maintenance represents a large workload. On each occasion that the program is improved and expanded there is the additional task of preparing existing material for transfer, and entering the new material which is to be stored. There is little evidence that computerisation will reduce the cost of record keeping, though it will lead to records which are more substantial and more flexible in their use.

Problems of error and topicality have come to the forefront. When the computerised system was used primarily for composite analysis, errors in individual entries could be and were tolerated, on the grounds that they would cancel each other out. Once the database starts to be used extensively for the interrogation of individual records, then the accuracy of those records becomes significantly more important. While accuracy of data entry must be viewed as the vital need here, there is some evidence that inaccuracies can creep in through minor program malfunctions. Topicality is similarly important, not only in the sense that each individual record must be up to date, but also in the sense that the database must be cleared of material which is no longer needed - quite literally, at times, of clients who have died! The work of Colin Barnes in Coventry Social Services Department offers a lead in these areas.

There is evidence that social workers and other professional service staff have often become disenchanted with the computerised client information system when they have been able to spot inaccuracies and out of date material. In part this is because there are much higher expectations of the accuracy of computer files than were ever established in relation to paper files (many UK paper files would fail miserably on any test for accuracy or comprehensiveness!). In part, however, accuracy and topicality have been found to be related to the attitude and behaviour of professional staff themselves. In the UK system they are the initiators of the data which goes into client information systems, and they have the power to ensure that it is correct, up to date and relevant.

Another problem from the UK experience has been that of access to terminals. Social workers often need to review client material at short notice, and they need immediate access to a terminal. Despite the rapid and substantial fall in prices, the hardware cost of giving professional staff good access to computer systems is substantial, though there are moves to provide laptop equipment. Training is a further issue. It is clear that any client information system that is to be well used should be introduced through extensive initial training, and diligent follow-up courses. Also, in agencies where professional staff have been involved from the start in discussions about the design, content and use of the system, it has been much more easily accepted and used. The context for these observations is that there is professional resistance to the use of computers, and measures must be taken to overcome it.

Discussion in this section so far has been in general terms about client information systems in social services departments. As noted above, there is no national system, so many in use are customised to meet the particular needs and procedures of individual agencies. This produces considerable complexity for maintenance once an agency customises its system beyond a point where any upgrade or enhancement from the supplier can be straightforwardly implemented. Nevertheless, a recent informal survey of English social services departments by one of the authors indicated a trend towards commercial 'big bang' solutions, though with a very mixed pattern of implementation. No individual commercial supplier dominates the field. Three applications warrant specific mention.

The first is ICL's **Social Services Information System** which utilises the ADABAS post-relational database management system and runs either on a corporate server or under the UNIX operating system. Its functionality includes a client index system, resource directories, needs assessment, care planning, financial assessment and management, all available at different levels of access. Second is Sheridan's **Social Services Information Database,** which is built around the Oracle fourth generation relational database and which again offers a comprehensive information system covering not only care and resource management, but also personnel and financial management. Again, this can run under a UNIX or corporate server. Thirdly, OLM Systems Ltd. supplies over twenty social services departments with its modular **Client Resource Management System**, which is also developed in Oracle.

Referral and assessment systems

The perceived initial IT need was to develop a system which gave the agency material about its clientele, their needs, and the services being offered to them. The data for each client file was primarily obtained at the point of assessment, and for that reason it has become commonplace for agencies to have structured assessment forms which can be transferred later to the computer system. While the assessment process was modified to aid the development of the information system, computer aided assessment did not initially develop beyond a small number of localised experiments (Client Questionnaire, DAESy, Driver). These and other programs mentioned later are described in the Resource Guide which is published as Volume 8, Number 4 of *New Technology in the Human Services*.

Recently the government developed the notion of a 'right to assessment' in the context of its community care plans, and both private companies and social services agencies are developing computerised assessment modules in this area. Many of these applications link assessment potential to the development and computerised costing of care packages (eg. Hampshire's Assessment and Care Management). They also make it possible to monitor how far the services being provided are meeting the objectives set out in the treatment plan. Such monitoring is available both at the level of the individual client, and more globally in relation to client groups or blocks of service provision.

Service provision systems

Except for benefits calculation programs, no decision support system has been put into widespread use, but there has been considerable development in this area of computer applications, particularly in relation to child protection. Britain has experienced a sequence of tragedies in which children in the care of a local authority have been killed, and subsequent reports have criticised the performance of social workers and other service staff involved with these cases. These events have focused concern on well informed decision making in child protection, especially relating to child abuse, which in turn has promoted computerised aids. SSRADU's **Child Care Information System (CCIS)** is licensed to approximately sixty social work agencies. This is a modular Windows-based system comprising: a database of child protection research with a facility for matching details of an individual case to relevant research findings; a database of signs and symptoms of child abuse with point and click body maps; and legal summaries of and commentary on child care and youth justice legislation. There are others in less widespread use, though none (CCIS included) would claim to be expert systems as narrowly understood within the domains of cognitive science and artificial intelligence. Rather, they are support and reference systems to bring research and legal knowledge closer to professional decision-making.

Individually based computerised decision support in such high profile areas as child protection may not come into use until professional social work attitudes towards the role of computers changes. There have, however, been a few developments in other areas, such as life planning for people with learning difficulties. There are some experiments in counselling support systems which are not based on client information (eg. **CARM, Balance** from Fred Yates). These are, in principle, usable both by a counsellor or by client for self-counselling. They also have potential educational uses.

CONCLUSION AND FUTURE DEVELOPMENTS

A careful scrutiny of recent developments suggests seven trends which should achieve growing importance during the remainder of this century:

- The use of small portable equipment to aid assessment for and delivery of personal social services, especially in those sectors where home visiting is a standard working pattern.
- The final establishment of computer files as the main client records, with documents largely serving archive purposes. Several factors are pushing in this direction in addition to improved technical capability, such as freedom of access to personal records, and pressures for greater staff productivity. At the same time we can expect to see a growing integration of systems linking clients records to contact data, assessments, records of advice, information and services provided, service costs, evaluation and quality monitoring, and case review.
- Inter-agency networking to overcome communication blocks between agencies serving comparable purposes in different geographical areas, and different agencies serving the same community. Growing links between health and social services can be expected (noticeably in developing community care services), and between probation, the courts and (more controversially) the police.
- Technology based learning, brought about partly by pressure to make more productive use of teaching staff rather than multi media developments.
- Clarification of quality standards and rules of conduct for the use of IT both at a general level and specifically to the human services. This is instanced by the significant increase in presentations addressing ethical issues at the HUSITA 3 Conference, a continuing trend at HUSITA 4 in Finland in 1996.
- The extension of smart systems, such as is already provided by Tunstall's PiperNet, which combine home alarm systems coordinated through a central control point with IT based service planning and monitoring.
- The rapid growth in the use of the Internet for a range of purposes: to replace or supplement existing in-house networks, to enable cross-agency communication (currently an area of serious weakness), to open up access to a new range of information, and to promote more extensive communication between agencies and user groups.

References

Glastonbury B and LaMendola W. *The Integrity of Intelligence: A Bill of Rights for the Information Age.* Macmillan. 1992

Sparks I. IT in the Voluntary Sector. In: Kerslake A and Gould N (Eds). *Information Management in Social Services.* Aldershot: Avebury. 1996

World Wide Web sites referred to in this chapter

1. Ferret Information Systems - Maximiser and other welfare benefits programs.
http://www.ferret.co.uk/index.html

2. CTI Centre for Human Services, Department of Social Work Studies, University of Southampton.
http://www.soton.ac.uk/~chst/

Author details

Professor Bryan Glastonbury is Research Professor at the University of Southampton and Director of the Centre for Human Service Technology. He is a former chair of ENITH and has been involved in organising three of the HUSITA conferences. He has published extensively on the use of information technology in human services

Dr. Nick Gould is a senior lecturer at the University of Bath and Deputy Director of the Social Services Research and Development Unit at the University of Bath. As well as undertaking consultancy to central and local governments, he has researched and published in the fields of professional education, social work with children and information management.

Contact: Professor Bryan Glastonbury
Centre for Human Service Technology
University of Southampton
Southampton SO17 1BJ
UK

Tel: + 44 1703 593536
Fax: + 44 1703 592779
E-mail: bryan@chst.soton.ac.uk

19 Rhythms of the future

Jan Steyaert, David Colombi and Jackie Rafferty

A MULTI-LAYERED ANALYSIS

This book provides a snapshot of the current use of information technology in human services across the world. It is a valuable snapshot that can contribute to societal learning. We can all learn from the experiences of other countries, either positive or negative, thus sharing ideas, allowing new ideas to germinate and safeguarding against possible failures. Fortuitously, this is not the only value of this book. It is a sequel to two previous overviews in the same subject area, even if those did not cover the same countries. This publication thus becomes part of a successive comparative survey, allowing a multi-layered analysis of the application of IT in human services.

The first of these surveys (Qvortrup, Glastonbury, De Graaf, 1992) was conducted in 1991 and covered nine European countries and established the basic framework for the surveys. It also provides the baseline for the comparative analysis over time. The second survey (Colombi, Rafferty, Steyaert, 1993) was undertaken in 1993 and covered fourteen European countries. It modified the earlier framework but broadened the scope by including more countries and topics. The present publication, based on information brought together in early 1996, covers seventeen countries - not only European but other Western and also non-Western countries. The wealth of information in these three surveys allows us to conclude this book with three different analyses. Firstly, we draw out themes, highlight significant initiatives, and pinpoint areas of concern across countries. Secondly, we compare the current nature and level of applications with the dreams of yesteryear and with the dreams of tomorrow. Thirdly, we analyse the available information in terms of shifting paradigms.

The report from Micronesia describes a social work conference in Guam in 1995. The conference was entitled *The Rhythms of our Ancestors* and this provided us with the idea for the title of this final chapter. At the start of this book, *Setting the Scene* laid down the rhythmic framework for the separate melodies from each country's report.

This chapter attempts to weave together both the rhythms and those melodies into a coherent orchestration of how the music now sounds and provides a glimpse into *the rhythms of the future*. We cannot provide a definitive analysis and the editors are aware that there are large areas of the world not covered. Nevertheless the seventeen reports provide a broader picture than previously existed. This breadth allows us to draw some conclusions on the state of the art of integrating information technology into the human services. The authors in each country do not claim complete coverage but have succeeded in the task of providing an overview of a complex range of activities.

DIVERSITIES AND COMMONALITIES

This section looks at themes identified in the different country reports under the headings of:

- Political and social diversity
- Cultural and ethical issues
- Integration of technology into civic and public life
- Embeddedness of technology supported services

Political and social diversity

There are some macro factors to consider when discussing how technology supports the human services. Whether or not a country is cohesive in terms of geography, population and politics defines the technological and social policy priorities. Societies organise themselves according to their political, demographic and historical make up. The Western societies conform to a macro model though there are major differences in how the model is delivered. For instance the USA relies heavily on insurance systems for the majority of its population, with a weaker net of services for those unable to afford insurance. Sickness and unemployment benefits follow the employment insurance model in many Western European countries.

Sophisticated systems have been developed to check rights and entitlement to services. Many such systems are in the throes of adjustment as countries undergo major shifts in policy, with consequences for the information technology systems that support these services. Even those countries with the strongest commitment to state provided welfare services are loosening their grip and diversifying their funding base. Denmark, Finland, UK, the Netherlands, USA and others are all reassessing how much they should keep of their safety net of services, how much should be further privatised, contracted to the voluntary or informal sector or become the concern of the individual and their family. Even within state and locally funded services, separation is occurring between purchasers and providers of service provision. Issues of quality and effectiveness of services come to the fore creating further challenges for information technology in terms of monitoring and supporting the role of care managers.

Within the above context the drive for the implementation of information technology is effectiveness, efficiency and cost cutting. The encouraging fact is that innovation and progress in information technology applications to support service providers and their service users is still taking place despite funding pressures. These societal adjustments appear relatively minor in the light of the examples of Romania and Russia who are in the midst of moving from one political regime to another and are just at the start of rebuilding social welfare policies and services. It will be interesting to see with all the technology transfer that is taking place between East and West, which societies avoid some of the technology traps that have befallen others.

Cultural and ethical Issues

Besides the obvious language issues which apply to any transnational initiative, the values and practice base of human services has to be sensitive to local culture and norms. Micronesia provides an extreme example where 220 islands each have their own culture and language. The UK report also highlights this issue: 'although the chapter is entitled the UK, it primarily concerns England. There are similarities with Wales, Scotland and Northern Ireland, but also differences.' The differences relate to legislation, practice guidance and local priorities, customs, context and history.

Synonymous with ethics and human service information technology is the question of data protection. Most countries have some form of data protection legislation in place but there are widespread concerns that the legislation will not ensure that the confidentiality ethos of the human services remains intact. Lindstrøm writes of Denmark: 'Confidentiality in public services might appear to be lost in a society where information floats freely'. He is concerned that regulations about who has access to what information is not covered by existing legislation and he proposes the need for ethical rules. This view is shared by Glastonbury and LaMendola (1992) who call for 'A Bill of Rights' covering personal data. Finland is currently pursuing this issue within the preparation of a law on customer's rights in social services. Belgium on the other hand enshrined the following in its March 1993 Regulation: 'Prohibition on data exchange between different databanks and on transnational exchange of data. The government can make exceptions'. There are tensions between protecting the privacy rights of individuals and using personal data for monitoring, social policy and research purposes, as outlined by Van Hove (1996).

Data protection is one aspect of an ethically based IT society. Some countries extend the debate to include issues around equity and discrimination, often worded in terms of disability but which also might include gender and race. More broadly still the UK report includes the need for debate about 'the role of computers in aiding or inhibiting consumer empowerment'. The differences across the world also need to be restated again and again. This book was made possible because of e-mail communication and file transfer between authors and the editors. In the midst of this process it is easy to forget that for much of the world a dependable telephone line is a luxury, let alone, faxes, electronic mail and other technology.

This section ends on an uncomfortable note for human service professionals who see secure employment as an essential factor of a stable lifestyle. Canada provides an example of the type of information technology solution which poses ethical dilemmas. In 1995 the Canadian government closed 150 offices, with the loss of 5,000 jobs, which were replaced by 400 electronic kiosks and self-service terminals.

Integration of information technology into civic and public life

The most marked difference since the Europe wide survey (Colombi, Rafferty, Steyaert, 1993) is the increased use of networked computers for communication and information gathering. This growth has impacted on all levels of the human services, including the service users and the general population. North America led the way with its cable telephone infrastructure in the development of bulletin boards (BBS). The World Wide Web may overtake or transform bulletin boards but they remain an area where IT has been used extensively, particularly within the self-help and advocacy movements. 'BBSs and the Internet are used for self-help conferences and providing consumer information. Local BBSs, available in almost every city, offer self-help conferences on addictions, mental health, and disabilities' (USA report).

Other countries are progressing rapidly with developing the use of the Internet and the World Wide Web. New 'digital cities' are regularly announced; for instance there are now ten digital cities in the Netherlands. Their goal is to use the Internet to strengthen relationships between government and citizens and between citizens. Denmark, Japan and Finland all have strategies for an 'Information Society'. The Danes intend to connect people and organisations through an electronic net on a model which builds on a value base of openness, democracy and responsibility for the weakest. The Ministry in Belgium has plans for more human service information to be accessible. Ireland opened *Ireland on Line* (IOL) in 1992. Japan provides 'information pillars' in convenience stores on child welfare information, etc.

There is often discussion of the rich-poor, North-South divide in terms of the use of technology. In Micronesia the island of Yap has a traditional lifestyle but the doctor has an Internet connection. This connection is at present extremely slow (300 baud modem) and relies on temperamental links through Hawaii. Romania, which is only at the beginning of developing IT for the human services, has had developments using the Internet, telephone and television since 1993 and now all universities and some agencies are linked. The Internet and the WWW may just be the platform which finally makes the notion of a 'global village' a reality.

Disability

Most reports talk about a range of technology related projects which aim to support people with disabilities. Germany, Greece, Finland and Spain in particular detail projects to support people with disabilities in terms of independent living, employment related initiatives and individual support. The technology is improving rapidly and disabled people are now able to employ very sophisticated systems to match their needs. European wide projects such as **Handynet** show the range of aids available. It is clear however, from the reports, that it is as vital to have effective processes in place to enable disabled people to find and afford the most appropriate support technology.

Embeddedness of technology supported services - Education

The *Setting the Scene* chapter laid out the potential and the problems of educational technology in human service education. The reports reflect more on the problems than actualising the potential. The Internet has made an impact on teaching and learning from the perspective of accessing e-mail and on-line databases.

The UK is moving rapidly into the arena of both Internet use and computer assisted learning (CAL) for the social work curricula. The Netherlands have been developing CAL for some time however they have now also moved into teaching about the process of using information (social informatics).

Canada reports on experiments in distance education: ‘The expansion of distance education seems focused on programmes with a higher job potential such as business, education, nursing and social work. Several use the Internet or conferencing software’. The Canadians also report that computer assisted learning materials seem to be more common among distance education projects. Normally competitive universities are co-operating in working on information technology-based distance education but that cost is still an inhibiting factor.

Other reports show there has been little movement in using educational technology with students being taught word-processing and computerised statistical analyses with some developments around the teaching of the ethical and data protection elements of using technology in practice. Israel has a more sophisticated strategy which has two ‘schools of thought’. In one the teaching is technologically oriented, teaching systems theory, decision theory and organisational theory; the second approach reviews major trends in information systems in social work and teaches evaluation and implementation strategies. Again Romania, by starting afresh has avoided problems like finding space on the timetable and has embedded an informatics course of one semester in their four year university qualifying courses. But as there is so little social work software the concentration is on generic tools. Spain reports that they used to have IT in the curricula but a restructuring of the curriculum dropped the IT component on the basis that basic IT literacy skills should be acquired independently.

In many countries the focus is still very much on teaching about IT rather than teaching about the use of IT in social work practice or using educational technology to teach the rest of the curriculum. It is possible to note differences which relate to whether there have been national initiatives in the use of educational technology as in the UK and the Netherlands. Different strategies can also be noted which depend upon the size of the country; the imperative for developing technology-based distance education for instance is greater when the country covers a huge land mass as in the case of Canada.

There are national networks in some countries of teachers interested in the use of information technology in human service teaching and ENITH provides a wider network for discussion on these issues. Given the cross fertilisation possible through these networks it is difficult to accept that social work education still falls so far behind other academic disciplines such as medicine in the use of the technology. Partly it is a question of the differential funding for disciplines but partly the difficulties teachers have of adjusting to the new potential. The future must hold more substantial changes which may be student and/or management driven.

Embeddedness of technology supported services - Practice

A common feature of the reports is the reliance on information technology to deliver financial benefits. Nearly all countries have large IT systems in place to deal with unemployment, sickness and pension payment administration. The arguments for identity numbers held on nationwide registers of populations has led to ethical debates about confidentiality. Arguments for greater security and perceived increases in efficiency are set against concerns about potential loss of confidentiality and threats to individual rights. For many countries the debate is history: Israel, Denmark, Japan, Belgium, the Netherlands and Finland are examples of countries with such registers and a person's identity number is a requirement for a wide range of services.

Apart from the use of IT for managing financial benefits the picture is much more diverse depending upon the autonomy of service providers at the regional and local level. Few countries provide locally run services with nationally developed IT systems. The common factor across a country is often the regional and/or national statistical reporting requirements. How individual services collect and analyse the required data is usually the responsibility of the particular service organisation. This, together with a lack of coordination across agencies, has meant the development of different information systems which are not compatible.

As issues of accountability, efficiency and effectiveness measures are prioritised alongside the idea of seamless services, so countries are tackling the large issue of data standardisation. Canada has already developed common data standards and quality assurance strategies, Finland and the UK for instance are just at the beginning of this process. Each report shows that the computer has arrived in terms of the administration of services, word-processing, databases, and spreadsheets. Most have implemented some form of client information system, a few have gone on to develop client information systems into case management systems. Canada has an example of a case management system in the field of community care for people with mental impairments. The project in Canada called **Accès-Di** began in 1989 and is still being tested: 'it seeks to both coordinate interventions among professionals and across services and facilitate the active participation of the clients themselves (or their representatives) in the decision making process'. There are other projects of this type in the reports, most of which are still under development and it will be sometime before they can be fully evaluated. However, they do show that it is possible to progress projects which aim to meet the needs of managers, practitioners and service users.

Information and Referral (I & R) systems, known in Belgium as 'social maps' have become common tools to support practitioners. Yet Schoech suggests that the North American software allows an unsophisticated I & R specialist to perform better but does not help the sophisticated specialist who requires more information than the systems can deliver. Although some developments in decision support software have been undertaken (see Israel's Juvenile Probation Service) there are few examples of note, most being experimental or in the early stages.

In terms of client information and quality assurance one initiative is the country-wide information systems for social work departments in general hospitals in Israel. Their use is qualified: 'While these forms were intended to replace all existing case records, their adoption for that purpose is limited. Total integration involves a more advanced and comprehensive use of information technology and a higher ratio of computers to social workers, which goes well beyond the aims of the project' (Israel report citing Steyaert, 1994). The drive for effectiveness and efficiency mentioned earlier have led to a substantial investment in social policy technology tools. Finland, for instance, with international projects supported by European Union funding, has developed **Evergreen** 'which includes the whole continuum of care for the elderly in the welfare and health sectors....making possible socio-economic monitoring and evaluation of the care system' (Finland Report).

Overall the applications described in the country reports are more sophisticated, easier to use than their older DOS counterparts, and they attempt to cover more of the service process, There are still barriers to full implementation and integration. The context in which they are used keeps moving, both in terms of changing policies and changing technology. It is easier to obtain funding for developing applications than it is to properly fund and support its implementation, maintenance and updating.

DREAMS AND REALITIES

The second layer of our three-tier analysis takes as its primary source the final section from each country report where the author(s) seek to identify future trends and developments. The aim therefore is to synthesise and summarise these views as a collective vision of possible future scenarios. There are notorious difficulties in 'future watching' even a few years ahead in such a rapidly changing arena as information technology. It is therefore salutary to set such an analysis in the context of examination of some earlier attempts to gauge the future. Our aim is first to ask how yesterday's dreams compares with today's realities and where and why they differ, in order to then cautiously anticipate how today's dreams might be realised.

Yesterday's dreams

Unlike many dreams that fade into elusive chimera as we wake, yesterday's dreams of the potential of IT are available to us in the literature. Some predictions were accurate but others over or under estimated the pace of change, were simply wrong or failed to identify the significance of particular developments. There is no shortage of material and it is all too tempting to selectively choose in order to ridicule and amuse. That perhaps is a good starting point. What happened to the prediction that television would fail as the average USA family is 'too busy to watch it'. There was also the business report at the end of World War II that predicted a future demand for only six computers for the USA and only three computers for the UK. More recently we had the prediction in 1993 of Personal Digital Assistants quickly becoming the essential tool of nurses, doctors and other health care professionals, all linked by infra-red sensors to a central hospital computer. In the latter case, prediction was also commercial hype to create that future, but the endless capacity of large companies to get it wrong is perhaps reassuring. Most notorious was the failure to anticipate the trend from mainframes to personal computers, and the significance of operating systems - marked by the fall of IBM and the rise of Microsoft.

A useful starting point for analysis in human services is Bryan Glastonbury's *Computers on Social Work* published in 1985 and properly recognised as a pioneering contribution to the literature. The final chapter anticipates paperless offices and first contact with services offered by a computer (and possibly) a receptionist. It forecasts 'sound databases' with knowledge of available resources, providing more effective services by analysis of similar cases and evaluating outcomes. It dismisses the 'robotic social worker' in favour of a partnership between computer and professional, the latter possibly working from home and able to 'telecommunicate'. Some of these predictions have been fulfilled. Some remain probable but still rather distant, such as the paperless office or databases filled with qualitative evaluation information that is systematically used to improve the quality of service delivery. Where the prognosis starts to unravel is in the prediction that the 'next generation of computers - that is, the computers for the 1990s - will boast artificial intelligence'. The difficulties were acknowledged but the anticipated qualitative shift from processing data rapidly into the ability to analyse and process it as useful knowledge remains elusive. An example is given of 'The computer could, for example, listen in to an interview, record it in full, and then provide a summary' (ibid, p.135).

Artificial intelligence quickly gave way to expert systems and decision support systems as carriers of ambitions for social work assessment and help through computers: 'Computers can rapidly develop statements of problems or diagnoses from symptoms, but they are dependent on quality input. Computers show promise as aids in the diagnostic process' (Schoech and Arangio, 1979, p.98). A decade later Schoech (1990, p.425) gives a detailed example of using a very simple expert system to test hypotheses about child abuse. Problems are acknowledged but there was an assumption that real progress would be achieved in social work by elaborating the rule base of expert systems - so long as the experts could agree what the rules were.

The knowledge base was the problem: 'Although not yet evident in social welfare, they (expert systems) will certainly have implications for the future because they raise issues surrounding the knowledge base from which welfare operates' (Smith, 1985, p.83). What is interesting here is the notion not so much that computer 'expertise' would have to adapt to social work knowledge but that the knowledge base itself would be questioned by the technology. As indeed it has, not least in the increasing use of computerisable check list approaches to assessing client problems.

However developers of expert systems quickly found that rule based expertise was difficult to apply to the complex world of social work interaction. Carlson (1993, p.339) identified some of the limitations of a rule based approach and identified memory as a source of social work expertise alongside analysis and logic. This led him to consider case simulations based on knowledge on the impact of interventions as an alternative approach to computer expertise. Ravetz (1993, p.351) focused on the nature of social work knowledge which he characterised as an ill-defined domain' which is dynamic, incomplete and fluid. However he argued that an acceptance of the limitations of knowledge acquisition may paradoxically lead to the design of usable expert systems'. The limitations of rule based systems in social work is a theme that Ravetz has returned to since (1996).

Decision Support Systems (DDS) incorporate expert systems approaches, statistical modelling, spreadsheets and/or database information into systems designed to assist professionals in decision making in complex situations. Hopes for Decision Support Systems playing a major role in professional practice have proved elusive, although we are now seeing some important developments in the area of social policy and planning as described elsewhere in this book. Believers in Decision Support Systems can be accused of naivety about the perseverance of actual decision making which is often based on personal and organisational interests, with information often used merely as a weapon. For example: 'the effect (of computerisation) on organisational structures was to move the location of decision making upwards in the hierarchy, generally resulting in a rationalisation of the total decision-making processes' (Smith. 1985, p.72). Similarly Abels (1975, p.27) argued that 'decisions concerning social policy will be made by computers and will be based on regional indexes of social problems, rather than by political manoeuvring'.

Setbacks of expert systems and decision support systems for social work practice are central in analysis of the overall progress of the last decade and casts a shadow over it. Where there has been much greater progress, as in medicine, it has come through investment of research and development funds. While the imprecise nature of social work remains a formidable barrier, progress may be elusive but is not impossible given funding. There is continuing work in human services at varying levels of complexity, including on neural networks, 'case based reasoning' and statistical modelling. However the potential remains largely unexplored and ill coordinated.

Another area of promising experimentation was the use of interactive video technology as an education medium with particular projects that produced high quality results (for example Seabury, 1993). However the alternative newer technology of multi-media effectively destroyed the future of inter-active video - showing some of the dangers in investing in new technologies. As a contrast to over optimistic views of the future we can note Fuller (1970) stating that 'present computer technology brings research within the range of almost every practising social worker..... Almost everyone can learn the basics of a computer programming language, such as Fortran, in a short time'. The idea of social workers learning Fortran to do statistical tests now strikes us as amusing and absurd. Whilst user-friendly and powerful software such as SPSS have democratised access to statistical analysis, their impact on the relationship between research and social work is far more complex than one could have anticipated.

From the start, the ability of the computer to manage and access large quantities of data was perhaps its most powerful feature. The relevance of this characteristic for information intensive human service organisations was clear. The issues, particularly in relation to client information systems, have rather been ones of whose needs and purposes would dominate and how systems would be controlled. However we are now also seeing the development of databases of academic and other resources that are relevant for social work education and social work practice. Alongside this we also have the gradual emergence of electronic information systems that provide valuable guidance to social workers on a complex array of legislation, agency policies, practices and procedures that underpin their work.

What was less anticipated was two features of computers that have dominated the way it is used. These are how it has developed as a visual medium and as a communication medium. The arrival of graphical user interfaces, initially on Apple 'Mac' computers and followed by Windows, has simplified using software once basic techniques are learnt. It has given us the security of check boxes and standard routines along with the power to run several programs at once and move data between them. The sheer enhancement of the quality of presentation, such as seeing on screen how printed text will look, and increasing use of photographs images and design has subtly transformed our responses to software. It is attractive, friendly, helpful and forgiving. Multi-media and CD-ROMs add substantially extended capacity and enhanced use of sound and moving images. Ever ingenious ways of enhancing software in conventional areas or word processing, databases and spreadsheets has perhaps inhibited their development into more unknown territories where success is less assured.

It is common to identify the rise of the Internet as an area of unexpected progress that 'future watchers' did not predict. It seems to have burst into bloom, almost from nowhere. Inevitably the truth is more prosaic and as early as 1972 we have the concept of the 'wired nation' (Parker and Dunn) which was identified as potentially contributing to fostering equal social opportunity. The notion of an idealised information sharing society was explored some years later by Vallee (1986) and the use of transnational networks for accessing information has an established history amongst a minority. The explosive popularity of the Internet came not with the infrastructure of network links to and between servers. It was rather the simplicity of access created by the World Wide Web using the friendly concept of a 'Home page' and the 'magic' of hypertext to make transparent jumps from one part of the world to another.

Future watching is not just about technological innovation but also about how human service organisations use the technology. The earlier *European Resource Book* (Qvortrup, Glastonbury and de Graaf, 1991) and the wider literature were concerned with issues such as office automation and use of client information systems. A consistent theme was about the processes needed in introducing technology into organisations and dealing with the staff anxieties and concerns. Valuable lessons were learnt, many of which are still applicable. However as technology has become familiar and established and the 'new managerialism' has taken over so organisational cultures have shifted towards acceptance of the computer in defined roles. The price however has all too often been that systems have been introduced primarily to achieve accountability and efficiency rather than quality of service. Social workers who see computers as primarily a tool by which they and their agencies are controlled, rather than as a helping tool, may have good reason to do so.

The mismatch between dreams and realities has its roots not just in slow or false technological trails. It is also a mismatch between the capabilities of the technology and the work characteristics and requirements of human services. Apart from the technical complexities of IT matching the subtleties of social work and personal interactions, social workers remain divided about its role. Many still instinctively resist the computer's intrusion into a direct helping role while growing numbers want the potential of the computer to be explored to empower both professionals and clients through better quality services. The latter group is supported by compelling evidence not only that clients like and respond to use of computers but that they often trust it more and feel confident enough to disclose personal information to the computer more easily. For a summary of this evidence see Colombi, Rafferty and Steyaert (1993, pp17-19).

This mismatch between needs and what the computer can actually do is compounded by lack of resources and poor coordination of initiatives. In turn this reflects a gulf between ideals about how technology can be used and the agendas of those controlling resources. In social work education the steady, if unspectacular growth, in using technology as a teaching medium is a direct consequence of resources being made available. Expert systems may be complex, but their slow introduction in part reflects the lack of provision of significant resources. Progress has often come through the work of committed practitioners and academics working alone, whose isolation also affects introduction of completed products into education and practice. Future watching is in part a process of watching the realities of our collective beliefs with sometimes the painful discovery that our values were only ever dreams and never realities.

Daring to dream

What then are our current dreams that may become tomorrow's realities or tomorrow's scrapheap? The first aspect of note is that each country identifies needs as well as making predictions. It is therefore an active endeavour to shape the future and not just to await it passively. Their contributions can be classified under headings of:

- Structural and economic
- Strategic - 'A shifting centre of gravity'
- Technical innovation
- Communications and the Internet
- Ethical dimensions
- Social work education
- Service provision

Before going on to consider these headings, reference should be made to the report from America (USA) which provides a detailed, brave and lucid exposition of future developments and their likely impact on human services in the USA. It is an account which deserves to be read in its entirety and no attempt is made to summarise it here, other than a brief reference in the section on technical innovation.

Structural and economic

A recurrent theme is how structural factors, such as geographic size (Russia, Canada, Micronesia and Australia); cultural and political traditions (Micronesia, Australia); or political and economic upheavals (Romania and Russia) will continue to shape how IT is used. For these countries communications technologies and the Internet takes on a specific relevance. However Australia cautions 'In many ways it is easier to link up with overseas colleagues. There is an insularity within the country which seems to carry with it the assumption that personal contact is the only real way of identifying with others'.

Economic factors are identified as critical, even in relatively wealthy societies - 'The most immediate and serious challenge for human service agencies in Canada will be in adapting to the increasingly restrictive financial situation as all levels of government attempt to reduce deficits.' In the Netherlands we have - 'the ultimate question: who is going to pay for all this? ... an absence of structural (financial) support for projects and experiments in the care and welfare sector'. Romania, Micronesia and Spain also all identify a low level of development related to economic factors which will affect their future development. Russia finds room for hope 'Although Russia faces a severe struggle with economic and social difficulties, there is a high level of technical skills and a strong willingness to apply technologies that can help to cope with the enormous difficulties'.

Strategic - 'A shifting centre of gravity'

Several countries identify the need for a more strategic approach to the use of IT in human services. Belgium welcomes the arrival of a coherent information policy for the human services which might have 'a major impact on the relationship between Belgian human services and IT applications'. Greece takes a similar view, looking forward to a European perspective based on the Bangemann Report. In Finland a nationwide approach is needed to 'avoid wasting resources', along with the need to avoid narrow views in which 'systems are useful in order to utilise statistics for state purposes, not for client services'. Canada takes up this theme - 'With front line workers becoming significant users of IT and representing the largest bulk of human service workers, the centre of gravity for IT within agencies will shift increasingly towards the front line worker needs. This should promote applications which are user-oriented and task directed'.

These views parallel Israel's expectation that systems 'will be geared to social worker needs thereby enabling them to use information technology as part of the work process. This will help counter the dominant managerial aspects of information technology use'. Romania neatly reverses the usual priorities - 'It is important to create client orientated applications in order to help social workers to guide and assist clients. Management orientated applications are also important ...'.

Technical innovation

It is perhaps surprising how few reports refer to further technical innovation. There is a sense of existing levels of technology setting a sufficient challenge and opportunities to occupy human services agencies for many years to come. There are exceptions. The UK mentions 'The extension of smart systems, such as is already provided by Tunstall's PiperNet, which combine home alarm systems coordinated through a central control point with IT based service planning and monitoring'.

The USA report takes a more radical approach and predicts 'a more important and fundamental change .... the integration of telephone, television, stereo, and computers into a universal information device .... This new device will be an integrated and inexpensive cluster of digital information technologies allowing information to be become a basic part of business and homes'. Geographic information systems, virtual reality and networked computers as the infrastructure of the global village are among the other ingredients of technological change identified.

The Canadian report refers to 'The notion of IT providing actual decision-support is becoming a reality'. The Netherlands refers to 'Work that is dominated by more or less fuzzy processes and interactions between human beings. In the next decade software developers and engineers will undoubtedly try to tackle this problem from a technical perspective. The first (demonstration) projects are now being carried out on topics which can be characterised as complex: decision making based on social security legislation; establishing the effects of (social) policy decisions; making diagnostic judgements on for instance delinquent juveniles or on people with multi-layered problems'.

Communications and the Internet

Perhaps not surprisingly, increasing communication and the role of the Internet featured in the anticipated future directions of most reports - a 'self understood daily tool in the offices' (Germany). The context varied from geographical isolation to empowering citizens and the 'hype' surrounding the information superhighway. The UK report refers to communication between agencies such as 'health and social services, ... between probation, the courts and (more controversially), the police'. The Internet is seen as replacing or supplementing existing cross-agency communication, although concerns about confidentiality are to the fore.

The following perhaps best articulates the hopes - 'connectivity or networking is emerging as the brightest star in the universe of IT applications. Given the enormous expanse of Canada and its range of diversities, IT offers the potential to break down many barriers and promote knowledge, awareness, tolerance and communication within the country, the new information superhighways like the Internet promise to add substantially to our connectedness at all levels, as we move to become truly citizens of the world'.

Ethical dimensions

There are a range of diverse ethical issues raised for the future. On a concern articulated in several reports, Japan notes - 'these social trends will widen the gap in the information available to information-skilled people compared to the information unskilled. The poor, aged, disabled, or less educated could be alienated from the world of information technology despite their severe social needs'.

Data protection is another area of concern. An interesting suggestion made in the Finland report is that information systems might not permit further documentation of cases until the record or plan had been signed by the client at certain stages. The Irish report raises concerns about social service unemployment and about the phenomenon of 'telecolonisation'. This is described as 'the process whereby urban employers use online circuits to tap the best talent in rural areas .... may swell the profits of metropolitan corporations, while contributing little to the well-being of the regions where they live' (Grace, 1991). One attempt to counter this trend is the 'telecottage' movement, which aims to channel IT resources into isolated regions.

The Canada report refers to the 'effect of computerisation on increasing depersonalisation within our society. People need individual help and counselling when they are out of work or in dealing with the system. All the computers in the world will not give you that'. Denmark suggests that we need to distinguish services provided by computer that can be offered on their own and those that should include an offer of counselling. A thoughtful contribution at the end of the Israel report refers to how computer applications can be seen as threatening professional standards, and the need to obtain support from professionals for introducing new systems. In a broader comment on ethical issues, the UK report identifies shared concerns for 'clarification of quality standards and rules of conduct for the use of IT both at a general level and specifically to the human services'.

Social work education

Social Work educational institutes are regarded as having a key responsibility - Romania sees them as the 'avante guarde of this profession' with a corresponding need for investment in IT and continuing exchange and collaboration between countries. Similarly the Netherlands sees social work educators as the driving force behind technological change - 'rethinking the changing content of professional acts should be a part of their core business'. Germany however sees a shift away - 'The future will bring a greater independence of IT development from the universities and schools of social work, which have been dominant in the past. This is because the software industry has discovered its interest in the special social work market'.

There is however consensus that 'computer literacy is becoming a necessity in social work education. Social welfare agencies realise that they need social workers who are familiar with computers and computerised information systems' (Japan). The UK identifies the economic pressures - 'Technology based learning, brought about partly by pressure to make more productive use of teaching staff rather than multi-media developments'.

Service provision

As noted earlier, several countries anticipate a fairly fundamental shift toward the needs of practitioners. Denmark notes the disappointment of many social workers with software but is optimistic for improvement 'Windows seems to be the answer'. It cautions however that - 'More IT is not the answer to professional questions and should be a tool for professionals in their other tasks. Information technology has the nature of being the answer, without anyone knowing the question. This trap demands that professionals be very clear about what to use and why. Clarification of professional aims and methods are key words here'.

The UK anticipates 'The final establishment of computer files as the main client records ..... At the same time we can expect to see a growing integration of systems linking clients records to contact data, assessments, records of advice, information and services provided, service costs, evaluation and quality monitoring, and case review'.

A particular area noted is the need to define social terms in a consistent way within a country in order to increase the compatibility of information systems both between different agencies at a local level and between the same agencies nationally. Denmark is one example but with reservations - 'it is hoped that professionals will be aware of the traps once development and implementation begin in earnest'. Finland refers to 'An unavoidable need to standardise the structures and terms used in social welfare work and IT practices'. Similar needs are raised by Japan, Spain and are implicit in national developments in Israel where the principle agenda is identified as 'Decentralisation is seen to be the dominant factor in the future development of information technology in the human services ...'.

Finally, to round off this section, the Netherlands summarises what may be a collective hope: 'A main objective for the coming years will be to answer the question of how to implement technology in a sensible way into the daily work of people concerned with our care and welfare'. If that goal is achieved then many dreams will be realised.

PARADIGM SHIFTS

A number of years ago, it was commonplace to refer to the human services as shivering on the brink when it came to using computers: 'Although computer technology and the field of human services may seem antithetical to many, a number of professionals have explored the potential usefulness of computers in social work' (Jaffe 1979, p.380). The early reticence has gone. No one is surprised to see a social worker using a computer these days, which is not unexpected if we consider how information technology oozes into every niche of our society and daily life.

Analysing how human services have applied information technology across time, we can distinguish between several generations. It starts with generations of hardware, the tangible aspects of information technology. First we had the big computers, like humming refrigerators, the number crunchers. For an excellent analysis of computer use in social welfare in this batch-processing era, see Smith (1985). Human services made little direct use of them as they required considerable investment, including a computer department with experts to 'talk' to the computer. Despite this, *Social Service Review* published an article in 1974 on computer assisted assessment including photographs of room-filling equipment (Thomas, Walter and O'Flaherty, 1974, p.173). Subsequent generations of hardware were smaller and cheaper but also more powerful and user-friendly. A typical modern PC has more computing power than an average university computer department of a few decades ago. And still the end of this development cannot be seen - buying a personal computer today means being out of date with technology tomorrow.

Generations of software can also be distinguished in the history of informatics. Few people recall the days of using Assembler as the communication language needed to get computers to do something for you. We look back with awe to the expert staff needed for the machine to even perform a simple calculation. They were the monarchs of the technology, powerful through their monopoly of the 'secret language'.

Fortunately, later generations of software came closer to the end-user with current software abandoning 'machine code' for flexible script-like programming facilities. Several country reports suggest that graphical user interfaces and ease of using the Internet have lowered the threshold to applying information technology.

It is intriguing to discern these generations of hardware and software as a form of industrial archaeology to shed light on possible future developments. It would however be similar to reading tea leaves, as the blueprints of future information technology products are well-kept secrets. A more fruitful form of analysis is to discern generations of applications and of relationships between human services and information technology. In discussing models of applications rather than chronologically successive generations, paradigms is perhaps a more appropriate label.

The technology efficiency paradigm

A first paradigm emerged ten to fifteen years ago when personal computers were introduced and word-processing software became available. Prices for hardware and software were substantial, but human services began to expand their administration with computers. Often using small grants, the first personal computers and printers were introduced - computers that bore little resemblance to current models. Screens were small, with green or amber angular characters. Printers produced dot matrix characters, typically at 9 or 25 pin resolution. Those with more funds invested in 'letter quality' daisy-wheel printers - but who could bear the noise generated, similar to chain-saws? Answering the telephone while printing a letter was impossible.

Notwithstanding these disadvantages, the benefits of word-processing were so apparent and overwhelming that the technology achieved considerable diffusion into human services. Gone was typing and retyping texts, the actual 'cut and paste' activity needed for producing reports. Manual indexes of clients (names, addresses and essential administrative data) which were previously held on systems like the Rolodex, were a perfect task for database software. Other information followed - without mistakes, without complaints, just that sonorous, steady background murmur, much like a purring cat.

Has this model changed in the subsequent years? Certainly. Mono-screens gave way to colour screens, daisy-wheel printers were silenced, ink-jet and laser printers took over from needle printers. And we went graphical. Graphics on the screen with Windows, and graphics on paper with desk top publishing, charts and even maps. Annual reports and publications improved in appearance (when design was not overdone). The question is, do these changes bring about another model? They increase the megahertz speed at which the computer works, increase a hundredfold the capacity of hard disks and enhance print quality. But essentially, the model did not change. The credo of this model, this paradigm shift is *increase of efficiency*. The relationship between human services and information technology was one in which computers decreased the time needed for administrative work. The associated dream was that, ultimately, time would be freed up for more client contact: 'provided the time benefits which accrue as a result of the computerisation of tasks are not taken over by other routinised organisational needs then it seems that more time can be made available for professional contact with clients' (Smith, 1985, p.113).

The effectiveness paradigm

A sequel, though not always a successor, to this paradigm of efficiency is our second model. The start at an international level can be located in September 1987 in Birmingham (UK): the first HUSITA conference. The title *Human Services Information Technology Applications* marked it as a new direction, a milestone in thinking about how the technology could be used. The first HUSITA offered ideas and presentations that went well beyond word-processing or simple databases. New concepts and applications were introduced such as automated client information files (Glastonbury, LaMendola and Toole, 1988), computerised assessment (LaMendola, Glastonbury and Toole, 1989) or expert systems. These were of widespread fascination, accompanied by complaints about practitioners not being interested in using computers - shivering on the brink, modern Luddites. The slogan of this second paradigm becomes 'take up the challenge', innovate and include IT in your practice. If not, you may be overwhelmed by it in the long run.

This paradigm is no longer concerned with greater efficiency - that battle has been fought and won. 'Increased effectiveness' became new key-words. The effectiveness of human services was questioned by funding sources following the strident criticisms of the late seventies and early eighties. Accountability of the quality of care provision became a key issue in the survival of human services - and computers could greatly contribute in that process. Not only did they provide the charisma of accuracy and reliability, but the use of client information systems is an intrinsic element of an accountability strategy.

Although this paradigm promised much, it left a sour taste. It has proved difficult not to focus on the technology itself. All too often descriptions of applications elaborated on the technological innovations involved, and it is tempting to go along with that trend. You achieve a mystical turbo-language, become distinguished from your colleagues and are needed whenever the computer malfunctions. However it remains a technology push that does not amount to a sound incorporation of IT into human service practice. Part of the problem was that the push towards accountability was set in the context of the 'new managerialism' with social work agencies adopting a pseudo businesses language and social work values displaced by corporate image making. Priority was placed on accounting and quantification of service delivery rather than enhancing the quality of the service provided to clients. The focus was on managing budgets, measuring throughput in different categories and quantifying 'success' on often rather arbitrary criteria.

Fortunately, the effectiveness focus is now shifting. Several country reports anticipate the information needs of service providers becoming more important. Applications are developed no longer just because the technology is available, but are more closely tied to information needs. Automated client information systems no longer just link databases to a word-processor. They become sophisticated, tailor-made packages meeting the information needs of the professional care provider at every stage of the process (e.g. see ADORA in the Belgian report, or GIRST in the Dutch report). Databases generating statistical analyses no longer do so only to generate data-cemeteries, but are more likely to be guided by carefully constructed information plans for both policy and professional needs. In these examples, we see the human service provider finally taking up the challenge of incorporating information technology in his/her daily work, not being led by technology but by information needs.

While we can be optimistic about how client information systems are developing, the evolution of the computer as a tool for assessment and direct support to clients within social work relationships remains uncertain. Many social workers still resist their use on principle. However the gradual evolution of better quality software, greater accessibility for front line staff to technology and new social workers trained and expecting to use IT will all play a part. Ultimately however it may be client expectations that have the greatest impact.

A characteristic feature of the effectiveness paradigm is the shift in focus from the technology to information itself. In five or ten years there may be no special attention to the use of IT in human services as the next generation of providers may no longer consider technology as something special. Computers will be seen as a normal facet of daily life just like the telephone or the fountain pen - and when was there ever a conference or a journal on the impact of the fountain pen on human services?

We can already see the first signs. A few years ago Steyaert (1992) compared the application of IT to decision processes in human services with using a flashlight in a dark room. They both serve to illuminate the surroundings, allow you to analyse your position and environment, to identify your target and the way to get there. Continuing this metaphor, up to a few years ago attention mainly focused on the construction of the flashlight, its parts, the energy used and its quality. Some research focused on the clarity and diffuseness of the light produced. Seldom was attention paid to the user, the way he or she used it to find their way and success in reaching targets. In that sense, the subject of 'i**T**' was approached as a very small 'I' and a very capital '**T**'. Technology was all the starting point of research, publications and applications. Fortunately, this situation has changed and the focus is now more and more on '**I**t' with a capital '**I**' and a smaller 't'.

Redesigning care delivery

In our third and final paradigm, concerns about efficiency and effectiveness in human services take on a new dimension. We find high levels of innovative activity from social policy makers, redrafting the core structures of the welfare state. The UK introduces the Community Care Act and separates the roles of service providers and purchasers. Local welfare services are suddenly competitors in the 'mixed economy of welfare'. Israel is another country that opened up care provision to commercial profit orientated organisations. The Netherlands seeks a golden mean, serving its citizens a mixture of decentralisation, case management and a profound shift in funding towards client based budgets.

These developments imply availability of rivers of information that can only be provided by intensive use of IT. The decades-old structures of the welfare state find themselves under close scrutiny and the new technology opens up new opportunities. For example, through developments in measuring effectiveness using client information systems, the relationship between government and service providers can drastically change. Overt central control gives way to closely monitored tasks seconded to lower levels. Elaborate data streams enable controlling organisations to keep a finger on the pulse. The process has been described as *business process redesign*. The concepts of 'social indicators' and 'performance indicators' take on a whole new meaning as they become determinants in allocation of resources. Unfortunately performance indicators are often limited to overall work flows leaving professional aspects and quality untouched. They also upgrade the mean to a normative status, giving it power based on nothing else but 'this is how everybody does it, why not you?'.

These changes are driven by a mixture of demographic problems of aging populations, political ideologies and new theories about welfare provision. The impact may vary from a neo-liberal adaption of the welfare state to a fundamental assault on its basic foundations. Not least is the impact on the role of social workers and the nature of their professional practice which shifts from service provider to that of purchaser and rationer often using an inadequate budget. These issues are crucial and are explored in more depth elsewhere (Glennerster and Midgley, 1991; Steyaert, 1996). The key point of relevance in the present context is how fundamental social practice and policy changes are only made possible through IT.

Within this paradigm there is a final further shift which has been a recurrent theme throughout this book. It is the growing role of the computer as a communication medium through local networks, area networks and the Internet. Such networks impact on the provision of all forms of information whether to citizens generally, to service providers or clients of welfare services. We can anticipate that this shift will have a continuing and growing impact provided that search tools and capacity match demand.

While previous technologies were non-interactive and originated from one source to many audiences, these networks are interactive enabling specific information needs to be met. Moreover, they allow citizens to initiate provision, searching for certain information whenever they wish to do so. It illustrates a shift from an information model towards a communication model in which the user is empowered and in control. Some observers have suggested that we should in fact now talk of ICT - information and communication technologies - in place of IT, to mark the extent of the change implied.

CONCLUSION

Within this multi-layered analysis we have examined some aspects of how the use of information technology is developing across the world. It is a snapshot in time as well of a range of countries that are inevitably more representative of the developed world than of the world as a whole. However the message is clear that technology is increasingly taking its place in human services and finding its role. The full nature and potential extent of that role remains unclear, with continuing and sometimes profound tensions between controlling and empowering aspects of our use of the technology. Our progress over the last ten years has been a mixture both of disappointment and setbacks on one hand and of extraordinary and sometimes unexpected success on the other. Technology is not an aim in itself, but is a tool to make use of information more efficient and more effective. We can safely predict continuing development of using technology to achieve those aims and we can anticipate some surprises in store as well. Perhaps the hardest question is whether we can find solutions to some of the ethical dilemmas that so far have been clearer in their presentation than in their solution. If information is power then we must continue to strive for it to be used to serve the needs of those for whom social work exists. Fortunately success in that endeavour is an achievable goal.

References

Abels P. Can Computers Do Social Work? *Social Work*: 5-11.1972.

Abels P. Terra Incognita: the Future of the Profession. *Social Work:* 25-28. 1975.

Carlson R. From Rules to Prototypes: Adapting Expert Systems to the Nature of Expertise in Clinical Information Processing. In Liederman et al (Eds.) *Technology in People Services*. The Haworth press, New Work. 1993.

Colombi D, Rafferty J and Steyaert J (Eds.) *Human Services and Information Technology: A European Perspective,* ENITH, 1993.

Fuller T. Computer Utility in Social Work. *Social Casework* 51: 608. 1970.

Glastonbury B. *Computers in Social Work.* MacMillan, London, 1985

Glastonbury B and LaMendola W. *The Integrity of Intelligence,* Macmillan Press, UK and St. Martins Press, USA.1992.

Glastonbury B, LaMendola W and Toole S (Eds.). *Information Technology and the Human Services*, John Wiley and Sons. 1988.

Glennerster H and Midgley J (Eds.). *The Radical Right and the Welfare State, and International Assessment*, Harvester Wheatsheaf. 1991.

Jaffe E. Computers in Child Placement Planning. *Social Work:* 380-385. 1979.

LaMendola W, Glastonbury B and Toole S (Eds.), *Casebook of Computer Applications in the Social and Human Services*, The Haworth Press, New York. 1989.

Parker EB and Dunn DA. Information Technology: its Social Potential. *Science.* 176. P. 1392. 1972

Qvortrup L, Glastonbury B and de Graaf H. (Eds.) *European Resource Book: Information Technology and Human Services*, ENITH/NIZW. 1992.

Ravetz J. Expert System Development in Ill-Structured Domains: The Application of Artificial Intelligence Technology to Diagnosis and Assessment in the Human Services. In Liederman et al (Eds.) *Technology in People Services*. The Haworth Press, New Work. 1993.

Ravetz J. Limitations of Rule-base Measures of Professional Practice in the Human Services. In: Steyaert J (Ed.). *Information Technology and Human Services, More Than Computers?* Utrecht: NIZW. 1996.

Schoech D. *Human Service Computing*. The Haworth Press. 1990.

Schoech D and Arangio T. Computers in the Human Services. *Social work:* 96-102. 1979.

Seabury B. Interactive Video Programs: Crisis Counselling and Organisational Assessment. In Liederman et al (Eds.) *Technology in People Services*. The Haworth Press, New Work. 1993.

Smith N. *Social Welfare and Computers.* Melbourne: Longman. 1985.

Steyaert J. Databases And Information Systems In Human Services: Where Do We Go From Here? *New Technology In The Human Services*. 20-29. 6:2.1992

Steyaert J. *The Use Of Client Information Systems In Israel*, Jerusalem, Ministry of Labour and Social Affairs, p.8. 1994.

Steyaert J (Ed.). *Information Technology and Human Services, More Than Computers?* NIZW. 1996.

Thomas E, Walter C and O'Flaherty K. Computer assisted assessment and modification: possibilities and illustrative data. *Social Service Review*: pp.170-183. 1974.

Vallee J. The Network Revolution: Promises and Pitfalls in the Use of Information Technology. In: Geiss G and Viswanathan N. *The Human Edge: Information Technology and Helping People*. 1985.

Van Hove E. The Legislation On Privacy Protection and Social Research, *Human Services in an Information Age*, Haworth, New York. 1996.

Appendix: Key Literature

Jan Steyaert

This book has a wide geographical coverage but it is only a small part of the extensive literature on using technology in the human services. The aim of this appendix is to provide information on some of that wider literature in its diverse forms. As such it can be seen as an appetiser to a substantial dinner. This dinner includes journals, books and virtual publications. Electronic sources feature as the dessert.

PROFESSIONAL JOURNALS

The core professional journals focus on the use of information technology in the human services. These are *New Technology in the Human Services* and *Computers in Human Services*. Both are published quarterly although Computers in Human Services often publishes double issues which are also available in book format.

New Technology in the Human Services (ISSN:0959 0684) is edited by Jan Steyaert and Ann Wilkinson and published by Causa (Eindhoven, the Netherlands) and the Centre for Human Service Technology (CHST, Southampton, UK). It contains refereed articles offering descriptions and analysis of key developments, policy and practice reports giving details on applications and issues in daily practice, book and software reviews to keep you up to date with new (virtual) publications/R&D projects and news. This coverage includes major conferences and forthcoming activities. It regularly publishes a resource guide giving an overview of software for the human services. Details are available on http://www.fz.hse.nl/nths/.

Computers in Human Services (ISSN:0740-445X) is edited by Dick Schoech and published by The Haworth Press. This substantial North American journal provides a platform for the publication of conference presentations, such as the successive

HUSITA (Human Services Information Technology Applications) conferences. Details are available on http://www.uta.edu/cussn/cussn.html.

Although these two journals are the main source of information about the application of information technology in the human services, articles on this topic regularly appear in other national and international professional journals. CD-ROMs of Social Work Abstracts (see http://silverplatter.com/) and CareData (http://www.nisw.org.uk/) are useful tools to keep track of articles.

BOOK PUBLICATIONS

This appendix identifies key book publications in English only and is limited to books directly related to information technology and the human services. This list is not comprehensive. Publications are listed alphabetically by first author/editor.

Cnaan R and Parsloe P. (Eds.). *The Impact of Information Technology on Social Work Practice.* New York: The Haworth Press, 211pp. ISBN:0-86656-825-5. 1989.
This special double-issue of 'Computers in Human Services' assembles academic articles that counter the primary focus in the literature on management applications and societal consequences of IT for human services. It contains descriptions of applications of immediate interest to practitioners, such as use of computer games and an expert system, how to monitor interventions and capture expertise, and use of computers for social diagnosis.

Colombi D. *The Probation Service and Information Technology.* Aldershot: Avebury, 213pp. ISBN:1-85628-953-2. 1994.
This book discusses the use of information technology in one specific area of the human services, the probation service. It elaborates the thesis that a critical success factor of computerisation is addressing the information needs of all stakeholders in an agency, and not only the information needs at the managerial level.

Colombi D, Rafferty J and Steyaert J. (Eds.). *Human Services and Information Technology: A European Perspective.* Antwerp and Southampton: ENITH, 208pp. ISBN:0- 854-32476-3. 1993.
The predecessor of this book had a similar sandwich structure in offering a substantial introductory chapter (described by one reviewer as a tour de force in conceptual clarity), a series of country reports and a final section with analysis and appendices. The scope of this predecessor was limited to European countries.

Geiss G and Viswanathan N. *The Human Edge - Information Technology and Helping People.* New York: The Haworth Press, 428pp. Pbk. ISBN:0-86656-407-1. 1986.

The product of a 1984 conference in Colorado, with a wide range of human services applications, opportunities and threats identified. Focuses on managing client information, service delivery and ethical issues with professional applications represented in their relative infancy. The term 'Compiling an Encyclopedia of Ignorance' captures the pioneering spirit. A seminal early marker in the shared endeavour to develop IT in human services, subsequently made international through the HUSITA conferences.

Glastonbury B. (Ed.), *Human Welfare and Technology*. Assen: Van Gorcum, 280pp. ISBN:90-232-2831-6. 1993.
Published at the HUSITA 3 conference at Maastricht in June 1993, this contains a selection of twenty four papers presented at the conference. Several of them have triggered debates and further research and belong to the much quoted publications of this field.

Glastonbury B and LaMendola W. *The Integrity of Intelligence - A Bill of Rights for the Information Age*. Basingstoke: Macmillan, 206pp. Pbk. ISBN:0-333-605-21-7. 1992.
This book addresses concerns about how 'the scale and rapidity of technological developments has outstripped the capacity of human services to absorb them into their everyday lives'. It focuses particularly on the global IT industry and its impact on different parts of the globe. The book ends with a proposed Bill of Rights regarding the ownership of data.

Glastonbury B, LaMendola W and Toole S. (Eds.). *Information Technology and the Human Services*. Chichester: John Wiley and Sons, 432pp. ISBN:0-471-92127-0. 1988.
This is the first of two books, by the same editors, of papers from the first HUSITA conference at Birmingham, England in 1987. This volume include 42 papers from the 150 presentations. The two books provide an important reference source as the first international perspective on IT developments in the Human Services. They also mark the start of the HUSITA movement as an international cooperative endeavour.

Kerslake A and Gould N (Eds.). *Information Management in Social Services*. Avebury: Aldershot, 99pp. ISBN:1-85972-293-8. 1996.
This edited volume brings together a number of British contributions on the use of information in social service departments. Its core thesis is that information is not on the edges of daily practice in these services, but the backbone of the organisations. Hence, application of information technology is not a cosmetic innovation, but touches the heart of social services.

Although this book builds from the experiences in Britain, its contents carry great relevance for other countries.

Kolleck B and Rafferty J (Eds.). *Both Sides: Technology and Human Service*. Berlin: Alice-Salomon Fachhochschule, ISBN 3-930523-60-4. 1996.
This virtual publication is the first one in this area in making contributions available in electronic format. The contributions originated from the ENITH conference in Berlin, September 1994. It groups sixteen articles in three sections on support for clients, support for agencies and education. This book is available as an electronic publication on disk and on the World Wide Web at address http://enith.asfh-berlin.de/.

LaMendola W, Glastonbury B and Toole S (Eds.). *Casebook of Computer Applications in the Social and Human Services*. New York: The Haworth Press, ISBN:0-86656-867. 1989.
This is the second of two books of papers from the first HUSITA conference at Birmingham, England in 1987. It includes 21 papers from the 150 presentations.

Leiderman M, Guzetta Ch, Struminger L and Monnickendam M (Eds.). *Technology in People Services: Research, Theory, Applications, and Ethical Issues*. New York: The Haworth Press. 519pp. ISBN:1-56024-456-9. 1993.
This books brings together a number of papers that were presented at the second HUSITA conference, in New Jersey, 1991.

Nurius P and Hudson W. *Human Services, Practice, Evaluation and Computers*, California: Brooks/Cole, 463pp. Pbk. ISBN:0-534-15090-X. 1993.
This book offers a unique balance of theoretical coverage on practice evaluation and the use of assessment scales and practical guidelines on implementation and instruments. It includes a version of the CASS software (Computer Assisted Social Services), limited to 20 client records. However, this is not a manual to the program. The book invites the reader to develop a clinical social work practice, offering a theoretical framework, practical guidelines and versatile software. In a way, it can be compared to the excellent manuals of the statistical software SPSS, which are being used as a guide to statistics, even by those using other software.

Phillips D and Berman Y. *Human Services in the Age of New Technology: Harmonising Social Work and Computerisation*. Aldershot: Avebury, 151pp. ISBN:1-85972-128-1. 1995.
Contrary to the common belief that information technology does not go along with the person-oriented value base of social work, this publication argues that 'computers, if appropriately used, can be a major asset to even the most

individualistic and person-centred social worker'. It argues this case by providing numerous examples of how computerisation may be to the direct benefit of clients.

Rafferty J, Steyaert J and Colombi D (Eds.). *Human Services in the Information Age*, New York: The Haworth Press, 372pp. ISBN:1-56024-768-1. 1996.
This publication joins the earlier book edited by Glastonbury in bringing together the most significant contributions to the HUSITA 3 conference in 1993 in the Netherlands.

Reinoehl R and Mueller B (Eds.). *Computer Literacy in Human Services*. New York: The Haworth Press, ISBN:0-86656-980-4. 1990.
This US book is a selection of articles which 'identify and discuss the issues and competencies in teaching the use of computers in human services or describe how computers can help faculty to teach about other aspects of human services'. It includes sections on the issues involved, program development, course development, computer assisted instruction and computer controlled video.

Resnick H (Ed.). *Electronic Tools for Social Work Practice and Education*. New York: The Haworth Press, 405pp. ISBN:1-56024-658-8. 1994.
This selection of papers focuses on the use of computer games, simulations and interactive videodisc programs both for daily practice as well as for educational purposes. Although much of the hardware and most of the hardware has been overtaken by developments by now, the core concepts and framework of this book are still relevant for today's situation.

Schoech D. *Human Service Computing*. New York: The Haworth Press, 614pp. Pbk. ISBN:1-56024-063-6. 1990.
This book sets out 'to provide human service professionals with a basic framework for moving into the information age. It synthesises available information in the field of computer analysis, information management and communication within the context of the human service environment'. An ambitious task which with detailed examples to illustrate themes and issues leads to a comprehensive and stimulating contribution for people at all levels of experience.
The three parts cover the human service environment, a detailed guide to hardware and software and analyses computer applications in the Human Services, issues involved and future trends. It ends with the view that the 'Infrastructure of the information age is being built ... human services professionals must develop the human service components of this..... central to the future is having the vision to avoid potential problems, such as privacy violations and dehumanising systems'.

Steyaert J (Ed.). *Information Technology and Human Services, More Than Computers*. Utrecht: NIZW, 202pp. ISBN:90-5050-372-1. 1996.